D1736297

Behind
The Muse

Pop and Rock's Greatest
Songwriters Talk About
Their Work and Inspiration

Behind
The Muse

Pop and Rock's Greatest Songwriters Talk About Their Work and Inspiration

Bill DeMain

Tiny Ripple Books
P.O. Box 1533
Cranberry Township, PA 16066

Published by:
Tiny Ripple Books
P.O. Box 1533
Cranberry Township, PA 16066
www.tinyripple.com
Copyright © 2001 by Bill DeMain   .
ISBN 0-9675973-2-3
Library of Congress Control Number: 2001095955
Printed in the United States of America

Contents

Preface

In Salman Rushdie's novel *Haroun And The Sea Of Stories*, a young man who wants to learn the secrets of storytelling encounters a water genie. This water genie is a cross between a muse and a plumber. He tells the young man of an ocean full of "story water," and how those storytellers who are serious about their art must have their own personal taps installed through which the story water can flow. "But how does the plumbing work?" the young man asks. "It's a P2C2E," the genie responds. "A process to complicated to explain."

Songwriting is also, to borrow the genie's phrase, a P2C2E. How does a songwriter get the perfect combination of melody, harmony and lyrics to flow through their instrument and pen to create a great song? While the plumbing involved may be too complicated to explain, this book attempts to at least provide a rough schematic. In the pages that follow, you'll be privy to inside information about how 40 great songwriters deal with their own water genies and how they've kept their taps flowing with some of the best songs of the past century.

The first songwriter I ever interviewed was Antonio Carlos Jobim. What a way to begin. It was 1991. I remember being extremely nervous, not only because I was a huge fan, but also because I was acutely aware of being a novice songwriter in the presence of one of the best songwriters ever. I mean, this was the guy who wrote worldwide standards such as "The Girl From Ipanema," "Meditation," "How Insensitive" and "Corcovado (Quiet Nights Of Quiet Stars)." Songs that Sinatra sang. I hardly felt worthy to call myself a songwriter in the face of that. And yet, during the course of our conversation, Jobim was candid about the difficulties he had with writing. At one point, he said with a sigh, "Maybe you have to write the more-or-less songs so the moment 'Corcovado' comes, you are there." What a revelation that was to me! Jobim sometimes wrote average songs? It was such an affirmation to hear him admit that.

Over the next ten years, I interviewed nearly 300 songwriters, from all walks of musical life, and time and again, I had these kind of affirmative experiences. I found that there were common threads that connected all writers. It doesn't make any difference how far along we are in our careers, we all seem to share the fears, doubts, worries and superstitions as well as the joys, excitements, enthusiasm and awe surrounding this most mysterious process. If there's an underlying theme of this book, it is this: You are not alone.

Whether you're Billy Joel or a beginner, you're still dealing with the same basic raw materials when it comes to songwriting – intros, verses, choruses, bridges – and you're still venturing into the unknown with every song. Who knows if the confluence of time, space, weather, C Major 7th chord, the blue shirt you're wearing, what you had for breakfast and what your girlfriend said to you on the phone last night will gel into a great song or an unfinished dud. It's an adventure every time.

Of course, it can be a lonely adventure, especially if you write by yourself. When I first started, I wrote exclusively by myself. I bought loads of books about songwriting, then found more at the library. Most of these books were by songwriters I'd never heard of. While there was some valuable information in those pages, I couldn't help thinking, "Why should I believe this person? I've never heard any of their songs. How do I know they've written anything good?"

Even now, when I look at what's currently available on songwriting, I don't see the kind of inspirational how-to book that I've always craved. A book that gives you insights and tips from those who've already proven themselves successful. *Behind The Muse* is that book. A songwriter once advised me, "Try to make records that you would want to buy." Well, this is a book I would want to buy.

In what follows, you'll hear from a vast range of songwriters. While the book cuts a wide breadth, both historical and stylistic, these are all artists who care deeply about the tradition of songwriting. No matter the genre, their songs have defined eras, enriched our culture and given voice to the collective thoughts and feelings of millions.

The book unfolds in roughly chronological order. Younger readers will enjoy meeting consummate old school professionals such as Burton Lane, Antonio Carlos Jobim and Hal David. These are men who didn't think in terms of creative angst or changing the world. They mainly believed in doing their job well. And they did. At the same time, those readers who are slightly older will be pleasantly surprised to learn that contemporary writers such as k.d. lang, XTC's Andy Partridge, and Aimee Mann proudly carry the torch of tradition. In fact, in an era when popular music is often more about image and envelope-pushing, the art of songwriting has found refuge in what are often called "cult" artists. Will it be a temporary detour? As Burt Bacharach reassures us, "I think there will always be room for a good song."

Songwriters and music fans alike will find plenty of fascinating tidbits here, as these artists lift up the hood on their creative processes and trace the evolution of their best-known songs. Did you know that Barry Gibb of The Bee Gees was inspired to write "Jive Talkin'" by hearing the sound of a car tire clicking over a bridge? Or that Justin Hayward of The Moody Blues had a dog named Tuesday, and the way he used to call her name inspired the opening bars of "Tuesday Afternoon"? Or that Dolly Parton refused to let Elvis Presley cover "I Will Always Love You," because Colonel Parker insisted she give up half her publishing? Or that Alan and Marilyn Bergman's classic movie theme "The Windmills Of Your Mind" was an attempt to rewrite "Strawberry Fields Forever"?

As I compiled the interviews for this book, I realized how helpful they've been to me in my own music career. I think of them as a kind of masters program on songwriting. My professors imparted these words of wisdom that I can look to as I make my own way. Neil Finn says, "Half of writing a song is believing that you can do it." Burt Bacharach says, "Get away from your instrument and look at the long line of the song." Jerry Herman says, "A song is like a freight train; it needs a great locomotive at the front to push it and a colorful caboose at the end to give it a twist ending." John Mellencamp says, "Play it like you feel it." Tori Amos says, "As songwriters, we have to put our hands on the 220 voltage and say, 'What do I want to write for?'" Sarah McLachlan says, "Read *Letters To A Young Poet* by Rilke." And on and on.

Whether you're a songwriter, a music fan, or just interested in living a more creative life, I think this book has something for you. I hope that it entertains you, comforts you, and most of all, inspires you. Enjoy!

Bill DeMain
September 2001

Acknowledgments

Behind The Muse would not have been possible without Lydia Hutchinson, who gave me the opportunity to interview hundreds of songwriters for *Performing Songwriter Magazine* (www.performing-songwriter.com).

Jeff Bleiel, my editor and publisher, has my gratitude for giving me the opportunity to bring this long-dreamed of project to fruition. His keen eye for detail and tireless work helped to make this book the best that it could be.

Thanks also go to Randy Schmidt, Paul Zollo, all the helpful managers and publicists who set up the interviews (especially Susan Swan, Bobbi Gale, Angie Jenkins, Anne Marie Roller, and Mary Melia), David Leaf, Paddy McAloon, Don Cunningham, Michael White, Ann Moats, Nicky Bleiel, and *MOJO* magazine. Special thanks to my parents, Jim and Nettie, and to Molly Felder for her love, support and friendship. And of course, I thank all the songwriters who talked to me about their art for this book.

Mitchell Parish

Stardust ☆ Sweet Lorraine ☆ Sleigh Ride

Interview conducted in 1992

"Nobody sits down and says 'I'm going to write a standard.' A standard evolves."

In 1929, Mitchell Parish wrote a lyric about "the stardust of a song" to a Hoagy Carmichael melody. "I had a gut feeling it was going to be an important song," he said. It's safe to say that history has proven him right.

Few adjectives remain to describe "Stardust." Most of the accurate ones – timeless, classic, beautiful, haunting – have been exhausted. The song has withstood not only the test of the years, but also the assault of countless bad lounge renditions and muzak arrangements. Pop chart chronicler Joel Whitburn has called it "the most recorded love song of all time," and National Public Radio included it on its list of the most important American musical works of the 20th century.

Born at the turn of the century in New York City, Mitchell Parish discovered his love for words at a young age, writing poetry and short stories. By the time he was 18, he was working as a song plugger and special material writer for the vaudeville houses. This apprenticeship led to his becoming one of Tin Pan Alley's most successful lyricists. In addition to "Stardust," his formidable catalog of standards includes "Sweet Lorraine," "Deep Purple," "Sophisticated Lady," "Stars Fell On Alabama," and "Moonlight Serenade." He also wrote the Christmas classic "Sleigh Ride" and the English lyric for the cocktail anthem "Volare."

1

What do you think makes a great lyric, as compared to a good one?

That's easy. The longevity of the song. A great lyric doesn't have to be a masterpiece of poetry. It can be written in the vernacular.

"Stardust" is one of the greatest popular songs ever written. How long did you spend on the lyric?

The writing of the lyric is not when the writer sits down at a desk or a table with a typewriter or pen and paper. He or she can be walking around with it for weeks, letting it percolate in his mind. When you sit down to actually write it at the typewriter, you have already written it in your mind weeks before. So when you ask me how long it took, I really don't know. I could have been walking around with it for weeks.

If I had to labor over a lyric too long, if it became an arduous task, where I sweated and toiled and really struggled with it, I would drop it. I'm not talking about any particular song now. I'm talking about an occasional tune in my career. You know why I would drop it? It's not that I shunned arduous work, or writing songs that required a lot of effort, but because I felt it wasn't fair to the composer. The lyric would show its toil, and the sweat that went into it, and that wouldn't be good for the song. The struggle would be too obvious.

"Stardust" would seem like a hard melody to put a lyric to, with its long, wandering form.

When I originally heard it, it was a swing tune, with a very fast tempo. I didn't like it and I didn't write it when it was that way! It sounded like just another swing tune. It was nothing like the way it is now, which is sweet, mellow, romantic, and all that. Then an arrangement was done by Victor Young, and it sounded the way it is known now. When I heard that, I wrote the lyric. It was an altogether different mood, a different feeling. Really beautiful. And it became what it became.

Did you think it would become the enduring standard that it is?

Nobody sits down and says "I'm going to write a standard." A standard evolves. It may be years later. But there is one thing I did know when I wrote the song with Hoagy. I had a gut feeling that the song was going to be an important song. It didn't become an overnight smash. It grew gradually. Many overnight smash hits saturate the ears of the listening public, then you never hear of them again. But certain songs, like "Begin The Beguine," things like that, they grow gradually and they become standards. Maybe it's because of the fact that they don't saturate the ears of the public to the point where people get fed up and forget about them.

Now with "Stardust," there were several things that contributed to its longevity. Walter Winchell, the outstanding newspaper columnist of the day – he had 135 million readers – well, I used to contribute little sonnets to his column and we became friends. And he fell in love with "Stardust." It became his favorite and he quoted lines from the lyric in his column. Every week he had something. Another contributing factor is that the title, "Stardust," appears in short stories, in advertising, magazines, novels, cartoons. It's constantly being used in every cultural aspect of our society. It's almost become a synonym for outstanding popular song. That makes me feel good! It's a nice feeling to know that you're not forgotten.

How did you get started as a songwriter?

I was always interested in writing. Even in elementary school, I was the editor of the school publication. In high school I was the editor of the school magazine. Then during a summer break, I got a job with the Beth Israel Hospital as a temporary secretary. While I was there, I got to know one of the resident doctors. And I wrote a few things for the bazaars, fund-raisers, you know. Well, this doctor said he really liked what I did, and he said he knew someone who was in the music publishing business. The name of the company was Jack Mills. So the doctor brought me up there and introduced me to a piano player who rehearsed acts for vaudeville. I'm talking about the year 1920 now.

I was going to be what was known as a special material writer. A special material writer in the days of vaudeville would write punchlines for comedy songs and novelty songs. A punchline was a two-line couplet [sings "How ya gonna keep 'em down on the farm, after they've seen Paree..."]. I didn't write that one, but that sort of

3

thing. I was writing these things for other writer's songs. The special material writer in a comedy song would retain the format of the song but change the punchlines. They varied. A singer who appeared at a vaudeville theater where her predecessor had done the same comedy song the week before wouldn't want to do the same punchlines. So my job was to write different punchlines. The songs themselves were written by different writers, not by me. I had not yet begun to write my own songs. It was sort of an apprenticeship for me, although I didn't realize it at the time. I also wrote special material like recitations for ballads, and double versions, which means boy and girl versions of the same song.

Who were the writers you looked up to?

Well, when I was a kid I'd go to the penny arcades. And inside these halls they'd have machines lined up, about 50 in a row. These machines had an Edison cylinder inside. You dropped a penny in the slot and the cylinder began to play and you had earphones to listen to the song. Above each machine there was a copy of the title page of a different hit song. For example, "Alexander's Ragtime Band" by Irving Berlin. Over time, I learned the names of the songs, the writers, and the publishers. Besides Berlin, I also heard songs by Lewis & Young, Walter Donaldson, Gus Kahn, George M. Cohan.

When you write lyrics, do you like to begin with titles?

In general, most songs are written in that manner. Usually the lyricist would think of a title. And if he got a good, catchy title, especially in a comedy song or a novelty song, half of the song was written. Let's say I got "Stars Fell On Alabama." I got the title and I went into the arranging room and there was Frank Perkins. He was an arranger, not a writer. So I said to him, "Frank, I've got a title, 'Stars Fell On Alabama.' Fool around with it and see what you come up with." So a few days later he comes in with [the opening bars of the song]. Well, the song was half-written! When I wrote a song that way, I'd give a title to the would-be composer and after he had the music all set, then I'd get the rest of the lyric in there. But there was no set formula where you had to adhere to certain rules. It was all done in an informal way.

Tell me about writing "Sweet Lorraine."

Sometimes after I perform at a college or at an ASCAP function, there'll be questions from the audience. And they'll ask me, "Did you know somebody named Lorraine?" I straighten that out by saying that a writer of a song that has the name of a lady as the title, like "Sweet Lorraine or "Sweet Georgia Brown," or even Stephen Foster's "Jeannie With The Light Brown Hair," they don't have to know anybody by that name. I didn't know anybody named Sweet Lorraine.

What advice would you give to songwriters?

I'm not in the position to give advice, because right now, if Irving Berlin were alive and writing songs today, he would have difficulty in getting a song published. We're living in a different kind of world today. Now, I'm not dead set against rock'n'roll. In fact, a good friend of mine is Jerry Garcia from the Grateful Dead. And I like country and western. Willie Nelson is a friend of mine. But getting back to your question, the advice I'd give you is to keep in mind that it's a tough struggle. It's not easy. It wouldn't be easy for me today. But I say if you enjoy writing, then keep doing it. That alone should be reason enough to continue. Remember, you never know when a hit song is going to come along!

Mitchell Parish died in 1993

Burton Lane

Old Devil Moon ☆ How About You?

☆ On A Clear Day (You Can See Forever)

Interview conducted in 1992

"I wanted to be absolutely true to the characters and the situation. I wasn't going to sacrifice quality to be commercial."

You may not immediately recognize his name, but any music listener in the 20th century is familiar with Burton Lane's wonderful tunes: the infectiously hummable "How About You?"; the enchanting score of the Broadway classic *Finian's Rainbow* ("Old Devil Moon," "Look To The Rainbow," "How Are Things in Glocca Morra?"); the pop standards such as "You're My Thrill," "Everything I Have Is Yours," and "On A Clear Day (You Can See Forever)." Recorded by everyone from Sinatra to Streisand, Lane's songs are timeless, as distinct as Berlin's or Gershwin's. Humorous, lilting, melancholy, and always full of unexpected surprises, a Lane melody has a way of quietly working its magic on the listener. In November 1991, he received ASCAP's highest honor, the Richard Rodgers Award, firmly establishing him in the pantheon of great American composers.

First of all, congratulations on the Richard Rodgers Award. How did you feel about being selected?

It was a very nice thing to have happen. I'm a great fan of Dick Rodgers and suddenly to be told that I got this award, that was more than anybody could ask for! I remember the first musical show my father ever took me to was a show called *Dearest Enemy*. It was written by

Richard Rodgers and Larry Hart. And that started a lifelong romance between me and the musical theater. And I've never gotten over it.

Do you remember writing your first song?

All I can tell you is that it happened when I was so young, that I didn't know what I was doing and I wouldn't call it writing a song. My father was a great song buff. He loved pop songs. Within a very short time after I started taking piano lessons and I was learning how to read music, he brought home a copy of a hit song of that day. I guess I must've been about eleven years old. I tried to read the music. Because it was all new to me – reading off the page – I struck a chord that apparently was not on the page and that led me into playing something else. And I found a kind of joyful experience in fooling around. I guess I was composing, but I would never have known what I was doing. Liking the sound of something I hadn't seen on paper, that was fun!

At 17, you were hired as a staff writer at Remick Music. How did that come about?

I was younger than that. I was 15! All these things happened through friends. That time, it was a friend of my family's. There was a team of lyric writers, Joe Young and Sam Lewis, and they were writing some songs with Harry Warren. Also, many songwriters in those days wrote special material for acts appearing in vaudeville. Anyway, this friend talked about me to Joe Young, and Young said, "I'll give him a test. Sam and I just finished a lyric for an actor. See if he can set a tune to it." So this guy called me and within, I don't know, four minutes, I had a tune for it and they liked it. Then Joe Young arranged for me to play for the head of Remick. They put me under contract for a year. And I got an advance of $17.50 a week. I was very proud of that because I later found out that George Gershwin had a similar contract, but he was getting $15.00.

Meanwhile, I was going to high school. I would go down to Remicks after school and I would end up plugging songs. You know, the publishers in those days had little cubbyholes where upright pianos stood. Acts would come in from all over the country, and a piano player, a song plugger, would take them into a room and play them the new songs that were being published. I started to do this because

I enjoyed it. I met Fats Waller. I was just a kid and he was many years older than I, but we enjoyed each other. I'd play for him and he'd play for me. I met a lot of actors that way and it was fun. I had one song published under the name Burton Levy – because my name wasn't changed at that time – called "Broken Butterfly." Nothing ever happened with it, but it was a good experience. I remember Harry Warren was the only other songwriter under contract to Remick. And I remember my father, when he met Harry Warren, saying, "Now take good care of my son." Because I was in an environment of grown-ups, there was no kid around my age.

Did you meet the Gershwins there?

I met George and Ira about a year later. I was a great, great fan of George's music from the first show I ever saw of his. And it was Ira Gershwin who introduced me to "Yip" Harburg [lyricist for some of Lane's biggest hits]. Then Yip and I wrote a couple of songs. I was still going to school, so I wasn't ready for a professional career and wasn't even thinking in terms of where I was going.

Tell me about your move to Hollywood to be a film composer.

It was 1933. Before my move to Hollywood, I started to seriously write songs and had songs in Broadway shows. I had music in four shows that were playing at one time, when I was 16 or 17 years old. I met Harold Adamson. He and I teamed up and we wrote some pop songs. A couple started to make noise, though we didn't have any real big hits. But one song, I guess it was the first American rhumba, a song called "Tony's Wife," was published by the Irving Berlin publishing company. It was Berlin who sent us to California in June of 1933, on a six-week contract, to see if we could place songs in pictures. I ended up staying there 22 years and Harold stayed there for the rest of his life.

What happened was a fluke. A day or two after arriving in California, we were invited to a dinner party by a friend of my brother's. Alan Rivkin, the screenwriter, was at the party. At the end of the dinner, Rivkin said, "I have a picture that's shooting now and we're desperately searching for a ballad." So I said, "Well, we started one. We haven't finished it yet." I played him half the song and he liked it. And it was "Everything I Have Is Yours." He said, "When can you have it

9

finished?" I said, "We'll go home now and finish it." We did. We called the guy and he arranged for us to come out to MGM the next day. Then there was a whole whirlwind of activity for two guys who'd been in Los Angeles for just a day or two. Suddenly we find ourselves at MGM, playing a song for David Selznick, the producer of the film, who takes us immediately to Joan Crawford's dressing room for her to hear the song, then we're invited to play for L.B. Mayer, the head of the studio, and then we're invited to Mayer's 50th birthday party, where every star in Hollywood appeared. This was within five days of our arriving in California. It was a wild, crazy experience.

Was there a camaraderie amongst the songwriters at the film studios?

There was a camaraderie. I met Rodgers and Hart at MGM. Walter Donaldson. Gus Kahn, Leo Robin and Ralph Rainger, when we went over to Paramount. I was under contract to Paramount with Ralph Freed, who was Arthur Freed's brother. Rainger and Robin were the outstanding songwriters there. Hoagy Carmichael was there. There was a spirit of friendliness. None of us were rivals. None of us felt like we were in competition with each other. And I know that Leo Robin was very helpful. He would advise us in any situations that seemed a little uncomfortable for us. He was very experienced, having been there many years. I found most writers very decent.

How does a melody begin for you? Do you have to be at the piano?

A melody can happen any way at all. It can happen in my sleep, and it has. I can dream a melody. When I'm working on something, music is constantly going through my head. I'll keep a pad of manuscript paper by my bed with a little flashlight and a pen, so I can get it down fast enough to capture it. I write mostly at the piano, although I've written many melodies away from the piano. The piano is my instrument, so no matter where it comes from, I'll end up at the piano to see whether I can improve it or develop it maybe in a different way. It makes no difference. I can write songs on the golf course.

Do you need a title or a completed lyric?

Again, it makes no difference. I like working to titles and I like working to lyrics. But most of the lyric writers I worked with did not write lyrics in advance. Yip Harburg never wrote a lyric in advance.

But he would come up with titles. Like "When I'm Not Near The Girl I Love, I Love The Girl I'm Near." Alan Lerner would come up with titles and sometimes write some lyrics. There might be four lines or eight lines of something that would get me going. Ira Gershwin would write a lyric first on some occasions. He also wrote to music. So I've written in all different kinds of ways.

Finian's Rainbow *was your biggest hit. Do you consider it your best work?*

I consider it my best work because I don't think of the music alone, I think of the whole project. I felt at the very beginning that *Finian's* was the best libretto I'd ever seen for a musical. I've never changed my mind about that. The show was handled in the right way. Casting was careful. Everything was done thoughtfully. And we wrote the show in a way I had never worked before, in that when the show was presented to me originally, it was the first draft of the libretto. As the score was being written and there were certain changes being made in the libretto, Yip Harburg would invite 20-30 people to his home and we would have readings of the play, with Yip and I doing the songs. And this is like workshopping. It was a wonderful way to work, because we really got a feeling of audience reaction, doing it this way. So much so that from the day we went into rehearsal, I didn't change one note of music. Yip didn't change one word of lyric. And the libretto, after we opened, had very, very minor changes. It came out the way we all dreamed it would. This is opposed to my working with Alan Lerner. On the two occasions we did shows together, we went into rehearsal with the book not finished, with the score not finished, people unprepared to do what they were supposed to do. Both shows were terribly affected by this kind of carelessness.

I've read that Finian's *was a turning point in your writing career, in that you decided to write for the book itself rather then to go for hits.*

When Yip gave me this script to read I was so ecstatic about the quality of the writing, that the first thing that entered my mind was that I wasn't going to try to force songs in, just to have hits. I wanted to be absolutely true to the characters and to the situation. I wasn't going to sacrifice quality to be commercial. And it turned out to be the most commercial show I ever wrote. Out of eleven numbers, there were eight standards! A great victory for me.

There have been some lengthy periods of silence during your career, between shows. Is this usually due to your own decision to wait for the right project?

It's been my own decision, not to be silent, but to only do shows that I truly believed in. There have been a couple shows I started and then resigned from, because I didn't like the way it was working out, and they were dreadful flops. Not that that means anything, because one can never guarantee what's going to be a hit, or what's going to be a flop. I only know that if it didn't please me artistically, or emotionally, or in some way, I couldn't write it.

How do you keep your composing skills sharp during these times?

In between shows, I write all the time and I keep looking and keep hoping that I'll find something that will work. It's very frustrating because in a world of music as it is today, the kind of music I write is not the kind that quickly gets recorded in the pop market. I'm not a rock'n'roller. The kind of songs I write will only get recorded if they appear in a show or in a film. I always have hope that the right thing will come along. I keep looking,

Are you familiar with what's current on the Broadway scene?

I'm up on all that's around now, yes.

What do you think of it?

I try not to. There hasn't been anything, not since *Gypsy*. I thought that was a wonderful show. I think *City Of Angels* has a wonderful book, I think Cy Coleman is a wonderful songwriter, I think he had a good idea in what he attempted to do – that is, use jazz as a style of writing. The opening is brilliant. And then the book takes over. I think it's the best show on Broadway. Most of the others, the shows that are passing for operas, I don't like. I love scenery, but I've never cried at scenery, I've never laughed at scenery and I don't think scenery is enough. And wall-to-wall music doesn't make an opera. When I see *Miss Saigon*, I think of Puccini and *Madame Butterfly*, which is so much better.

What's a day in the life of Burton Lane like nowadays? Do you still compose?

I manage to write all the time. I need to release the tensions that build up in me, because I am very frustrated at not being able to work on a show or have some assignment. I play golf and that helps to release tension. And I'll listen to good music, because that's always a pleasure. I listen to the classics. I read a lot, hoping to find something that will work into a musical. I've currently got an idea of mine in the hands of a writer, and I'm hoping that something good will come of it. The promise is there. I'm keeping my fingers crossed.

Burton Lane died in 1997.

Paul Weston

Day By Day ✮ I Should Care ✮ Shrimp Boats

Interview conducted in 1992

"I think a melody has to flow, without any ugly skips in it. The harmony is almost as important as the melody."

One glance at Paul Weston's musical resume and you may think you're reading about not one man, but four or five. Such are his accomplishments over the course of six decades in the business.

As a songwriter, Weston has penned standards such as "I Should Care" (one of Frank Sinatra's early signature songs), "Day By Day" (a hit for The Four Freshmen), "Autumn In Rome" (recorded by Tony Bennett and Johnny Mathis) and "Shrimp Boats" (a #2 hit in 1951 for Paul's wife, the great Jo Stafford). As a composer – Weston makes the distinction – he is responsible for two symphonic suites ("Crescent City Suite" and "Mercy Partridge Suite"). He has also written two masses and a number of published hymns.

As an arranger, Weston cut his teeth with 1930s musical stars like Rudy Vallee, Tommy Dorsey and Bob Crosby, then went on to write distinctive charts for Fred Astaire, Nat King Cole, Jo Stafford, Doris Day, Frankie Laine, Sarah Vaughan, Ella Fitzgerald, and others.

As a recording artist, between 1945 and 1954, Paul Weston and His Orchestra racked up over 20 hit singles for the Capitol and Columbia labels. Weston has also been dubbed the "master of mood music" for his pioneering "Music for Dreaming" projects (such as the landmark 1955-56 albums *Mood For*

12 and *Solo Mood*), which combined lush melodic strings with a big band rhythm. With Stafford, Weston also enjoyed a Grammy-winning masquerade as one half of the lovably horrendous lounge duo, Jonathan and Darlene.

In the 1930s, when you started as an arranger with Joe Haymes' band and Rudy Vallee's band, did you have specific musical goals? Did you know you wanted to write songs?

No. I had gone to Dartmouth, majored in economics and was Phi Beta Kappa. In those days, after college, you went into business. Except in 1933, there wasn't any business. So I decided, instead of staying in Pittsfield, Massachusetts and working for the General Electric Company, I'd go down to New York and do some graduate work at Columbia in advertising. That's where I was when Joe Haymes and Rudy Vallee got me started. My father would make periodic trips down there to tell me I had to get out of this filthy business and get a decent job. Finally, one day I had a Rudy Vallee check for $75, which was monumental in those days. I didn't have a bank account in New York, so I sent it home to Pittsfield. When my father went in to cash it, he became a celebrity because he had Rudy Vallee's autograph. I never heard another word about show business. Everything was cool from then on.

Tell me about working with Tommy Dorsey. What kinds of things did you learn from him?

I learned how to be a leader; that you had to be charitable sometimes, and very aggressive and demanding at others. Tommy was a great leader in that he would never get upset at an honest mistake. If a trumpet player went for a note and missed it, he wouldn't yell at him or anything. But if he left out three bars, he'd hear from Tommy. He didn't suffer omissions gladly. I enjoyed my period working for him. He left arrangers alone. He wasn't like some of the band leaders who would take the arrangement, fiddle around with it, then make the guy do it over again three or four times. It was an easy relationship with Tommy.

Were you writing songs at this point?

Well, Tommy had always been after Axel Stordahl [a fellow arranger] and me to write songs, because he said that was the best racket in the business. So the two of us had been fooling around with a melody. I

16

had about four bars and we expanded it into a song. Then one day Sammy Cahn came in our room and said, "What's that?" We told him it was just a song we'd been fooling with. And Sammy locked the door and wouldn't let us out until he finished the lyric. That song became "I Should Care."

How does a melody begin for you?

Most of the time, it begins with hearing something, writing it down and then taking it to a lyricist. Although, I've done it the other way where somebody's brought me a lyric and I've written music to the lyric. It happens all different ways.

What makes a great melody?

I think it has to flow, without any ugly skips in it. I think the harmony is almost as important as the melody and that has to follow sequentially. Being singable is important, and that's also part of the lyric. Writers like Sammy Cahn were always very sharp in that they tried to get an "ooh" sound on the higher notes. That sound is easier for singers to handle.

You were good friends with Johnny Mercer. Did the two of you ever write songs together?

Yeah, he wrote lyrics to two or three things of mine. One, "Conversation While Dancing" was on Capitol Records. I could've written a lot with him because I was with him for three years on almost a daily basis. But there were millions of guys coming to his house, bringing him lyrics and driving him crazy. I saw that side of it, so I just stayed where I was, and did the arrangements for his records and for the radio shows. I enjoyed that and I never bugged him much. He was a wonderful guy and I think the greatest songwriter ever in America.

Paul Weston died in 1996.

Antonio Carlos Jobim

Interview conducted in 1991

"It is not my intention to write ephemeral pop songs that are on the hit parade for three months."

In Brazil, there is a beautiful word that is peculiar to the country's native language of Portuguese. The word is "saudade" (sow-DAH-djee). While it is difficult to translate, it means, roughly, a longing, yearning and sadness, all felt simultaneously. It's often associated with homesickness, but it can also apply to a feeling for a person or thing.

To best understand "saudade," you only have to listen to the songs of Antonio Carlos Jobim, father of the Bossa Nova and composer of "The Girl From Ipanema." The feeling finds its expression in his soft, sensual melodies, sophisticated chord changes and gently poetic lyrics, whether sung in English or Portuguese. Even when Jobim's songs turn joyful, it's a fragile joy tempered by melancholy. In the chorus of his song, "A Felicidade," there's the telling line, "Saudade never ends but happiness does."

Born in Rio de Janeiro on January 27, 1927, Tom Jobim (as he was known to friends and family) was, like many boys, a reluctant piano student. His early influences were classical masters Chopin, Beethoven and Debussy, along with the American big-band sounds of Duke Ellington and Count Basie. The tropical environment of Brazil was also a major influence on his songwriting.

That environment included many beautiful girls, and one in particular, from Jobim's hometown of Ipanema, became immortalized in his most famous song (one of the ten most recorded songs in the world). The 1964 hit, credited to saxophonist Stan Getz (who introduced bossa nova to the U.S. charts via a version of Jobim's "Desafinado" in 1962) and vocalist Astrud Gilberto, but also featuring Jobim on piano and Joao Gilberto on guitar, made the U.S. Top 10 amidst the British Invasion, and soon thereafter the whole world could envision the "tall and tan and young and lovely" girl from Ipanema as she went walking along the beach.

The prolific Jobim quickly followed with a succession of standards, including "Quiet Nights Of Quiet Stars (Corcovado)," "Dindi," "Meditation," "One Note Samba," "How Insensitive" and "Wave."

For Jobim, the initial splash of Bossa Nova (literally "new wave;" Jobim defined it as "cool and contained . . . it tells the story, trying to be simple and serious and lyrical") rippled into a solo recording career, live performances and cover versions by a veritable A-Z of pop and jazz illuminati.

Frank Sinatra was so taken with Jobim's gifts that he built an entire album, the essential *Francis Albert Sinatra & Antonio Carlos Jobim* (1967), around the Brazilian's songs. It is considered one of Sinatra's best albums, and it remained one of Sinatra's favorites of his own recordings.

In his later years, the "saudade" of Jobim's songs turned toward the disappearing natural beauty of his native country. "I'm a woodsman, a son of mother nature," he said. "I know all the birds, all the trees, the animals, and I always try to protect these things." Indeed, the last full studio album he recorded, 1987's *Passarim*, was a beautiful paean to the natural world and a plea for universal ecological awareness.

Although Tom Jobim always scoffed at being called the inventor of Bossa Nova and laughed off his legendary status, he took his work as a composer seriously.

How did you get started in music?

I played harmonica when I was a kid. My mother led a school, and one of the people she hired was Joachim Koellreutter, a German composer/conductor, and he gave me music lessons. My mother rented an old piano, a Bechstein, so I started to play. At first, I thought piano was something for girls. I wanted to play soccer, so I went to the beach. But when I returned I'd play some sounds. Some sounds would clash. Some sounds would harmonize. I started playing by ear. I heard much North American music and South American music and Caribbean music. Also the classics – Chopin, Beethoven, Brahms, Bach, Debussy. These things led me to study classical piano.

When did you start to write your own songs?

I was not very conscious of that. I used to go to the beach, and the water was clean, less people. It was a wild place with crabs and gulls. Nature was big and very powerful. The shrimps, the pompanos, everything was there. I believe that helped me to write songs, you know, the forest and the mountains and the sea. Looking at it, meditating on it. Also, the girls passing by. I believe that girls are part of the ecology.

Was there a girl from Ipanema?

Yes. The girl that originated the song was a very beautiful girl – blond and dark, with green eyes. My partner, Vinicius de Moraes, who wrote the Portuguese words to the song, and I used to drink at a bar with chairs on the sidewalk, one block from the beach. The name of the bar today is The Girl From Ipanema. But we didn't bug her. She would go to school and to the beach and we would see her. Now she has a daughter, who is also very beautiful.

Do you like to start with a title?

The title usually comes last. Maybe some words, some phrase, some thing from the song itself gives me the title. I believe this also happens with writers when they write a book, then suddenly a word or a sentence becomes the title.

Do you keep a writing schedule?

Yes, I believe I'm disciplined in spite of the chaos. I'm a tenacious man. I'm a man from Aquarius. I still like to work. When I started to play, to pay the rent, I became a nightclub piano player, but now I'm an early bird.

Will you finish everything you start?

No, but I have to be in constant touch with the music. If you aren't there, you won't be there when the song comes. It's a big mystery. Maybe you have to write the more-or-less songs so that the moment "Corcovado" comes, you are there.

How long does it usually take you to write a song?

Some songs I did in five minutes, some songs took me ten years. Never got them quite finished, you know. They are all my children. I have no favorites, but naturally there are some songs that the response has been much stronger from the public, like "The Girl From Ipanema."

One of my favorites of yours is "How Insensitive."

Those lyrics were written by Vinicius, my friend, a poet who became a big lyricist. The translation, Insensitive, is not exactly Insensatez. It's not what the Portuguese title means. Insensatez means lack of sense, senseless. Something that you do without thinking, and you hurt someone because you've been foolish. But I like both the Portuguese and English lyrics.

Is songwriting still a big part of your life?

I think it's a lot of work. Today my life, I have children and problems, so many things. I have to think about the car, the flat tire, the dentist, the school, the kids, the colds, the viruses, the telephone. Everytime I go to the piano, I'm wanted on the telephone. Everytime I do a new record, I have to answer 25,000 calls. Artists strive to be known, and then they go to the mountain and hide themselves.

How do you hope you'll be remembered?

When you do something you love it lasts. It is not my intention to write ephemeral pop songs that are on the hit parade for three months. I always had the intention to be faithful and serious. I want to be eternal.

Antonio Carlos Jobim died in 1994.

Jerry Herman

Hello, Dolly! ☆ Mame ☆ I Am What I Am

Interview conducted in 1995

"I didn't sit down and say I'm going to write a song called 'Hello, Dolly!' The first thing I wrote was 'Hello Harry' after my father, then 'Hello Manny' after my uncle."

"There's nothing more rewarding than a life in the theatre," says composer/lyricist Jerry Herman.

For Herman, those rewards have been bountiful: everything from winning multiple Tony and Grammy Awards, to overhearing his songs on the radio while riding in the back of a taxi, to watching his Broadway musical comedies grow into American institutions. On any given week, in theatres around the world, you can safely bet that actors and actresses are belting out Herman's songs.

Herman burst onto the scene in 1961 as Broadway's youngest composer/lyricist with *Milk And Honey*. The New York native followed with *Hello, Dolly!*, *Mame*, *Dear World*, *Mack & Mabel*, *The Grand Tour* and the Tony Award-winning *La Cage Aux Folles*.

What's remarkable is how Herman has been able to adapt his songwriting, in a chameleon-like manner, from Yiddish-flavored tunes, to 1890s Americana, to French-style melancholia and everything in between. "I'm really proud of that," he says. "Because I try to be a musical playwright and I don't give a damn about writing in my style. I try to write in the style of the piece."

Whatever style he chooses, Herman has consistently delivered unforgettable melodies, in songs such as "If He Walked Into My Life," "I Won't Send Roses,"

"Before The Parade Passes By," "I Am What I Am," and of course, "Hello, Dolly!" Because of their universal appeal, his songs have been covered by a who's who of pop vocalists, including Barbra Streisand, Louis Armstrong, Tony Bennett, Frank Sinatra, Bobby Darin, and Eydie Gorme.

Were there certain events in your childhood that made you want to write songs?

Absolutely. What really started me off in that direction was the fact that I had parents who loved the musical theatre. When I became old enough, they started taking me to musicals. That was their Friday night entertainment. It cost like four dollars and forty cents, or six dollars and sixty cents for good seats to a musical in those days, so it was a luxury they could afford. The first thing they took me to was *Annie Get Your Gun*, and seeing Ethel Merman on that stage belting out those great Irving Berlin songs affected the whole rest of my life. I came home, and because I'm able to play by ear very fluently, I went to the piano and I played half of "They Say It's Wonderful" and "There's No Business Like Show Business" and I had never heard these songs before. I was a kid, but it hit me that Irving Berlin had given me a gift – songs that I could remember, hum, and play at the piano. I didn't realize it that night, but it shaped the course of my life.

Do you remember writing your first song?

Yes. My first song was called "It's Not My Fault," and it was a very uninspired ballad. It was just a way to begin. I always wrote my own lyrics and my own music. Of course, my mother thought it was wonderful and encouraged me. But I always thought that songwriting would be a hobby. So I went to the Parsons School of Design, and I wanted to be an architect and an interior designer of things like hotels and airports. I was doing very well there when my mother said, "You know, these things that you're writing are getting better and better, and I want you to take them to a friend of a friend," who happened to be Frank Loesser. Of course, I was a stubborn kid and I said, "You're my mother, of course you think they're good, but I'm not going to go." And she said a line that I'll always remember. She said, "would you please waste a half hour of your life?" You can't really say no to that. So I packed my little bag and I went. That changed my life also, because Frank kept me there all afternoon and said to tell my parents that he believed very strongly that I could make it in this business if I gave myself the chance. And I came home very starry-eyed and announced that this was what I was going to do. My father was not pleased at all. He thought I would starve somewhere in an attic. My mother was absolutely thrilled, because she was the musician in the family and she really stirred this whole thing up.

Along the way, while you were writing songs, did you study a lot of composers?

Yes, I went to see everything. I spent every penny that I made playing cocktail piano in nightclubs to see everything on Broadway, good or bad. I studied without realizing that I was studying, but every show taught me something. I was gathering up a world of knowledge just by experiencing these shows. I really gave myself a cram course in musical theatre. I read everything that was available, to find out about how musicals started in this country. Without going to class for it, I just sort of got more into it. My piano playing got more and more fluent, and my writing got much more sophisticated, much more interesting, which is natural.

Before your first big show, Milk and Honey, *were you writing pop songs?*

No, they were always revue material songs. They were always songs that were theatrical. I was never interested in pop songs, even though people laugh at me when I say that because so many of my songs became pop songs. But I didn't intend them to. I have never sat down and tried to write a *Billboard* chart song. My songs always came from characters or situations in plays. I really call myself a musical playwright, that's what I am. The fact that they come out sometimes as "Hello, Dolly!" or "Mame" is because I want to write for a mass audience. I purposely aim to write simply and melodically. That way, it's possible for people to take those songs, like the way Sammy Davis, Jr. took "It Only Takes A Moment" and it became a big song, and he didn't need to explain to his audience that this came from a courtroom scene in a musical. The song stood all by itself. But the answer to your question is that I've never sat down to write a pop song. I'd be a total failure if somebody said they wanted me to write a song for Madonna. I wouldn't know how. I had no idea "Hello, Dolly!" would become a popular song, because it was very 1890s to me.

Using Mame *as an example, can you talk about the first steps you take in writing a score for a show.*

I always try to go to the heart of the character so that I get a feeling and a sound that goes with the character. In *Mame*, the first song I wrote was "It's Today," because I thought it was her whole philosophy – that life was a party and you don't need a reason to throw a party. It just gave me the exuberance and madcap-but-sane juxtaposition of Mame's character. In *Hello, Dolly!*, the first song I wrote was "I Put My Hand In" because it was very garrulous to me, and the character never shuts up, so I wrote a song that just went on and on with practically no place to breathe. And that said Dolly Levi to me. So I always try to go for the character, something that will give me a hook. Then it gets easier. Once I get the musical idea for the first song or two, I'm usually flying and I can usually write faster than anyone in the business.

Do you tend to work from titles?

A title usually comes from a situation. One of the toughest songs I ever had to write was an anti-love song for Mack Sennett, because he's not a man who says "I love you." The idea of "I won't do all the things that you deserve to have done, so I'm warning you, you really should stay away from me, because I won't send roses." When I came up with that line of "I won't send roses," that song was written in twenty minutes. It was a great, joyous experience to write that song because it was an unusual ballad. Titles usually come from those central ideas. "If He Walked Into My Life" came from just the first lines of the song. I didn't sit down and say I'm going to write a song called "Hello, Dolly!" The first thing I wrote was "Hello Harry," after my father, then "Hello Manny," after my uncle. I just started working on the first chorus, where this woman is saying hello to these different men, and it doesn't have those words in it. But then of course, "Hello, Dolly!" was the natural thing for them to answer to her. I realized I had a title not only for the song but for the show. So I don't really work from titles. Titles come out of what I'm trying to do.

What do you think makes a great melody?

I think it's impossible to put it into words, or else I could teach everybody else to do it. Then I'd be in big trouble. I think when I write a melody, if it stays in my brain or if I find myself humming it in the shower and I can't get it out of my brain, I keep it. If I write a melody and that doesn't happen, I usually discard it. I still play "I Won't Send Roses" to amuse myself, so I consider that a successful melody. But I really can't define a great melody. There isn't a secret or formula, because as you can tell from my work, I've written Hebraic melodies, minor key melodies, very Frenchy things, 1890s things. *Milk And Honey* doesn't sound like it was written by the same man who wrote *Hello, Dolly!* I think that's been one of my strengths, but it's also not given people a good strong idea of what my style is.

One of my favorite lyrics of yours is "I Wanna Make The World Laugh" from Mack & Mabel. The rhymes are really brilliant and effortless. How do you approach that kind of writing?

Again, that came from the idea of trying to explain to the audience what this man was all about. Making the world laugh was more important to Mack Sennett than loving this woman, and so it was a very important statement. I just came up with this real razzmatazz show business melody and then I thought about all the things that Sennett did in his movies: the car chases, the slapstick, the fly on the nose. I tried to conjure up all these things. I find that I've written a lot of my lyrics once I have a melody formed in my head so I have something to attach them to. The rhyme scheme of that song came to me while I was walking. I write a lot of my lyrics while walking. I walked the streets of New York for forty years, and I loved writing while walking because ideas would just pop into my head.

When you're between shows, how do you keep your chops in shape?

I sometimes do little exercises. I wrote a song for the character Lenny in *Of Mice And Men* with no idea and no desire to musicalize the whole piece. I just thought, gee, this is a lovely character to write a song for and I wrote a song. It's just in my trunk and no one will ever hear it. So I do that or I experiment. I play a lot of other people's material – everything from Sondheim to Berlin, the whole gamut. I love Kander and Ebb. I become a fan of the musical theatre when I'm not working and I play other people's stuff. I have another hobby too, which is buying and redesigning houses. That hobby keeps me interested because it's also artistic and creative. It's very similar in a way. It's getting hundreds of diverse elements together and creating a whole, which is the finished house with the green sofa and the this-and-that, the chandelier that goes with it. A show is that same thing. You take thousands of diverse elements and you get into costumes and orchestrations, and it either comes out to be one piece like *Hello, Dolly!* or *Mame* or it comes out to be kind of confused, which one or two of my shows have been. They're very similar arts I think and I'm very grateful that I have both in my life.

Can you comment on the current state of the Broadway musical?

Not without depressing both of us. I think it's obvious that it's in deep trouble. It's in deep trouble for about 20 different reasons. First, financial. It's just too expensive. My first musical cost $300,000 and was a sumptuous show, filled with Howard Bay sets, Miles White costumes, and Hershy Kay orchestrations. It was the works and it cost $300,000. I know that people will say, "Well, lettuce was cheaper then too," but the difference between $6.60 and $75 changes the entire perspective of who's going to go to the theatre and how often. My parents, if they were going today, couldn't go every Friday night. Not for $150. The theatre today has to be an event, and that's what I think is the saddest part of the state of our theatre. People only go on an anniversary, or go to a very special event like if a *Phantom Of The Opera* opens and everybody's talking about it. They'll order tickets six months from today, and they'll wait and look forward to it. When I was growing up, going to the theater was like what we do today in going to the movies. It cost exactly the same thing. That's the biggest change.

Also, music has changed totally. There was a time when all the recording artists waited for the new score, for the demo record of *South Pacific* or whatever, then everybody would record their versions. That doesn't exist today at all. We sent out demo records of the songs from *Hello, Dolly!* and Eydie Gorme did "If He Walked Into My Life" and won a Grammy for it. And I have to say, that with all the great talents involved in that show, Louis Armstrong gave the show the biggest kick, just took it over the moon. And who would've dreamed that a jazz musician would've taken an 1890s production number and made a hit out of it. That's a phenomenon. But that doesn't happen today. It's just that musical theatre has become less and less a medium for the public. It has a very esoteric group of people that follow it.

What's the best advice you've ever been given as a songwriter?

I think Frank Loesser, in that wild afternoon I described to you, gave me the best advice. He drew me a picture of a freight train, using different colored crayons that he had on his desk. And he explained that a song to him has to have a great engine, a great locomotive that pushes it. And then it has to have a caboose, a colorful red caboose with a twist or something that ends that song in an unusual way. Then the cars in the middle are the filler. It was a wonderful, child-like lesson, but it's very good advice. I can't tell you how many songs don't do that, don't give you a beginning, a middle and an end, and don't surprise you along the way. Frank drew different colored cars to show that there could be surprises along the way. He was a fascinating, charming man and I'll never forget that lesson.

Richard and Robert Sherman

Super-cali-fragil-istic-expi-ali-docious
✯ It's A Small World (After All) ✯ You're Sixteen

Interview conducted in 1992

"We don't think of them as little stuffed teddy bears, we think of them as personalities."

During the 1960s and early 1970s, Richard and Robert Sherman, two brothers working as top staffers at Disney studios, wrote classic songs such as "Super-cali-fragil-istic-expi-ali-docious," "Chim Chim Cheree," "A Spoonful Of Sugar," "I Wan'na Be Like You," "Let's Get Together" and "The Age Of Not Believing" for much-loved family films including *Mary Poppins*, *Jungle Book*, *The Parent Trap*, *Winnie The Pooh*, *The Absent Minded Professor*, *The Sword In The Stone*, *The Happiest Millionaire*, *Bedknobs And Broomsticks*, *The Aristocats*, *That Darn Cat*, and *The Monkey's Uncle*.

Encouraged by their father, Al Sherman, a composer who made his mark in the Tin Pan Alley days, Richard and Robert began collaborating in the early 1950s. Despite having a well-known father and some connections, the brothers toiled in obscurity, learning their craft and getting used to the sound of doors being shut in their faces. Then, in the early days of rock'n'roll, they scored with hit singles such as Johnny Burnette's "You're Sixteen" (successfully revived by Ringo Starr in the 70s) and Fabian's "Got The Feeling."

In 1958, after the Shermans penned a ditty called "Tall Paul" for everybody's favorite Mouseketeer, Annette Funicello, destiny stepped in courtesy of Mr. Family Entertainment himself, Walt Disney. Pleased with the talents and upbeat attitudes of the siblings, Disney hired them to write music and lyrics for all things Disney over the next decade. This included not only the aforementioned films but music for Disneyland and Disney World attractions (such as the ubiquitous "It's A Small World," which has been called the most translated and performed song on earth), as well as songs for Disney TV shows. Their association with Disney continued into the 1980s, when they wrote two songs for the opening of Epcot Center.

Along the way, the Shermans also wrote songs for many successful non-Disney films, including *Chitty Chitty Bang Bang*, *Snoopy Come Home*, *Charlotte's Web*, *Tom Sawyer* and *The Magic Of Lassie*.

With a multitude of gold records, Grammy Awards, and Academy Awards, the two brothers, who prefer to be called Dick and Bob, could comfortably rest on their supercalifragilistic laurels, but instead, their love of songwriting propels them onward.

What attracted you to music and songwriting initially?

Dick: I think it was something in both the environment and the genes, because our dad, Al Sherman, was a wonderful songwriter, and he wrote some great hits in the 1920s and 1930s like "Now's The Time To Fall In Love," "You've Got To Be A Football Hero" and many, many others. Music was in the family. My mother was an actress, but she played piano beautifully, classical piano. Dad was always playing his pop songs and beautiful melodies.

How would you describe your first songs?

Bob: Trite. Either they were trite or a little too esoteric, a little too clever with inner rhymes and things. Our dad had a secret for writing songs. He said, "You've got to have them simple, singable and sincere." He called them the "Three S's."

D: You can add to that original and inventive. I think those are the things that make songs. The "simple, singable, sincere" within the realm of creative, inventive and original. Those things have to be part of it.

34

B: Soon, we learned that a song has three parts. The music, the lyrics, and the most important part, the idea. Everything revolves around the idea.

D: That's the hinge upon which the door swings. Usually it's either a great title or a concept, a reason for the song to be written. So many times our songs have novel ideas behind them. Sometimes there's stuff that you don't expect. One of our early pop songs, for example, was a little play on words called "Pineapple Princess" [a 1960 hit for Annette Funicello]. It's a nice little sound. It was the first time a Hawaiian song was done to a samba beat. Nobody had ever done that. Another thing, "You're Sixteen," was a 1935 shuffle beat, like "Shuffle Off To Buffalo." We thought, nobody's done this in 30 years. It hadn't been done in rock songs.

When you were writing pop and rock'n'roll songs like "You're Sixteen," did you feel like you'd found your niche?

D: You know, in those days we were just trying to make a dollar. We were doing the best we could and we got lucky with a wonderful little girl named Annette Funicello. She was 15 years old, she had five months to go on her Disney contract and they were looking around for some material she could sing for the pop market. And a little song we wrote called "Tall Paul" came across the eye of a fellow called Mo Preskell in New York City, who was working for Disney. Annette made this record and it was tremendously successful, and the guys who ran the record company were wonderful. They called us and asked for more material for Annette. Nobody had ever asked us for a song in our entire lives. It was ten years of writing pop music and all we'd ever heard people say was, "No, we don't need that; thanks very much, but no."

B: Anyway, to make a long story short, we started writing songs for Annette. In fact, we wrote 35 songs for her over seven years – from "Tall Paul" to "The Monkey's Uncle" [a 1964 recording on which she was accompanied by The Beach Boys]. Then Walt Disney said, "Who are these two brothers that are writing songs for Annette? She's going to England to do *The Horsemasters*, maybe we can get them to write a song for us." So they told us on the telephone they wanted a song for a girl who was learning how to ride a horse.

35

D: And she was singing in a rec hall at the end of the day and they said, "Write a little song for kids who are coming together from all over the world to learn horsemanship." So we wrote a song called "Strummin' Song." And we brought it into Walt's office . . .

B: And the first thing he said was, "Now these two sisters have never met. They're twins and they meet in summer camp." And we looked at each other kind of puzzled and said, "Look, Mr. Disney, we brought a song here for Annette Funicello."

D: Boy, was he ticked. He was describing *The Parent Trap*, which we knew nothing about. All we knew was that here was a living legend who we'd met for the first time who was ticked as hell because we came in with the wrong song.

B: Anyway, after we demonstrated our song for him, he said, "Yeah, that'll work." We didn't know at the time that that was the nicest thing that Walt Disney ever said about anything [laughs]. That was his way of complimenting you.

D: Then he said, "Now that I've wasted a lot of time on these other things, I want you to take this script home and see if you can find some song spots." He handed us a script called "We Belong Together," which was the working title of *The Parent Trap*. We took it home and we wrote a ballad called "For Now, For Always." We brought it in to him and he said, "Yeah, that'll work, but that's not the name of the picture. We can use that in a certain sequence, but we need a song where the kids are hinting to the parents."

B: We had a great title called "Let's Get Together." He said, "That'll work, but that's not the name of my picture."

D: We put that into the picture and Hayley Mills had a huge hit with it. By the way, the "Yeah, yeah, yeah" was before The Beatles did "She loves you, yeah, yeah, yeah." But we wound up writing four songs for *The Parent Trap* and we were off and running.

How did you get involved with Mary Poppins?

B: Walt said one day, "Do you know what a nanny is?" And we said, "Sure, a goat." He said, "You read this book and give me your ideas on it."

D: And that book was *Mary Poppins*. We read it and got very excited. We thought we could do a couple of things to make the book work a little better. First of all, there was no story line at all, so we took about six chapters that we thought were really juicy ones, the ones with the most colorful stories and characters, and we wove a little tentative story, and we changed the period. It was written in the mid-30s, a depressed time. We changed the period to 1910, which gave it a lot of color and sort of took away that veil of disbelief, so you could actually start believing that a nanny would fly in on a west wind. We got our actual invite to become staff members at Disney the day we brought in our outline and six song sketches. Walt liked our songs and our idea for the story. He pulled out his copy of the book and he had underlined the same six chapters that we had. That's when he said, "How'd you like to work here?" And we found ourselves under contract. We were there for a very happy eight-year period and we've had a connection with Disney for the past 30 years.

What's the story behind "Super-cali-fragil-istic-expi-ali-docious"?

D: We drew from our childhood. As kids, we were in summer camp in the Adirondack Mountains in New York state. And there was a contest in our camp. Anybody who could say "antidisestablishmentarianism" was a super-genius. But if you could make a bigger word than that you were a super super-genius. Years and years later, when we were working on *Poppins*, we said, "Let's get the children in the story a souvenir from the chalk drawing experience – something they can take with them that will make them feel good." We remembered the crazy word contest and we thought, "Let's make a really atrocious word." And then we thought, "Well we can be real precocious if we were atrocious and that rhymes with docious, so we can have a super word ending in docious. We put in the "califragilistic" in the middle and added the "expiali."

From the same movie, what about "Chim Chim Cheree"? It's such a lovely melody. Almost like an ethnic folk song.

D: We wanted it to have a folky quality, but originally the harmonics in it were not quite as sophisticated. To be specific, it has a downward chromatic movement, a shifting major-minor sound. Then we started playing with the word "chimney" - breaking it up. We had the music and it was very heavy, almost with a middle eastern sound, and both of us started disliking it. It was a straight minor. We thought, "We've got to lighten this thing up. It's English, it isn't Russian." So we were thinking and thinking and then we reharmonized it, and that's when the chromatic downward movement started in the harmony. All of a sudden the song came to life. Another thing happened. There's only sixteen bars of music. We had to have more than that – maybe a bridge, a different phrase. We were constantly tortured about that, but then we thought, "Maybe a folk song is about repetition." So what we did was change the treatment, so sometimes it's a recitative, sometimes it's sung. The lyrics change every time around. It became a running theme in the movie, taking on different guises.

One of the wonderful things about your songs is that they reach both kids and adults without shortchanging either.

D: Bob and I have never written down to kids. We've always written up to kids. We want them, if they're curious like we were, to find out what things mean. Or if there was a double meaning within a statement, let the parent get it on one level and the let the kid get it on a second level. We write for family audiences, that's our thing. We try to write with a broad spectrum of meaning. You can listen to "Feed The Birds, Tuppence A Bag" and one person will say, "Oh, it's a guy that's trying to make a pitch to buy breadcrumbs and feed pigeons with them." And somebody else might say, "Oh maybe it's more a song about being kind and giving a little love to people that need it." There's a double way of looking at it.

What was the most difficult assignment you ever had at Disney?

D: I think the pressure that we were put under at the time when Disney was doing the World's Fair.

B: We were invited by Walt to go down to a factory in Glendale where they made all the rides and things, and we walked through a mock-up of a ride called Children Of The World, and they played music – kids from all over the world singing their national anthems. These were the animatronic dolls singing and it was a mess, one horrible cacophony. Walt said, "You see our problem. We have the World's Fair pretty soon and we need a song that can be sung in every language."

D: So we wrote a little song that was too simple. It was very sweet, a nice little song, but we were writing it under terrible pressure because they kept calling to ask if we had anything written yet.

B: Then we wrote a song that was too sophisticated.

D: Then we wrote a very pretty ballad that we thought would be nice . . .

B: Then Walt's secretary said Walt was coming down to our office and he wants a song now.

D: We heard him hacking and coughing down the corridor, coming towards us and we both looked at each other and said, "Let's do the simple one." It was "It's A Small World." And what did Walt say? "That'll work." That was a tough assignment because it had to be simple and translatable, and yet it had to be repeated so often over a fourteen minute ride that it couldn't be boring – that was the counterpoint. It had to be malleable so it could be played with a Latin beat, it could be played with little Dutch shoes clicking to it, it could be played in a little French march.

Tell me about Jungle Book. *Did you know that you were writing "I Wan'na Be Like You" for Louis Prima?*

D: No, we didn't know that Louis was going to be the voice. We wanted to write a song for a swinger, make a comedy song about the king of the apes, the king of the swingers. The whole idea was to do a Dixieland jazz, scat-singing song, and we came up with "I Wan'na Be Like You." At a certain point, after we were demonstrating this song in the story conferences, the idea of who will do it came up. Louis Prima and Sam Butera and the Witnesses were holding court at that time down in Las Vegas, so we thought, "If he would go for this, it would be great."

B: So we went down there and we played it for them, and they had very serious looks on their faces and when it was over, Louis said, "You want to make a monkey out of me? Well then, you got me!"[laughs]

D: These guys were so marvelous. On stage, they were the wildest thing you've ever seen, jumping around. Louis Prima was magnificent; he was all over the place. In fact, when we recorded the song on the soundstage, the Disney animators came down and filmed them in black and white so they could get their movements, and they included a lot of the movements that the musicians were doing in the monkey sequence.

When you write for an animated picture, are you aware ahead of time what all the characters look like and sound like?

D: Many times, they do give you sketches. The artists have already conceived the character personalities visually. We don't know what their voices are but we do know the physical precepts. Like with Winnie the Pooh, we knew he was a little stuffed Teddy Bear and we knew that Tigger was a stuffed tiger that bounced around a lot. So you could sort of feel them . . .

B: But we don't think of them as little stuffed Teddy Bears, we think of them as personalities. We write for them the same as we write for anybody.

D: Oh yeah, they have feelings, they have emotions, they have heart, they love, they're afraid. They're just as real to us as if we were writing for a live actor.

In between projects, what kinds of things do you guys do to stay in touch with your creativity?

D: We just let the muse sort of nurture itself. We've been writing for so long that when an assignment comes along or we have something we want to work on, the juices start flowing again.

B: We don't have to keep in touch with it, it keeps in touch with us.

What's your definition of a great song?

D: Bob and I are from the old school. We believe that a great song can be sung by one guy or one gal with a guitar or a piano. You don't need to have all this synthetic crap to make it sound like something. There was an album that came out a few years back called *Stay Awake*, which was the title of a song we wrote for *Mary Poppins*. And Suzanne Vega sang it a cappella and to me that was a big compliment. It takes two things, a great melody and a great lyric. Then you put it together with a great singer. You don't need all this hogwash to make it happen.

What advice would you give to a songwriter who wants to write for the movies?

D: You have to write what's right for the situation or character. You have to write the best that you possibly can every time out of the box. You always try to be original, and try to be different than the next guy. The same cliched phrases, you hear them so often. Don't do that. Do something different that's your own thing. You have to keep trying. The harder you try, the luckier you'll get.

Alan and
Marilyn Bergman

The Way We Were ☆ You Don't Bring Me Flowers
☆ The Windmills Of Your Mind

Interview conducted in 1995

"The world

certainly

doesn't need

one more

song...unless

you can find

an original

way of saying

something."

From the stage of the Tennessee Performing Arts Center, renowned husband and wife lyric writing team Alan and Marilyn Bergman have the audience entranced. Neither one is what you'd call a glitzy star performer. Nor are they dynamic vocalists. Instead, their magic comes from a genuine, self-effacing charm and a catalog of some of the best-loved American standards from the past 40 years.

Tonight, those award-winning beauties are on parade – finger-snapping swingers, rich emotional ballads, and movie themes, all speaking to the heart and mind: "Nice And Easy," "The Way We Were," "The Windmills Of Your Mind," "How Do You Keep The Music Playing?" "What Are You Doing The Rest Of Your Life?" "You Don't Bring Me Flowers," "It Might Be You" and more. These songs have earned the Bergmans three Academy Awards, three Emmys, two Grammys, cuts by Barbra Streisand, Frank Sinatra, Tony Bennett, Dusty Springfield, Neil Diamond, and countless others, and a permanent place in the pantheon of great American songwriters.

43

In the late 1950s, while working with the same composer, Alan and Marilyn met, fell in love and married. After penning lyrics to children's songs, material for TV variety shows, and a hit for Sinatra ("Nice And Easy"), Alan and Marilyn were asked to write songs with Quincy Jones for *In The Heat Of The Night*. That began their long and fruitful association with the world of motion pictures. Collaborating with composers such as Henry Mancini, Marvin Hamlisch, Dave Grusin, Michel LeGrand and John Williams, the Bergmans contributed songs to numerous films, including *The Thomas Crown Affair, The Way We Were*, *Tootsie, Best Friends*, *Yentl* and more recently, *Sabrina* (which included the Grammy-nominated "Moonlight," performed by Sting).

Were there specific events that led both of you to want to write songs?

Alan: Yes, my folks took me at a very early age to a Broadway show and I was mesmerized. It was *Porgy And Bess*, and it was just terrific. I saw a lot of the early shows by Irving Berlin, Cole Porter, and Rodgers & Hart. Then I remember one of the first pieces of sheet music I got was "Lost," by Johnny Mercer. By then, I'd decided to become a songwriter.

Marilyn: I was always a music student. I think I started taking piano lessons and studying music when I was about six. All through those early years, my prime extracurricular activity was music and I went to a special high school in New York for music and art. By the time I finished high school I realized I would never be good enough or disciplined enough to be a classical pianist and make that a life's work. So I became pre-med and kind of flitted from department to department. Then by accident, I fell down a flight of stairs and I broke my shoulders and I had to come to California where my parents had moved during my college years. The only friends I had in California were a lyric writer and his family. Bob Russell was his name. I was in a body cast and didn't know what to do with four months of my life, so he said, "Why don't you write songs?" I said, "How can I play the piano, I can't even turn the pages of a book." He said, "Well then, talk lyrics into a cassette player." So I did. And the very first song that I wrote with some young composer that he put me together with was recorded by Peggy Lee two days after I wrote it. And I thought, "Wow, this is like taking candy from a baby." So, I was a lyric writer. I've often thought if I'd broken my legs, I might've written tunes.

Alan, what kinds of things did you have to do to get your foot in the door?

A: I was very lucky. I also studied music from a young age and I was a music major in college. In high school I wrote a couple of shows for the drama department, and then in college I wrote a show. When I got out of college, I met Johnny Mercer. I was writing both music and lyrics in those days, and he took a liking to me and kind of became a mentor. For about three years, he listened to what I was writing and he'd criticize it, but also be very encouraging. In order to support my songwriting habit, I was a television director for two years. I got a job writing music and lyrics for a big variety show on television, then the following year I met Marilyn and we started to write together. We were very lucky that in 1958 there was a big Calypso craze in this country. With Norman Luboff, who had a very successful choir with Columbia Records, we wrote eleven Calypso songs for his *Calypso Holiday* album. But the biggest break was when we wrote the title song for a movie called *Nice And Easy*.

Did you know you were writing that song for Sinatra?

M: Yes. They asked for a title song for an album of rhythmic love songs, lightly swinging songs.

What would you say are the advantages of being husband and wife and co-writers?

M: We don't have to waste time with all kinds of disclaimers. You know, when two people sit together in a room to write, in order to be productive, you have to almost free associate with each other, you have to throw out whatever comes into your mind and not worry whether it sounds stupid or not. Because sometimes through a series of stupid things, it's distilled down to what becomes a good idea. So we don't have to worry about sounding stupid in front of each other. And also, the element of trust and respect in a collaboration is very similar to the trust and respect you get in a marriage.

Have there been times when there have been difficulties, when you can't leave the lyric writing behind?

M: I'm able to stop when I stop. Alan carries it around with him a little bit more. I look over at him every once in a while when we're watching television or something and I see that look on his face and

I know he's working. He'll come back from the tennis court and I'll know that while he was on the court he was working. I'm able to turn it off.

When a composer gives you a melody, what are the first things you do to set lyrics to it?

M: We've always felt that a good melody has words on the tips of the notes. You know, Michelangelo talked about starting with a block of marble, and that his job was to keep chipping away to release the form that was inside the marble. I think that when we're fortunate enough to get the kind of music that we get from people like Michel LeGrand and Dave Grusin and Marvin Hamlisch and John Williams and all these extremely talented composers, that we're turned on by the music and if we listen to it and internalize the piece of music, more often than not, we'll get an idea. The music will say something to us and then once we get the idea, it's a matter of craft, and inviting the muse to stay a little longer in the room.

In those early stages when you're tossing ideas around, is it important for you to find a title?

A: No. If you hear some of the songs, in a lot of cases, it's the first line, then we'll repeat it and that's what we call the song.

Tell me about "The Windmills Of Your Mind."

A: That was written in the context of a movie, *The Thomas Crown Affair*. There was a scene in the picture where Steve McQueen was flying a glider and he had just masterminded the robbery of a bank, and flying gliders was what he did as a hobby. During this scene, you could see that he was very anxious and grim, and the director, Norman Jewison, shot the sequence knowing he wanted a song. He said, "I would like you to write a song that underlies the anxiety the character is feeling." He played us the temp track [a temporary piece of music that indicates the general feel of what the director wants].

M: In this case, Norman had put in "Strawberry Fields Forever." He said, "I don't know why this feels right to me, but something about it does." Clearly, what felt right about it to him was that it was some kind of mind trip, some restless thing going on in this guy's head that he couldn't turn off.

This was the first picture song that we wrote with Michel LeGrand. He was staying with us at our house and I remember he wrote about eight melodies. It's like turning on a faucet with him. Each melody was different from the next and they were all very interesting and good. None of the three of us could decide which was the right melody, so we decided to sleep on it. The next morning, we all came to the breakfast table having all decided on the same melody, which would've been the least likely, because the picture was kind of jazzy and used split-screen techniques and multiple images and it was very angular. What we selected was this kind of baroque, long ribbon of a melody which was more related to the glider, I think, than the movie. When we got through with the lyric, we didn't know what to call it, and the line "the windmills of your mind" only appeared once. When we looked at the song, we said, "That's an interesting phrase, let's see if we can plant it one or two more times."

How about "The Way We Were"?

M: Sydney Pollack came to us and showed us this wonderful script and said that he needed a song prior to shooting the movie, because there was a scene early on in the picture where he wanted the melody established coming from a dance band. So he had Marvin Hamlisch write the melody, and if you listen carefully to the picture, the melody that's played by the dance band is not exactly the same as the song melody. There are one or two notes that are different that became altered during the writing. So we wrote the song with Marvin, then played it for Sydney and Barbra and the other producers and they loved it.

"It Might Be You"

A: Well, on *Tootsie*, we were again working with Sydney Pollack, who knows about music and its relation to images. There's that scene where Dustin Hoffman looks at the baby and at Jessica Lange and she's cooking, and he's wishing he could tell her he was really a man.

M: Also it's a guy who, clearly from his relationship with the Terri Garr character, could never make a commitment. Because the song is all iffy, with all the mights and ifs, you know that this guy is getting ready to make a commitment.

47

With both of you having been in the business for years, what kind of perspective can you offer between how it is now for a songwriter and how it was then?

M: I think it's easier now. It seems to me that when we began writing, the places where one could go with your music were limited for non-established writers. The doors were not open as wide as they are now. I think that now, people don't know where the next sensation is coming from. I know that in music and in film, they're much more receptive to new faces and new names than they were then. The audiences are becoming younger and younger, and the tastes are becoming less establishment. So from that standpoint, I think it's easier. It's probably more difficult in the sense that there's such a glut of product. Unless something sticks to the wall right away, it just fades very quickly.

A: Also, when we started our career, there were many more interpreters of songs. Today, you have mostly performing songwriters, singing their own songs. That makes it more difficult for people like us, who write songs for other people. It's a vanishing breed, song interpreters.

What would you say, at this point in your careers, are the recurring obstacles for you as songwriters?

M: One of the things that we have to look out for is complexity. We have to watch that songs don't tip over into being art songs – which are fine, and we love to write them, very often just for pleasure. But if you're writing for a film or trying for a hit record, I think you have to keep in mind who the audience is. There's a line in "How Do You Keep The Music Playing?" that says, "How do you think of new things to say?" That's the thing. I've often thought, what the world certainly doesn't need is one more song. Unless you can find an original way of saying something. Most songs are love songs of one kind or another. But to find that variation that maybe is a little different than all the literature has dealt with, that's the challenge. To not repeat what came before you, which is why you have to know what came before you, I think.

What do you think about the freedom of language in today's lyrics?

M: I think it's great. The whole freedom that songwriters have now that we didn't have when we were starting out is wonderful. They can write about anything and express it almost in an unlimited fashion.

People were kind of gasping the night of the Grammys when Alanis Morissette sang her song with some of the profanity in it. And I thought, what are they carrying on about? Why is it all right in movies and in television but it's not okay in a popular song? I don't see anything wrong with it. If you don't like it, don't listen to it. But these new women – Joan Osborne, Alanis Morissette – I find great. It's not only the language that's becoming more free, but the form and the structure is opening up, too.

Marvin Hamlisch

What I Did For Love ☆ The Way We Were
☆ Nobody Does It Better

Interview conducted in 1995

"If 'The Way

We Were'

hadn't come

from a movie,

and Barbra

Streisand

hadn't sung it,

it would have

been a great

song that no

one ever

heard."

Scoring movie soundtracks, writing Broadway musicals, penning Top 40 pop hits, conducting and composing full classical symphonies for orchestras, accompanying Liza Minelli, Barbra Streisand and Groucho Marx – you name it, Marvin Hamlisch has done it.

Hamlisch's film scores include *Save The Tiger*, *The Sting*, *Ice Castles* and *Sophie's Choice*. He's written chart-topping hits such as "Nobody Does It Better" and "The Way We Were." Perhaps his most-acclaimed achievement was writing (with lyricist Ed Kleban) the score for the long-running musical hit *A Chorus Line*. Two of the songs from that show, "One" and "What I Did For Love," have entered the rarefied world of Broadway standards.

Hamlisch was born on June 2, 1944 in New York City. At seven, he became the youngest ever student at Julliard School of Music. But while he was studying Bach and Beethoven, he discovered he had a talent for making up his own songs. In time, he came to prefer the fun and creativity of songwriting to the intense classical piano competitions that used to wrack his nerves.

Encouraged by his first hit, Lesley Gore's "Sunshine, Lollipops And Rainbows," written when he was 20 years old, Hamlisch turned to composing full-time and soon found himself in Hollywood, where his first assignments included scoring the early Woody Allen films *Take The Money And Run* and *Bananas*.

In 1974, Hamlisch became a household name when his adaptation of Scott Joplin's ragtime material for *The Sting* yielded a million-selling hit, "The Entertainer." A year later, he swept the Grammys and the Academy Awards with "The Way We Were," a song he co-wrote with frequent collaborators Marilyn and Alan Bergman. More success followed with movie scores and the Broadway shows *A Chorus Line* and *They're Playing Our Song* (the latter written with his then-companion Carole Bayer Sager).

While Hamlisch hasn't repeated the incredible success he enjoyed in the 70s (two of his more recent musicals, *Smile* and *The Goodbye Girl*, were, despite well-written scores, fraught with difficulties), he has continued to grow and challenge himself as a musician. I caught up with him after he conducted a special Rodgers & Hammerstein concert with the Pittsburgh Symphony.

Were there specific events early in your life that made you want to write songs?

I don't know if there was an event per se, but when I used to go to the piano as a very young child, about five or six, for some reason, even though I was taking piano lessons, learning the basics of Bach and Beethoven, I did enjoy making up songs. I remember the first song that I wrote when I was seven years old. It was called "Billy Boy." I know that as the years progressed, there were two reasons that I liked writing. First of all, I loved the idea that you wrote it and then someone else interpreted it. Also, I was very nervous when I had to perform Bach and Beethoven, and I wasn't nervous at all when I was writing, so it was a very great way to cure any nerves that I had. In fact, the whole process of writing has always been the most enjoyable process for me.

What kinds of things did you do to learn how to write songs?

I've never really taken a composition course. The one I did take at Julliard was more a course about writing serious-type music. I think that the fastest way to learn how to write songs comes from your enjoyment of listening to songs, because I think that as you listen to songs and you hear all the great ones, you absorb it. I had a job as a rehearsal pianist for a very famous television show years ago called *The Bell Telephone Hour*, so I was really open to a lot of different kinds of music. I think for songwriters particularly, it's important to know what repertoire existed before you, and to get a sense of melodic structure. It's hard for me to talk about songwriting, because most of the songs that I find to be not very enjoyable or not very good or whatever, usually are hits. I find that what I love about songwriting is not necessarily the most successful thing. Of course, there's a big difference between writing a one-off song and a show. I consider myself much more a person who writes in context for a show, and that's a whole different way of writing. But for the normal 32-bar song, in today's market, I think it's very important to listen to a lot of music and try to think what artist it is that you really like a lot, so you can write with someone in mind. I think that always helps. Whether or not you get that artist to record the song, I think it's very good to write a song with someone in mind.

I've read that when you begin a song, you like to start with a rhythm. Can you elaborate on that?

What I like to begin with really is a title, or an idea for a song. It's hard for me to just sit down at the piano and noodle along and come up with something. But when you are given a gift of a title like "The Way We Were," which is such a great title, you're off and running. Certain titles are just very, very strong. Sometimes a lyricist might have an idea for a song, maybe they don't have a title but they have a feel for it. So I like to do it that way. I also work best if the lyricist and I are in the room together.

Using They're Playing Our Song *as an example, can you describe the first steps you take when writing a musical?*

I think the most important advice I can give someone – because I've made this mistake – is if you're going to write a musical, it's very important that you absolutely love that musical. And that the reason you're writing it is because you really love it, as opposed to writing it because you have a possibility of getting it on. There are a lot of people around who can get things on. There aren't that many who can love what they're getting on. So if you're going to have to make a decision one way or the other, go for the one that says "I love doing this and I must get this out of my system," as opposed to "I'm not really crazy about this, but they've got the millions of dollars for it, so we might as well do it." In the case of *They're Playing Our Song*, it was a situation in which we had Neil Simon and a very funny book. Carole [Bayer Sager] and I basically tended to write a song almost every weekend, and we would think almost chronologically. We started with the first song and went on. That was probably the easiest show I've ever written in my life, but I didn't have the sort of total commitment and love of it that I had for *A Chorus Line*. Though, having said that, so many people come up to me all the time and tell me how much they loved *They're Playing Our Song*.

Tell me about writing A Chorus Line.

I was very blessed on *Chorus Line* with a lot of things. First of all, I knew that Michael Bennett was a genius, so I felt very confident. If you walk in and you know the director is brilliant, you figure to yourself, if I make a mistake, he'll tell me I made a mistake and he'll get me back on track. Number two, he put me with a brilliant lyricist that I really adored. That's a very important thing. I think you have to like the person who writes the lyrics, not just like his work, but genuinely like him. That was a very character-driven show. It wasn't written in the normal way where you write everything then come to rehearsal. We went into rehearsal with maybe one song, and as the show was put into workshop, we just kept coming up with new ideas for it.

I recently spoke to Jerry Herman and he talked about trying to capture the sense of a character musically.

Absolutely. I think that's something that show composers do innately. If you ask a costume designer what they do first, they tend to think, where's the setting, what's the period of the piece, then they get all the books about Paris 1930 or whatever, and that's how they see it. In a way, that's what composers do. They have to dress their characters in the musical language of the period. It's trying to get a certain rhythm of the characters so that when you go in and out of dialogue, you don't feel like two people have sung as opposed to one. It's a continuum. One thing that's happened that's a big difference between the shows of today and the shows of before, whether it was *Carousel, Oklahoma,* or *My Fair Lady,* is the importance that was placed on the music and the lyrics. There's been a total change, and it's not a change for the better, whereby now the book of the musical has become much more important than the score. A show can now come out with a book that people care about, but with a so-so score and it will be a big hit. But a show that comes out with a wonderful score and a so-so book, I don't believe is going to be a hit.

Why is that?

People care much more about the characters in these shows. They care about whether there's a song they can take away from the theatre, but if there's not, it's forgiven.

What do you think makes one of those melodies that people can take away from the theatre?

I think there are two things. Most good melodies have a certain yearning quality to them and a certain leap towards something. They tend to be melodies that look upward and try hard. They keep searching. But I also think there's a magic between a good song and the person who does it. "Some Enchanted Evening" – when Ezio Pinza did that, it was perfection. As much as I love "The Way We Were," and I think it's a great song, I truly believe that if it hadn't come from a movie and Barbra Streisand hadn't sung it, it would've been a great song that no one ever heard. There's a marriage between song and performer. A good song doesn't necessarily mean that you're going to hear it. It just means it's a good song. I sometimes go to clubs to listen to singers. Someone like Barbara Cook, she picks out great songs, half of which I've never heard. So the criteria's not always if it's a great song, but if it's an accessible song. Is it something that someone can hear just once or twice and go, "God I want to hear that again"?

If a songwriter wanted to improve his melody writing, what kind of advice would you give?

I think the best way to get better is to somehow get into a workshop, be it ASCAP or BMI. I'll tell you why. The best thing that can happen to a songwriter is to hear the song sung by somebody else. When a songwriter finally sits down and writes a melody, and the lyricist says, gee, this is great, and his mother says, oh this is great, and they bring in the neighbors and they go, oh this is great. Now that's easy. But if you're in a class and you bring in a song, and then you have a professional or semi-professional singer sing your song, and you're sitting in the audience and you see how it goes – that's the quickest way to know what you're doing right and what you're doing wrong. For me, it was trial and error. I must've made about a hundred demonstration records of songs before anything even resembled a hit.

Were you trying to write in all different styles?

When I was young, I was writing everything that I thought would be a hit, which was based on whatever was number one at the time. Unfortunately that doesn't work, because you tend to be writing like somebody, but you're not writing yourself. It's like trying to write a Hemingway novel.

You know, these are very tough times for a composer. I don't want to give a rosy picture because number one, a lot of performers do their own songwriting, so that hurts most of the writers. Again, to circumvent that, you either have to write a show, or a theme for a movie, or a theme for a TV show. It's not so simple anymore. In the old days, it used to be you wrote a song, Sinatra recorded it, Tony Bennett covered it, Rosemary Clooney did a record of it – but that's a whole era that's gone. So I would say to someone who wants to be a songwriter, be sure you have another job in case this doesn't work out.

Does it worry you as a theatre composer to consider the state of the Broadway musical?

I think the Broadway musical is, at this moment, just about dead. I think we're now into this world of revivals. New shows are very difficult because unless they are brought in from England and have all that wonderful backing behind them, it's very tough. I hope to bring a new show to New York eventually that I think is really wonderful. I'm working on it now. Again, it will be one that I really care about. But I think that we're going through a very rough time. Most composers know that if they go to Hollywood and they're lucky enough to do a Disney animated film, they get tons more money and they won't go through the hell they have to go through in New York. Don't get me wrong, I adore Broadway. It's my favorite place in the world and I don't want to hang up my shoes until we at least do another show, but it is a very difficult process, and it's been made more difficult by the fact that these shows are so expensive. I'm talking about eight or nine million dollar investments.

Are there things you'd still like to accomplish as a songwriter?

I really want to accomplish a few things. I want to write another hit show. I want to accomplish some major compositions, perhaps even a ballet. But I enjoy what I'm doing now. I'm doing a lot of conducting with different orchestras. I'm the conductor with the Pittsburgh Pops Symphony. I like that, but I hope to be able to look back and say, oh, there was one that got into the top five.

Tim Rice

Don't Cry For Me, Argentina ✴ One Night In Bangkok
✴ Can You Feel The Love Tonight

Interview conducted in 1993

"You wouldn't

ordinarily

compare it

with a Cole

Porter gem,

but I think

'Blue Suede

Shoes' is a

great lyric."

A chess grandmaster, the flamboyant wife of a South American dictator, a wisecracking genie, and a messiah from Nazareth. What do these assorted characters have in common? They've all sung the distinct, memorable words of lyricist Tim Rice. With his gift for both the witty, sardonic turn of phrase and the heart-wrenching emotional lyric, Rice has successfully combined modern attitude with tradition.

The recipient of multiple Grammy and Tony Awards, Rice has enjoyed worldwide popularity ever since he and his composer/partner Andrew Lloyd Webber turned the musical theater world on its ear in the 1970s with ground-breaking shows like *Joseph And The Amazing Technicolor Dreamcoat*, *Jesus Christ Superstar* and *Evita*. The latter two yielded the worldwide hits "I Don't Know How To Love Him" and "Don't Cry For Me, Argentina."

In the 1980s, Rice joined composers Benny Andersson and Bjorn Ulvaeus of the pop group Abba to write *Chess*, a dramatic musical based on the Bobby Fischer-Boris Spassky matches. Two songs from that show, "One Night In Bangkok" and "I Know Him So Well," also became hits.

Rice has also enjoyed a very successful association with Disney. With Alan Menken, he wrote songs for the biggest animated feature of all-time, the Academy Award-winning *Aladdin*, including the smash hit, "A Whole New World." Rice collaborated with Elton John on the soundtrack for 1994's blockbuster, *The Lion King*, which produced the hits "Can You Feel The Love Tonight" and "The Circle Of Life." That partnership continued on Disney's feature-length animated version of *Aida*, which also became a hit Broadway show.

What made you decide to become a lyricist?

I don't know really. I was always interested in popular music, but I was not particularly gifted at writing the actual tunes. Even though I already had a couple of songs published and one recorded, for which I'd written the tune, when I met Andrew Lloyd Webber, I was more happy having a go at the words. Andrew was better at tunes, so it kind of set me concentrating on the lyrical side of things.

Did you know from the start that you wanted to write for the theatre?

No. I had no interest in theatre at all [laughs]. My interest was almost exclusively rock'n'roll and popular music. I didn't live in London and had hardly been to the theatre at all. It simply was not part of my life. My parents had several albums of great scores which I always enjoyed, but I never thought of actually going to the theatre. Maybe once a year we might go to a pantomime or a Christmas show.

On the early shows you wrote with Andrew Lloyd Webber, do you think that you approached your work more as a pop lyricist or a theatre lyricist?

The very first thing I wrote with Andrew was a show that never got performed. And that was a very conventional piece, rather like *Oliver*. It was not that original. I think when I stopped trying to imitate a form, which I didn't know much about anyway, we began to have success. With *Joseph*, *Superstar* and *Evita*, I wasn't consciously trying to fall into any pattern. I was just doing what I liked lyrically and what I thought I might like if someone else had done it. Obviously, there were influences from rock'n'roll and that end of things. But equally, I was trying to write something that would work in the theatre. I didn't really have a particular theatrical hero whom I was trying to follow. One of the reasons Andrew and I got lucky, I think, is that he was very much steeped in the theatre and I was more interested in rock'n'roll and records - that combination of experience and ignorance helped us to be original.

Can you think of a few lyricists who you admired then or admire now?

One was Jerry Leiber. Sammy Cahn, Alan Jay Lerner, W.S. Gilbert. There was a very good lyricist named Michael Flanders, an Englishman who wrote lots of comic songs. And another English writer called Paddy Roberts. I liked Tom Lehrer. I think from a very early age, I was always attracted to songs that had good lyrics. And to this day, if a song has a terrible lyric, however good the melody, I really can't get into it.

Could you describe your first steps when undertaking a project on the scale of something like Chess?

On that particular one, the very first step was to find a composer. In that instance, by chance, I heard that Bjorn and Benny of Abba were thinking of trying a musical and I was a great fan of their records. Through a mutual acquaintance, we were introduced and they became interested in the idea.

How much research did you do before you actually put pen to paper?

Quite a bit. I went to a world chess championship. I got to know several people in the world of chess - former players and commentators. I read some books about it and began to learn about characters like Fischer and Spassky and all that lot. I was very interested in it, so it wasn't very much of an ordeal.

From there, would you come up with an outline for the songs?

Yes, this is true with *Evita*, *Superstar* and *Joseph*. I would come up with an outline, a storyline that was the basic structure, then hope that each scene or each section would inspire a tune from the composer, which normally it did. The composer wouldn't necessarily know what the lyrics were going to be or even what the title was, but he would know what the song was going to have to say. So Bjorn and Benny in *Chess* would know that it was a comic song or a romantic ballad or a patriotic anthem or whatever. So they would write the right kind of tune. Obviously, sometimes we would say maybe that tune would work in a different place, or perhaps that tune isn't quite right. There's a lot of fine-tuning. The principle though is basically story-music-lyrics.

Most of your shows have begun life as recordings first.

Yes. On *Superstar* we discovered that was a very good way of getting a show on - to make a hit record first. We did it on *Evita*, and *Chess* as well. When you do it this way, and you get a hit, then it becomes hard for the most powerful director to say, "I'm sorry, we're going to make major alterations." You can tell him, "No, you can't, because the public knows the work as it is."

Do you prefer to work from titles?

Yes, I think if you get a good title, it's a great help. But I don't necessarily feel I have to give a good title to a composer. I often find that it's easier to come up with a title if you've got a great tune, because you're thinking perhaps in a rhythm that you wouldn't think otherwise. "Don't Cry For Me, Argentina," which turned out to be a very good title, emerged after the tune.

Did you expect that song to be the hit it was?

No, we certainly didn't. After the record was released, everybody said, "That's the one."

Did most of your writing with Andrew involve fitting lyrics to a melody?

Yes, every bit of it had the tune first. But before that, plot came.

Was it different with Benny and Bjorn?

No, we adopted pretty much the same procedure. The one that was different for me was working with Elton because he likes lyrics first. He likes virtually the complete song. I enjoyed that, because it gives you a bit more freedom.

What is the most difficult lyric that you've ever had to write?

The ballads and the love songs are always harder than the comic ones and the uptempo ones because your vocabulary is generally much more restricted. Some have taken a very long time. With the "Don't Cry For

Me, Argentina" melody, I got the "Oh What a Circus" lyric fairly quick. It took longer to write the ballad lyrics and even longer to come up with a title. The whole thing was written without a title. In fact, I'd already written the line "Don't cry for me, Argentina" in an earlier scene, the funeral scene. When it came to the scene with her on the balcony, we wanted to use the same melody, but it didn't seem to make sense saying "Don't cry for me, Argentina." Yet it fit perfectly. Once we actually put it in, it worked really well. By and large, most ballads and love songs are difficult because everything's been said a hundred ways before.

What makes a great lyric?

I don't know. It's like what makes a great picture. It somehow works. I think for me, first and foremost, it has to make sense. And it has to be unpretentious. I mean "Blue Suede Shoes" is a great lyric, beyond any shadow of a doubt. You wouldn't ordinarily compare it with, say, a Cole Porter gem, but I think "Blue Suede Shoes" is really memorable. It's a great image, very simple and direct. "Tutti Frutti" I would argue is a good lyric, though perhaps that's going a bit far. It doesn't necessarily have a rhyme or scan. It can be irregular and break rules. But by and large, if it's well constructed with a solid form, it tends to be better. Many great lyrics, like "Some Enchanted Evening" or "Moonlight In Vermont," don't rhyme. One thing I don't like is lyrics where you can tell the chap is trying to rhyme but didn't quite get it right, like rhyming "fine" and "time," or "mind" and "wine," or "tough" and "such." Again, that doesn't matter so much in rock'n'roll, but I find it annoying. I've certainly been guilty of it in the early days. Now I try to avoid it.

What advice would you give to an aspiring lyricist who wanted to write for stage and screen?

I think my first advice would be get your work performed, under any circumstances. It's better to get it performed somewhere modest than not to get it performed on Broadway. *Joseph* got us going and we did that in schools. If a piece is any good at all, once you get it going, it will gather it's own steam, and gradually go up. Two would be don't copy anybody else. Try to evolve a new style, which is the hardest thing in the world. And three, make sure if you're a lyricist, that you get equal billing and you have equal rights in perpetuity with your composer and partner [laughs].

Burt Bacharach

The Look Of Love ✳ Raindrops Keep Fallin' On My Head
✳ I Say A Little Prayer

Interview conducted in 1996 and 1998

"I think you learn the rules so you can break the rules"

It pulses with staccato dabs of color, then pauses dramatically. It stirs, leaping gracefully, stretching, yearning up the scale, then worrying down. It charges forward in a breathtaking gallop then suddenly quiets to a demure whisper. Rousing itself, it builds and builds, finally detonating in a dazzling fireworks display.

What is this dynamic thing? A Burt Bacharach melody.

For over thirty-five years, Bacharach has been lighting up contemporary pop music with his unforgettable and unconventional melodies. The list of classics stretches to staggering lengths – "I Say A Little Prayer," "Do You Know The Way To San Jose," "Always Something There To Remind Me," "Alfie," "I Just Don't Know What To Do With Myself," "Twenty Four Hours From Tulsa," "What's New Pussycat?" "Wishin' And Hopin'," "Wives And Lovers," "Promises, Promises," "The Look of Love," "(They Long To Be) Close to You," and "Raindrops Keep Fallin' On My Head," to name a few. When musicologists look back at the American music of the 20th century, Bacharach will surely have earned his place in the pantheon of greats alongside Gershwin, Berlin, Porter and Rodgers.

65

Born in Kansas City on May 12, 1928, Burt Bacharach started piano lessons while in elementary school. When his family moved to New York, the aspiring young musician fell in love with jazz, especially the complex rhythmic sounds of be-bop. To this day, Bacharach cites Charlie Parker and Dizzy Gillespie as two of his shaping influences.

After serving in the army, he studied theory and composition at McGill University and Mannes School of Music with famous teachers such as Henry Cowell and Darius Milhaud. Then came Bacharach's professional apprenticeships in the mid-1950s, when he served as pianist/arranger for Vic Damone, the Ames Brothers, Polly Bergen and Steve Lawrence, and musical director for Marlene Dietrich. His songwriting ambitions led him to a fateful meeting in New York's Brill Building with lyricist Hal David.

Bacharach paints a picture of the time: "We'd work together in a room with a window that didn't open and a kind of beat-up piano, both of us smoking. You know, your typical image of how songwriters wrote in a room at a publishing office."

From that small, smokey room came the seeds of the music that, along with The Beatles, The Beach Boys and Motown, would help define the era of the 1960s. It was a breezy sound, gently propulsive, irresistibly melodic and full of sensuality. It was a sound that challenged listeners with its time changes and dynamic shifts. It was a sound to stir the imagination.

In all, the successful duo penned a string of 39 consecutive chart hits, most of them for their favorite chanteuse, Dionne Warwick. Their songs have been covered by an A-Z of 20th century artists, including Frank Sinatra, Barbra Streisand, Dusty Springfield, Tony Bennett, Gene Pitney, The Fifth Dimension, The Carpenters, The Stylistics and Aretha Franklin. Beyond that, Bacharach and David also wrote a hit musical (*Promises, Promises*) and several award-winning movie soundtracks (*Casino Royale, Alfie, After The Fox, What's New Pussycat?* and *Butch Cassidy And The Sundance Kid*).

But in 1973, after the commercial failure of their movie musical *Lost Horizon*, Bacharach and David split amidst an ugly exchange of publishing lawsuits. The rest of the decade proved a very lean one for

Bacharach, who kept a rather low profile and didn't chart again until 1981, as a co-writer of the Christopher Cross hit "Arthur's Theme (The Best That You Can Do)."

That same year, Bacharach married lyricist Carole Bayer Sager and the two began to collaborate professionally. During the 1980s, they topped the charts twice with "That's What Friends Are For" (Dionne Warwick and Friends) and "On My Own" (Patti Labelle and Michael McDonald).

In the 1990s, Bacharach enjoyed a huge revival in popularity, which resulted in a 3-CD box set (Rhino's *The Look Of Love: The Burt Bacharach Collection*), a TV special (*One Amazing Night*, in which contemporary performers such as Sheryl Crow and Barenaked Ladies covered his songs), and most significantly, a collaboration with Elvis Costello on 1998's *Painted From Memory*, an album of new material that echoes Burt's best work of the 60s.

When you started playing piano as a kid, did you enjoy it?

To me, it was just something I had to do because my mother wanted me to do it. I had to take piano lessons and I was very non-interested in it. It was a real effort to come back from high school and have to practice for a half an hour before I had a chance to go out to play roller hockey or whatever, basketball. Really, it was something I never looked forward to.

Was there a turning point that made you consider becoming a professional musician?

I don't know about becoming a professional musician. I heard a couple of things that really influenced me very much – attracted more than influenced – and one was the Ravel "Daphnis & Chloe Suite." I thought it was very beautiful and very different than the kind of classical music that I'd been listening to on drives back from Philadelphia. Suddenly I was hearing something that was really lyrical and beautiful. That kind of turned my head around. Of course, then I heard Dizzy Gillespie's big band, with Charlie Parker, in New York and I'd never heard anything like that before.

Had you written your first song at that point?

No, that was still high school. I don't think I wrote my first song until I was in college and that was not a very good song.

Do you feel like there are things that you learned in your college composition courses that applied to your pop songwriting?

I think all the technical study – learning how to be able to read music and write it down – was very helpful. If I was hearing something in my head and I couldn't get to a keyboard to check it out, I could take a scrap of paper in a hotel or a restaurant or something and just write it out. I think that's very important. I think you learn the rules so you can break the rules. What else did I learn? It's hard to teach classical composition, I think, because I don't know that there are any set forms that one has to follow. With Darius Milhaud, that was an important thing with me. He heard this one piece I was working on and told me that it was very good. It was very melodic and the rest of the class was writing very dissonant music, and he really encouraged me to tap into the melody. It's nothing to be ashamed of, he said.

When you're given a title or a bit of a lyric, what are your first steps in approaching a melody?

I think I just try to see what it means to me first of all – if it's an attractive thought, an attractive idea. I don't dislike writing to a lyric. It takes you in another course that you might not go into if you were just writing a straight melody. It kind of sits out on a road and then you have to follow it in a general direction. Sometimes that's a very attractive direction.

Do you prefer just getting a fragment to a whole lyric?

That depends. Maybe a whole lyric. Like "Alfie," I think Hal gave me a whole lyric on that. A lot of stuff from *Promises, Promises* had lyrics first. I think it's a good framework to start with things that have something to say lyrically. With a musical like *Promises, Promises*, the words have to step right off the Neil Simon book, you know?

You've said you like to get away from the piano as soon as possible when you're composing. What are the main advantages of that?

You can hear a long line that way. You can hear the whole song. You can hear it evolve, and not to be as concerned with what the fingers and the hands are playing, where they're going. It's short term with my hands on the piano. It sounds really good for that one bar, but I'm trying to hear the whole thing, and hear how it would sound just coming at you as a listener. You can hear the long line. I can anyway. Certainly that applies to orchestration as well, to hear what comes in when. I just get a better picture when I'm away from the piano. You can also get trapped by pretty chords when you're at the piano. I mean, guys have written great songs and continue to do so while sitting at their instrument, whether it's guitar or piano. Not to say I don't sometimes start at the piano, then get away from it. But I have to have a long-range picture of the whole scope of a piece. I get a sense of balance that I wouldn't get if I were sitting at the piano. I can't say enough about where your hands tend to go, because they've been there before.

If a songwriter wanted to improve his or her melody writing, what kinds of things would you suggest?

Try to get away from your instrument and work that way. It's very tough nowadays, because you can be duped by the technology we have. I can have my two-and-a-half year old go to one of my MIDI keyboards and play a couple of notes and it'll sound great. If you have a keyboard that's MIDI'd with a couple synthesizers, so you have strings and horns, you can sound glorious. But when you take it all apart, when you peel back the cover, what do you have? Do you really have a song; do you really have a melody? It's like the same principle when you take something you've recorded and play it on a little, cheap tape machine. If it's there, it's there. I remember Quincy Jones playing his album *The Dude* one night at his house for a group of friends, and he played it on a small boom box. I guess Quincy was thinking, if it's good, it's going to sound good on the least expensive equipment.

To whom did you listen to help develop your sense of drama in your melodies?

I don't know that I listened to anyone consciously. When I was doing songs with Dionne, I was thinking in terms of making miniature movies, you know? Every second counts. Three and half minute movies, with peak moments and not just one intensity level the whole way through.

When you composed melodies without words or titles – say something like "Close To You" – did you have a mental picture of what you were writing about?

I'd put words to it. I'd make up dummy words. I've always been a big believer in words with notes. I used to write for the trumpet players, or the flugelhorns or the reed players, anybody that would have a singular statement to make on a record, I'd write the lyric underneath. So they'd be playing melody notation but they'd try to speak through their instrument the actual lyric.

So the introductory melodies in your songs actually had words?

Yeah, or even the solos. I just put in imaginary words if it wasn't part of the song. People that I worked with in the studio who knew me didn't think it was so crazy, and whether they thought it was crazy or not was unimportant to me. There was a reason I did it. There are certain things that can't really be notated in an orchestration. It's maybe two eighth notes, a sixteenth note and another eighth note and that's the way it should be notated, but that's not the way it totally feels. But if you put words with it, or even vowel sounds, it does make a difference.

When you'd give a melody to Hal David, would you be careful not to have the dummy words in there?

Not really. The dummy words have to be in there sometimes so you have the right length, the right amount of syllables, the right amount of words, all to take home with him. I know one example, on "Raindrops Keep Fallin' On My Head," I kept singing that title. Even though he tried to change it, we never came up with anything that felt as good. Hal made it make sense overall, though he tried some other ways first because it's not the most natural way one would think to write that lyric. If I'd done that as an instrumental, I'd have put that lyric under the first phrase. It sang great, fit great.

If you find yourself in the middle of composing a song and you keep coming to a brick wall at a certain point, what kinds of things help you move through it?

I'm not so good with an answer like that because I tend to have it dominate me and I take it everywhere with me. If I'm going to the theatre, then I think about where I am with that melody and I don't enjoy the theatre, nor do I solve the problem because I'm split-ting off in two different directions. But I don't like to leave things undone like that. One thing that does help me sometimes is to try playing whatever I'm stuck on in another key.

Do you have any recollections about writing "Wives & Lovers"?

It was an assignment for a movie. It was a song for hire. It was just a promotional song. So Hal and I wrote it. It's a shame it didn't make the picture, but it has probably had way more value than the picture in the long run.

Whose is the definitive version in your opinion?

I'm not sure I have one. I like Dionne's record. I think she did it more like I thought it should be. I like Jack Jones' record too, though I had to get used to it. It was very different than what I'd imagined. But it started to do really well and became a hit, so I thought, "I can get used to it that way."

When you wrote "Close To You" were you disappointed it wasn't a single?

You know, I made the first record of that with Richard Chamberlain and it was terrible. I had a terrible arrangement and a terrible con-cept. I think the concept that Richard Carpenter and Herb Alpert came up with, the flow on that record, was very different than the way I had thought of it, and much more appealing.

How about "The Look Of Love"?

"The Look Of Love" was really targeted for that one character in the movie [*Casino Royale*], for Ursula Andress. It was really written just watching her on my moviola. Very sensuous, sexual theme. I treated it as an instrumental first, then Hal put lyrics to it. We got the ideal singer for it. I love working with Dusty. She's just great.

So many groups from the 60s, when I listen to them now, sound very stuck in that time. Yet the stuff that you guys did with Dionne still sounds fresh. Any thoughts on why?

I can't say it was a little ahead of its time, because it wasn't. It was right in the time. Take "The Long And Winding Road" – it was incredible then and it's incredible now. Maybe it's got something to

71

do with a substantial song to start with. What the song says, and how it's treated, and if it's not surrounded by a dated arrangement – maybe then it will hold up 30 years later. That's my only read on it. Ballads, ballads, you know. Uptempo tunes, maybe because of the very framework they had to be in, maybe didn't have the same chance to grow.

I've always detected a Brazilian influence in your work. Were there certain composers you were attracted to?

Yes. Milton Nascimento, Djavan. It's marvelous stuff. I think it's better when they're singing in Portuguese than in English. You don't know what it means, but it's definitely more romantic.

Were you a Jobim fan?

Yeah.

I wanted to get your impression on the difference between Hal David and Carole Bayer Sager as lyricists. Do you feel like Hal's lyrics brought different kinds of melodies out of you than Carole's did?

I'm not sure. I think it's very possibly a different time as well. They're both great lyricists. Carole is one of the fastest lyricists I've ever seen. Too fast for me, the way she writes, just because I'm that far behind. I'm still working on one note or something like that, and she's basically got the song done. Hal was more like the one who would take it home, work on it, bring it back the next day, and we'd look at it. Then he'd go back and I'd go back and we'd work alone a lot. Then together.

Hal seems like he might be a less sentimental person than Carole. Is that true?

You know, one is a woman, a beautiful woman and the other is . . . if you look at Hal, then you listen to the lyrics, you've got to be stunned at the insight that Hal has in those lyrics. Brilliant stuff. And Carole too. I was lucky to have worked with them both.

"God Give Me Strength," the song you wrote with Elvis Costello for Grace Of My Heart, *sounds more like the stuff you were writing in the 60s. Was that a conscious choice?*

No, not at all. The picture was about that time, so I think that has influenced the way people think about it. I don't think I was writing backwards, or trying to put it in a timeset.

Do you have the sense that some of what you wrote will last 100 years from now?

I think there's a chance that some of it will, because it's lasted 30 years. I think at that time, you could make songs that had a chance to last. I don't think we would be having hits with songs like that in today's market.

And yet kids are really tuning into your music.

I think it's terrific. I'm not sure I know why it happened. It started in England, started with some of the younger bands and artists, like Noel Gallagher. Last year, Noel came on stage with me and sang "This Guy's In Love With You" with me and the symphony orchestra. It started for me in England the first time, 30 years ago. First time around, I was more successful there than in the States. These kids that like these songs, this music, they weren't even born when it came out. They're hearing it for the first time. Is it a need for a melody? I think so. For melody, for romance, for love songs. So however it happened, it started again in England, then came to the States and they're kind of rediscovering me.

What are the things that you haven't done yet as a songwriter that you'd still like to do?

I think I'd like to do another musical. I'd like to write something for a symphony orchestra, other than the way I did with The Houston Symphony. I still want to keep writing and have hits, but I find it very hard now, because it's just a different kind of scene. It's much tougher for good, solid songs to get through. But I think there will always be room for a good song.

Hal David

What The World Needs Now Is Love
✫ Do You Know The Way To San Jose? ✫ Alfie

Interview conducted in 1996

"There were eleven floors in the Brill Building. You'd just start at the top and work your way down, playing your songs as if you were selling your wares."

When the songs of Burt Bacharach and Hal David first hit the charts in the 1960s, they captured the experimental spirit of the times with their urgent, often complex rhythms, daring melodic leaps and unusual, rule-defying forms. Yet Bacharach and David crafted their songs so expertly that listeners weren't distracted, but instead enchanted by this bold new sound. At the heart of each of the team's songs was a heartfelt lyric – graceful, elegant, and always memorable.

Thirty years later, it's amazing how fresh those songs still sound. It makes sense when you consider that David's major influences are the great American composers such as Cole Porter, Rodgers & Hart, and Irving Berlin, whose works also remains vital despite changing fashions and trends. David once said of his favorite, Berlin, "He had the ability to take the most complex things and turn them into songs. And he made it look so damn simple. His work is like a textbook of great songwriting."

Hal David was born on May 25, 1921 in Brooklyn, NY. Inspired by his older brother, renowned Tin Pan Alley lyricist Mack David ("A Dream Is A Wish Your Heart Makes," "I'm Just A Lucky So And So"),

Hal began his lifelong passion for writing when he was a teenager. While serving in the army during World War II, he wrote lyrics for military revues. After he got out, he wrote special material for nightclub acts. He scored his first hit when Mel Torme took "The Four Winds And The Seven Seas" into the Top 10 in 1949.

In the 1950s, David collaborated with a number of different composers and made the hit parade with songs such as "American Beauty Rose" (Frank Sinatra) and "Bell Bottom Blues" (Teresa Brewer). Then in the late 50s, while writing for Famous Music in New York City's Brill Building, he met Burt Bacharach. Working together on recordings, movie soundtracks, and an acclaimed Broadway show, they became one of the most respected and covered songwriting teams in pop music history.

After the team split in the early 1970s, David went on to collaborate with several other composers, turning out hits such as Ronnie Milsap's "Almost Like A Song" and the Willie Nelson/Julio Iglesias duet "To All The Girls I've Loved Before." Over his long, illustrious career, David has collected almost every major songwriting award, including a Grammy, an Oscar, and election into the Songwriters Hall of Fame. David sums up his successful approach to lyric writing this way: "I search for believability, simplicity and emotional impact."

What were some of the things, early on, that attracted you to writing lyrics?

My older brother, Mack David, was a very successful lyricist, so that became a part of our family life early on. What may have seemed like an odd profession to someone else seemed quite normal to me.

How much were you able to learn from watching and listening to your brother?

I grew up listening to songs, being involved with music, playing with little bands. I played violin. I guess I learned an awful lot, but it's hard to know what you learned. I don't recall watching my brother write. I don't know to what extent he did that at home, at least when I was around. I think I learned by osmosis, by listening and watching and I probably did ask questions, but I don't recall. I learned by writing. Most of us are collaborators – there are very few Irving Berlins and Cole Porters and Frank Loessers around – so we learn from our writing partners too.

When you were first starting out, what kinds of things did you do to get your foot in the door?

I did what was the usual and normal thing in those days. Music publishing and writing took place, for the most part, in New York City, except if you were doing films, then it was Los Angeles. The publishers were, to a large extent, in the Brill Building on Broadway and 49th Street. So you wrote your songs with various collaborators. Most of the publishers had piano rooms, and you usually had some kind of relationship with a publisher where you'd be able to work in one of their rooms. Then you'd go and play your songs around from publisher to publisher. There were 11 floors in the Brill Building. You'd start at the top and work your way down, playing your songs as if you were selling your wares.

How did you meet Burt Bacharach?

We were both working at Famous Music in the Brill Building, and in those days everyone in the music business seemed to know everybody else. There was always a great mixture of people writing together. You'd write with one composer in the morning and another in the afternoon. A lyric writer would work with a lot of composers over a period of time. So I met Burt, and we liked each other, and we liked the songs we wrote. I was very hardworking, as was he. I was always writing lyrics; he was always writing melodies. Either my lyric would set him off to write a melody, or vice versa.

You were both very prolific.

Even as we worked together on one song he'd give me another melody or I'd give him another lyric, and very often we were writing three songs at a time – a song together, a song to his tune, a song to my lyric. So we had a number of things going.

Can you describe your first steps in approaching a lyric?

The first step is to listen to the music very closely, not so much to learn what the notes are, but to see what the music was saying to you. If you're a lyric writer, you should hear the music talking to you. That's what I'd be doing initially.

While you were doing that, would you be taking notes or scribbling ideas?

I'd often write dummy lyrics, and I still do that. It helps me retain the melody, particularly if the melody is a little complex.

How about finding the placement of the title?

Well, I think a title is where you ordinarily go. But very often I'd start off with lines that would take me to a title. The placement of it was often obvious, but sometimes it wasn't. For "I Say A Little Prayer," the chorus section goes "Forever, forever, you'll stay in my heart and I will love you." That's ordinarily where the title would fall in that song but for whatever reason at the time, it seemed to me that the title should come in the less obvious place – in the verse after "The moment I wake up, before I put on my makeup." That's where I decided to put the title.

Do you keep a log of possible titles and lines?

I don't know if I keep a log, but I have notebooks full of lyrics, lines, titles. But it's not something that when I get an assignment, I go through and look at them, no. Every once in a while I do look at them to stir my memory and energize me, but I don't use them as a log in that sense. I pretty much attack everything in a fresh manner.

How was writing songs for Promises, Promises *different from writing pop songs?*

Show songs are somewhat easier to write because you have a story to deal with. When you're writing a pop song you've got air to deal with, blank paper to deal with. You have to create out of nothing-ness. When you do a show, there's a story, there are characters, there are scenes, there's a tree on which to hang your songs. Writing a show song of course, while in some respects it may be easier, is also more challenging because it deals with subjects that you wouldn't deal with very often in a pop song

Why didn't you and Burt do more shows?

Well, I've sometimes wondered the same thing. Burt lost his feeling for writing shows after that. His experience was different from what he had expected it to be. He came out of a record background, and every time you play a record back it comes out the same. It doesn't change. But if you do a show, the tempo can be too fast, too slow; the singers or actors can change lines or notes. The audience doesn't know these things, but you do. And if you're a perfectionist, and of a mind to let it drive you crazy, you don't enjoy it. So Burt didn't want to do another one. I have been trying recently to do some things with Charles Strouse [*Bye Bye Birdie, Annie*].

"Whoever You Are" from Promises, Promises *is a beautiful ballad with a lot of inner rhyming. How much do you labor over a lyric like that?*

Well, I do labor over my lyrics. That's one of my favorite songs, to begin with. I think it's a great melody and I like the lyric a lot. But I work very hard. I work on every word. I spend inordinate amounts of time deciding whether "and" or "but" is the right word [laughs]. To a certain extent, lyrics flow easily, but no matter how much they flow at a given time, by the time you really get it finished and refined to the best of your ability, it's a lot of work. It'll probably go through two or three drafts. You may even go back to something that's close to the very first draft you had, but you're trying the others just to see whether it can be improved or not.

What's the story behind "Do You Know The Way To San Jose?"

I'm not really sure. I think your work is obviously influenced by your life experience, and I did spend time in San Jose during World War II. I was at Fort Ort, California, and possibly because I had spent time in San Jose in those days, that may have been the natural outgrowth of that.

How about "One Less Bell to Answer"?

Burt and I were in London working on a project, and I was invited to a dinner party. The hostess said to me, "When you arrive, don't ring the bell, just come in. It'll make one less bell for me to answer." And at least I was wise enough to know it was a good title.

When you listen to today's music, do you hear any lyrics that impress you?

Yeah, I'm sure I do, but I couldn't name specific ones. Lyrics seem to be less important today than 30 years ago. Very often the melodies seem to be less important. More often than not, the sound and production seems to be more important. There are certainly some terrific songs written today, there just don't seem to be as many of them.

What advice would you give to a songwriter?

Firstly, make sure it's what you really want to do, because there's an awful lot of rejection that takes place, particularly early in your career. And secondly, what you've got to do is get yourself to the places where music is written and published, like Los Angeles, New York and Nashville, depending on what you write. Meet the people there, start writing. I think you learn by writing and you succeed by being where things are happening.

Jimmy Webb

MacArthur Park ☆ Wichita Lineman
☆ By The Time I Get To Phoenix

Interview conducted in 1995

"I've never been a slave to any of the rules and regulations of writing music."

From the time Jimmy Webb exploded onto the scene in the mid-1960s as the writer of hits such as "By The Time I Get To Phoenix," "Wichita Lineman," "Up, Up, And Away," "MacArthur Park," and dozens of other modern pop standards, he has been hailed by listeners and performers alike as a musical genius. In the songwriting community, the mere mention of his name elicits awestruck reactions, from "He's the best I've ever heard" to a speechless shake of the head. Webb's songs have been covered by a wide range of artists including Frank Sinatra, Glen Campbell, Donna Summer, Art Garfunkel, and Amy Grant.

I've been listening to your song "What Does A Woman See In A Man" over and over. The chord progression and the melody are so rich and full of unexpected turns. Can you describe your first steps in approaching a song like that?

Well, I believe in writing interesting melodies, and the reason that I do that is mostly for my own entertainment. If I'm not singing something interesting, I get bored very quickly. I lose interest in doing it. So it's always been my musical nature to try to point the melody in a different direction, or to change directions unexpectedly. When I do that, it leads me towards substitutions and unexpected chords. So really I let the

81

melody lead me toward unusual chord changes. I follow the melody. So if I want the melody to go to a certain note, and if I can't find a chord that fits, I go off in search of one. It usually takes me to an unusual place, because that's the kind of stuff I like.

I assume from your composing and arranging skills that you're fairly schooled. So when you're searching for those chords, does that involve any sort of turning off of your knowledge?

No, not really, because the truth is I don't know very much. I started playing piano when I was about six, and for the first few years, I played exclusively by ear. I taught myself to write the music down and I taught myself the technical aspects after the fact. I learned to play first, then I learned to write it down. It's really instinctive with me. I've never been a slave to any of the rules and regulations of writing music. I'm very, very glad that I learned to read music, because I think in a sense, to read music is to automatically know how to write it. It's a very obvious connection that apparently is very easy to miss, because people ask me, "When did you learn to write?" Well, I learned to write about the same time I learned to read.

So learning other people's songs has helped you write your own?

Yeah, but it also helps you write your own down. If you can play something on the piano, and you know how to read music, you can write it down for lead sheet purposes, or to write down chord charts for a session, or to do some simple orchestration or whatever. It's really obvious when you think about it. When you learn how to read someone else's music, you can write your own down. But in answer to your previous question, I don't really turn much off when I write a song. I tend to open up and engage all the possibilities.

The reason that I asked is because I've read that you sometimes approached the keyboard as a mathematical grid when you were composing.

I think you can look at it that way. Definitely the way to learn the nature of music is to approach it graphically or almost mathematically. That's the way I've taught my sons to play. I have five sons and a little girl. My three oldest sons know how to play and are already writing their own songs, and are really excited about it. With all due modesty, they're pretty advanced. But the time I spent with them has been minimal. I just went in and said, "Look, this is the piano keyboard and here's how can you make a triad out of any note on the piano." I just start right there. Once the mathematical aspects of the keyboard are explained, it's such a graphic display of what's going on because it's right there in front of you. It's more difficult on a guitar, I think, because it's much more abstract.

In those first steps of writing, is it important for you to have a good title or a concept?

That depends. There are two ways to approach writing a song. The most fashionable way to do it, particularly in country music down Nashville way, is that people get a snappy or catchy title and build a song around that. Make the whole song serve that. I think the positioning of a title or a catch phrase in a song is important, whether it's at the end of the verse or whether it constitutes the chorus of the song or the end of the chorus. That is one way to do it, and maybe that's an easy way to do it. But I have also sat down with an abstract concept in mind, thinking I don't know exactly what the title of this song is going to be, but I know it's going to be about this. And then I've gone off into the song in search of the title. I think sometimes you can start out without knowing.

Can you think of an example?

There's a song on my *Suspending Disbelief* album called "Sandy Cove," where I started out to express an emotion, a deeply felt emotion about loss and about how we relate loss to material things, even though that's not really the nature of loss. I felt like it was a common emotion we all shared, and it was something I was feeling very deeply. I didn't start out with a catch phrase or snappy title. It was the emotion that began the process, and then by the time I was a couple of verses into the song and had accomplished some of the things that I had set out to do, I began to realize that the song was probably going to be called "Sandy Cove." But I didn't start out saying I'm going to write a song with that title, because a song called "Sandy Cove" could be about anything.

When you're venturing into that kind of songwriting, do you have much of a map structurally of what you want to do?

To some degree, I think a song tends to shape itself. Every songwriter of any expertise at all knows that if it's a verse-chorus-verse-chorus song, once the first verse is written, the second verse is going to be the same essentially – unless it's some kind of experimental form. It's going to have the same melody, chords and it'll scan the same. The rhyme scheme will be almost identical. This may be one of the things that we try to do, make it identical, because we're trying to match a traditional form. We're not writing a recitative, we're writing a pop song. Really in a sense, a song will write it's own form. There are some big decisions we can make sometimes. Well, we want an ending or we want a fade. We don't want a bridge in this song or we don't want a chorus. Those are big decisions. But once the first element, or the first piece of the picture is in place, the song is pretty much writing itself in regards to form. To me, it would be an artificial act to say "This is going to be the shape of this song." And it's very premature to do something like that before I'm halfway through the first verse, before I've gotten a feel for certain aspects of the song. For instance, how many lines are in the first verse. If what I've written is a very long first verse, maybe there won't be a chorus in this song. Maybe it'll be a two-verse song. Maybe I'll accomplish my goal in that way. All those decisions are made on the fly. To confine one's self to strict a form early on in the song is probably a mistake.

One of your songs that really knocks me out is "Still Within The Sound Of My Voice." How did that begin?

It started out as something from my childhood. My father was a Baptist minister, and we used to drive along at night down in the panhandle of Texas and down in Oklahoma, and my dad would always be listening to these radio preachers. There was a certain surreal quality to it – late at night, out on an empty expanse of prairie with little or no traffic, within the cozy confines of the car, listening to this disembodied voice coming out of nowhere. There was a phrase this one guy from Del Rio, Texas used to say – "For those of you who are within the sound of my voice." That phrase stuck in my head, and the analogy was pretty simple, yet it runs towards the complex. It's the actual recording artist singing the song. They're singing to someone they love whom they haven't seen for a long time or haven't been with for a long time. They're saying if I can reach you through this recording, I want to tell you, wherever you are, that I still love you. That's the idea of the song. Many times I find myself thinking of a phrase or a fragment of a thought that might go back decades, and begin to turn it over and look at it in a slightly different way. Sometimes they turn out, sometimes they don't. I thought that one did turn out.

Aside from the music you heard in the Baptist church services, what influenced you as a songwriter?

The first major influence that really excited me was the Bacharach-David songs. Both because of interesting song structure and chord structure. At times, soaring orchestral things. Overall just a very original, distinctive style of writing that I wanted to emulate. I liked the chords, the quirky melodies, and I liked that they were different from everything else on the radio. After Bacharach and David, probably when the *Revolver* album came out, and I began to hear these two hot British songwriters. When I heard "Yesterday," that was a big milestone in my life. I started paying very careful attention to Lennon and McCartney, because I realized they were off in some very interesting directions. Suddenly here were guys who were using string quartets for accompaniment and seemingly had no restrictions on what they would entertain as usable in the pop context, and notwithstanding were still writing very solid, accessible music. Virtually at the same time I was influenced by Holland-Dozier-Holland and all the Motown stuff, particularly the Four Tops' "Baby I Need Your Lovin'." Also, Phil Spector, Barry Mann and Cynthia Weil. At the time I graduated high school in 1964, there was a lot of stuff out there that was earth-shaking.

Some of the people you mentioned have been great experimenters with song form. Is that something you set out to do in your own work?

When we did "MacArthur Park," we did it pretty much as an experiment. I remember that I was asked to do that by [producer] Bones Howe. He said, "Can you do something that suggests movements, in the classical sense that a symphony or sonata has movements?" And I understood exactly what he meant, and the idea kind of caught fire with me and I thought that would be fun to try that. That's the only time that I can remember consciously setting out to do something like that, just for the exercise of it, to see if it could be done. I think that this experimentation with form that we're talking about occurs in Joni Mitchell's music and The Beatles' music.

85

The reason that I have goofed around with form, or altered it, has been to serve the song. It's been to get the listener's attention, thinking if I do this this way, it will get the message across in a more poignant way. It will make this person listen to me. Because when we do songs the same way over and over again – and we really are in a rut with the three minute song – I think half the time people are only half listening, because it is so predictable. You know where it's going to go. It's just been done the same way so many times for so many years, and I think if you're trying to get your message across, sometimes it's very wise to say, why don't we stop here and have a moment of silence, then go in a completely different direction for these few lines, because these lines are important. Let's change the chord structure completely, change the orchestration, or put it in a completely different place.

By the way, within the limits of the three-minute song, I think you're severely limited in terms of what you can do to alter form. But within the boundaries of being cognizant of having people have any idea what you're talking about, I have tried to do that. "By The Time I Get To Phoenix" has three verses. It has a beginning, middle and end, like a short story, in a way. It wouldn't have that linear story quality if there was a chorus in there. "Highwayman" has four verses, because there's four incarnations, and in the case of the record, there were four different guys singing it. This is the same guy, but he's come back in four different guises. That's a way of playing with form to make your point.

When you're writing lyrics to a song like "The Highwayman," which is so rich in detail and inner rhyme, do you let it flow or is it a meticulous line-by-line process?

My technique is always at the beginning to be as open as possible. Let things flow and try to get the meaning of the thing down on the page. Real meticulous attention to inner rhymes and matching rhyme schemes between verses, which is almost a game you play with yourself, is really something that can come a lot later. Too early on, if your nose is in the paper with your eyes all squinched up going, "Now let's see, that doesn't rhyme or that's a false rhyme," then you're really doing what Quincy Jones used to call "strangling the baby in the crib." I think you have to be more open. Sometimes put a line down if it says what you want to say. If it doesn't rhyme exactly, or if you're involved in a more complex endeavor like trying to match another verse at that point, I think you don't worry about that for the time being. I know that I'm going to do two rewrites, or three, sometimes four or five. I know I'm going to be on that lyric for a while until I get it exactly the way I want, and I know that during that process a lot of neat things are going to happen. Lines will change, things will occur to me, I know it'll get better. So I don't worry about it too much. My advice to someone, if anyone cares for my advice, would be to concentrate on content, on the message you're trying to get across and save the finer points of rhyme and scanning and perfect meter and inner rhymes for at least until halfway or close to the end of the process.

Does it take you a long time to finish a song?

I think from beginning to end, it does. I may have the song roughed out in a couple of days, but I'll still be thinking for a long time about some of the overtones and how to make it better. Even when I'm demoing it, I may run across a couple lines that I think could be better or pointed a little more towards a deeper meaning and change them right there on the spot. If I demo that song, and it isn't recorded for a year or a couple of years, I may come back to it and say, "That's not exactly right." I will never stop working on it. When I play in public appearances I will often play a song the way I want to hear it, and someone will come up to me and say, "Why did you change it?" I just kind of shrug my shoulders and say "Because that's the way it goes now."

How would you like to be remembered a hundred years from now?

I definitely don't have one eye on history, so that's a very difficult question. But, as I said, I do have all these children at home and I guess the best way I could put it would be in terms of how I would want them to remember me. I would like them to remember me as someone who stayed true to some of the traditional values of songwriting and didn't change directions every time the wind did. Someone who helped preserve some of the techniques of the great songwriters – some of the chord structures, some of the ways of working, some of the sophistication of lyrics. Someone who was always musical and always literate.

Smokey Robinson

My Girl ✮ The Tracks Of My Tears
✮ The Tears Of A Clown

Interview conducted in 2001

"I believe from the bottom of my heart that when you create, you are being used by God."

Nobody knows love like Smokey Robinson. For over 40 years, the Motown legend has given the world songs of unparalleled heartfelt sentiment and soulful tenderness. Even a small sampling of his catalog reads like a history of pop music: "You've Really Got A Hold On Me," "Shop Around," "Ooh Baby Baby," "I Second That Emotion," "More Love," "The Tracks Of My Tears," "The Tears Of A Clown," "Quiet Storm," "Cruisin'," "Being With You."

When not writing for himself or his group, The Miracles, Robinson was one of Motown's most prolific songwriter/producers, penning classics for Mary Wells ("My Guy"), The Temptations ("The Way You Do The Things You Do," "My Girl," "Get Ready"), Marvin Gaye ("Ain't That Peculiar," "I'll Be Doggone"), The Marvelettes ("Don't Mess With Bill," "The Hunter Gets Captured By The Game") and many others. His songwriting was so respected by his 1960s pop peers that he was even covered by artists (The Beatles, The Rolling Stones, The Mamas & The Papas) who typically wrote their own songs.

By the time he reached his teens, Robinson had written over a hundred songs and joined his friends in a doo-wop group, The Matadors. In 1958, they auditioned for a young entrepreneur named Berry Gordy, who had started his own record label. "I didn't know how to construct a song until I met Berry Gordy," Robinson says. "He was the one who taught me how to write professionally, to make it be a real song that meant something."

The two became friends and partners in the empire-to-be, Motown Records. The company's imprint, "The Sound Of Young America," wasn't just hype. Along with The Beatles, The Beach Boys and Bacharach & David, Motown was the soundtrack of the 1960s. The three-minute R&B romances that rolled out of Motown with staggering consistency remain some of the best-loved songs in the world. Smokey Robinson's name and magnificent falsetto are on many of them.

"Everything's good in the world when Smokey sings," proclaimed the British pop group ABC in their 1987 tribute hit. It's a sentiment that music lovers across the globe agree on.

As many times as I've heard your songs, I'm still amazed by how fresh and inventive your rhymes are. What were the beginnings of that lyrical flair?

From the time I was a little kid, I've always loved songs, and I always loved what they call the standard tunes. You know, Cole Porter, Irving Berlin, the Gershwins. I grew up listening to that kind of music. I had two older sisters and they were into jazz, like Ella Fitzgerald, Sarah Vaughan, Billy Eckstine. And these are the kinds of songs that they sang. I was always into that kind of writing too, and I was always good at rhyming.

Did you do much learning of those standards?

I must have, because I always enjoyed their rhyme schemes and how they would take two or three words, then rhyme it back so it would rhyme with one word that they had used prior or vice versa. You know something, that's what I love about today's rap. Young rap artists are doing the same thing. They're taking two or three words, and they're rhyming it back with one word. I think that's a throwback to the old writers.

Do you recall writing your first song?

I was about six years old. I was in a school play, and I was portraying Uncle Remus. My teacher had this melody that she was playing at the opening of the play and the end of the play, and there were no words to it. I went to her and asked her if I could sing some words to it. She said, "Oh yeah, William." And that was my first song.

Was that an isolated incident or did that start you writing all the time?

It must've started me writing all the time, because I've been doing that ever since I can remember. I was always trying to write songs.

What do you recall about that initial meeting with Berry Gordy when you played him your songs?

The most outstanding thing was that he never got bored or tired. If he did, he didn't show me that. He never said, "Okay, man, that's enough" or "Okay, I've got to go." I must have sung 20 songs because I had a book of about a hundred songs. He'd patiently listen and critique every one and tell me what was wrong with it, what I could do to make it better, what I could do to enhance it.

Was there an early song that was a breakthrough, one that made you feel like you knew how to do it?

I don't know that there was a song that made me think, "Now I know how to do it." When I first used to write, my songs had no continuity, because the first verse had nothing to do with the second verse, nor did the second or first verse have anything to do with the bridge. They were all different stories within the same song. Berry taught me to make my songs have continuity. He said to think of songs like a short story, or a short film, where everything tied in. He used to say that a song should have a beginning, a middle and an ending that tied together. Ever since that time, I always try to be conscious of writing a song, rather than writing a record, or trying to write something that I think is going to be a hit right then. Of course you do that as a writer, you want to write a hit. But I'm saying that I always try to make sure that it's a song, because perhaps it might not have the right treatment the first time people hear it. It might not take off, or it might not be accepted widely. But if it's a song, it has a chance to live on and on and on, and perhaps somebody will give it the right treatment.

How did the weekly Quality Control meetings at Motown affect your writing?

It made me more conscious of what I was doing. It made me more competitive. It made me want to do better, because that was the purpose of those meetings. All the guys who were producers or writers at Motown were in there with their stuff, trying to push their stuff, trying to get a record on any artist they could get it on. Everybody was recording everybody. I'll give you an example. I had been recording The Temptations. When they first came over, they were like my project. I recorded a few songs on them. No hits. And then Berry recorded a few songs on them. No hits. Holland and Dozier, before they were Holland-Dozier-Holland, recorded a few songs on them. No hits. Norman Whitfield. No hits.

So one day, I was coming in off of a tour with The Miracles, and I was thinking, The Temptations have such great harmony, and I want to write a song where they sing in harmony. At that time, Curtis Mayfield & The Impressions were having a lot of big hits where they were all singing in harmony. So I came up with this idea, "The Way You Do The Things You Do." That song was their first big hit. I used Eddie Kendricks' voice to sing the lead – they had three or four lead singers – so then, all the producers and writers at Motown jumped on The Temptations and started using Eddie Kendricks' voice. We'd go into those meetings, and even though I wrote their first big hit, it didn't matter. I didn't have any guarantee that I was going to get the next hit on The Temptations, if in fact I did not have the best record. That's what those meetings were about. We came in, played our stuff, and chose what we thought were the best records. Many times, not only did we do that, but we would call people in from off the streets. "Hey, we're going to play five records for you, and you just write down which ones you like the best."

Did "The Way You Do The Things You Do" begin as a title?

No, I think I fascinated myself with that first line, "You got a smile so bright, you know you could've been a candle." And then that led me to the title.

There must have been some great songs that didn't make the cut in those meetings.

Yes. And then there were some songs that I didn't like when I heard them and I didn't think they were going to be hits, and they turned out to be smashes. I recall the first time I heard "Reach Out" by The Four Tops, it was a raw kind of record at that point. I thought it was terrible. Berry liked it. He said, "Have Levi [Stubbs] re-sing it, then bring it back." Huge hit. I grew to love it. It's one of my favorite songs now.

Tell me about writing "My Girl."

That was a project song. I was doing an album on The Temptations. I knew that they had three or four lead singers, and I knew that they had two killer lead singers other than Eddie Kendricks: David Ruffin and Paul Williams. I knew if I got the right song for either one of those guys, it was going to be a big smash hit. I wrote a song called "Don't Look Back," and I had Paul Williams sing the vocal. When I first started to record The Temptations, I used Paul's voice more than anyone, because he's a great singer. I wrote "My Girl" specifically for David Ruffin's voice.

Since you were the writer and the producer, did you have a clear concept of how you wanted the record of "My Girl" to sound?

I didn't have that clear of a concept, because I worked with a great arranger named Paul Riser. I worked with him a lot in the early days of Motown. I had my basic chord pattern, my basic rhythm, the melody, the lyric, and then I just gave it to him, and pardon the expression, he kicked ass [laughs]. Also, the house band, who we called "The Funk Brothers," always added a lot. There was a guy named Robert White, a guitarist, who played that opening lick. That might have been his idea. We had a lot of terrific arrangers and musicians, and they all contributed so much to the sound of the records.

Talk about writing "Ain't That Peculiar" for Marvin Gaye.

That was inspired by my guitarist, Marv Tarplin. He's still with me today. Whenever you see his name on any song, he was responsible for the beginning of that song. Before there were any words or ideas, he would come up with these great musical riffs. He would put these riffs on tape for me, and I would listen and see what I could come up with. He had the riff for "The Tracks Of My Tears," "The Love I Saw In You Was Just A Mirage," "Cruisin'" – hits right down the years. "Ain't That Peculiar" was his lick. All that is Marv Tarplin.

We were on tour in Europe, and a couple of the Miracles helped me finish up that song. I used to encourage them to write, because when we were at home, they were just off and I was not only a vice-president of the company, but I was writing and producing. I still had a job and had money coming in whether we were on the road or not. In order for me to stay off of the road so much, I tried to encourage them to write songs. I was giving them songs that I'd started to finish and stuff like that. With that particular song, the first lyrics that I had led me to "ain't that peculiar." I didn't have an ending to "I know flowers grow from rain, but how can love grow from pain?" And then one day, there it was. "Ain't that peculiar" popped out. It was such a different title, a different expression for a song. I'd never heard a song that used that phrase. When that line came out of me, I said, "Oh man, this is a hit!"

Do you have memories of producing Marvin Gaye on that song?

Oh yeah. Marvin was one of my favorite people to ever work with. First of all, I loved him. Marvin and I hung out, Marvin was my brother. We did everything together. But Marvin was always late for his sessions. He was always late for everything really [laughs]. But he would come running in there at the last minute, and I would sit down at the piano and say, "Okay man this is how it goes." Then he would proceed to what I call "Marvin-ize" it. He would sing your song like you could never have imagined someone singing it. By the time he got through with it, you'd say, "Damn, I wish I'd thought of it like that!"

What did you think of The Beatles when they came on the scene?

At first, I was not that impressed by The Beatles and their sound, necessarily. But what I loved about The Beatles was the fact that they became so huge, so fast, and when they did, they were the first white artists to ever admit that they grew up and honed themselves on black music. I loved the fact that they did that. I loved the fact that they were that honest. They in fact recorded some Motown songs. Over the years, John and Paul became some of the greatest writers to ever write in this business.

How did "The Tears Of A Clown" come together?

Stevie Wonder came up to me at a Motown Christmas party and he said, "I've got this track, man, and I know it's a smash." A lot of times in those days, a guy might have a great piece of music but no words for it, and they'd get with somebody who could help, and vice versa. So I took the tape, brought it home, and I started to listen to it. I heard the circus in it [sings opening riff]. That melody is from the circus. The track was so driving and killer. I wanted to write something about the circus that would touch people's hearts. And so I thought about Pagliacci. He was the clown who made everybody laugh, made all the kids happy, all the grown people happy, and then he'd go back to his dressing room and he'd cry because nobody really loved him as a man. They loved him as a clown, but not as a man. So I wrote the song about him.

A lot of songwriters I've talked to say they feel like songs come through them from an outside source, as if they're receivers. Others say it's something they create on their own. How about you?

I don't know who said they create them on their own, but I think they're highly mistaken. I believe from the bottom of my heart, and from the depths of my soul, that when you create, you are being used by God. You are a catalyst. For me, everyday of my life, I hum a new melody. Or I think of some new words for a lyric. Many times I don't even write them down. I don't act on them. If I'm in the car, and I come up with something that's killer, I'll call my answering machine, so I'll know that I have it. But I know that God is the source. I know that God allows me to create. He allows me to do what I do, because it's not a job.

If you were teaching a workshop, what would you tell your students?

First, make sure that your song is a real song. A song is going to be your future. I'm sitting in my office right now doing this interview with you, but I'm making money because I've written some songs that are constantly being re-recorded and aired. So that's what I would tell young songwriters. Make sure your song is the best it can be, that every part of it is working.

Brian Wilson

Good Vibrations ✫ Surfer Girl ✫ Help Me, Rhonda

Interview conducted in 1996

"I try to measure up to my best stuff, but sometimes I can't."

Once upon a time in the small town of Hawthorne, California, a 19-year old boy named Brian Wilson took his favorite things in the world – The Four Freshmen, Chuck Berry, Phil Spector, cars, girls and laughter – added his innate genius for melody, filtered it all through a loving, gentle spirit and created a beautiful sound. It was a sound of freedom, promise and everlasting youth. A sound of warmth and eternal love. A sound that reverberated in the hearts of teenagers across America and around the world. A sound that forty years later still has the power to conjure the perfect summertime paradise.

The slice of pop mythology that Brian Wilson and his group The Beach Boys created – tanned California surfer gods and goddesses, endless sunshine, woodies, hot rods, hamburger stands and good vibrations – was so towering that it cast a shadow over a simple fact: Brian Wilson was a songwriter. Not just a songwriter, but one of the most gifted and original this country has produced in the 20th century.

In fact, songwriter may not be the appropriate word. Brian once referred to himself as a "song architect." That seems an apt description, for most of his compositions are multi-storied, complex structures. Whether it was "Surfer Girl," "I Get Around" or

"Wouldn't It Be Nice" the blueprint was always based on a gorgeous, flowing melody. Building on that foundation, Brian the arranger/producer would construct his grand mansions of pop splendor.

Fat bass lines and echoed rolling drums provided the solid framework onto which were layered twangy guitars, churchy organs, and a cornucopia of instrumental textures including flutes, brass, strings, banjos, accordions, vibraphones and harmonicas. Decorative flourishes were added, sometimes taking the odd form of theremins, bicycle bells and plastic water jugs. And topping it all off were the lush, meticulously arranged vocal harmonies. Towering in majestic chords, cruising on smooth strips of "oohs" and "aahs," swooping and chasing each other through inventive contrapuntal lines (just listen to the middle break on "God Only Knows"), these masterful vocals were the flourish of the signature Beach Boys sound.

Brian's prowess for this musical architecture bloomed at an incredible rate. Between 1962-65, The Beach Boys recorded and released ten albums, an amazing feat made even more unbelievable when you consider the quality of the songwriting. Hardly a month went by when the group wasn't climbing the charts with hits such as "Surfin' Safari," "Surfin' USA," "Little Deuce Coupe," "In My Room," "Fun, Fun, Fun," "Don't Worry Baby," "Help Me, Rhonda" and "California Girls."

It's sadly ironic that a man who has brought so much joy, pleasure and love to the world has found so little of those qualities in his own life. In the stormy years after the landmark *Pet Sounds* album, and the legendary unfinished *Smile* album, Brian wrote some great songs, but much of his energy was consumed struggling against personal demons: a cruel, manipulative father, a lack of self-esteem, paranoia, overeating, a failed marriage, estrangement from his children, tensions within the Beach Boys.

In the 1990s, the clouds finally began to break for Brian Wilson. Healthy and happily remarried, he celebrated the turn of the century by touring with a 10-piece band and a 55-piece orchestra, performing *Pet Sounds* in its entirety, plus other Beach Boys favorites. It was a personal and professional triumph.

Brian Wilson has never been comfortable being interviewed. Talking to him, I realized that his language of preference truly is music. I could sense that he was just as nervous as I was. So if a few of these answers seem frustratingly brief, you can always put on some Beach Boys music and listen to Brian expound at length in his one-of-a-kind, eloquent style.

What do you think makes a really great melody?

That it totally consists of notes that don't sound like they're bunched together; they sound like they flow together. The better the flow, the better the melody.

When you're first sitting down at the piano to begin a song, what are good ways for you to open the door?

A lot of times, it depends on the chords you're playing. The chords that you play inspire the melody and you sort of scat with the chords. You scat, you start singing anything, you know? Start in on any kind of song, with any interval and you write a song that way.

When you're scatting, are you singing dummy words?

Sometimes yeah. Sometimes just "da da da" or "doo doo doo" - it's usually like that.

Will you ever play old songs of yours to get in the mood?

Yeah, I do that a lot. "God Only Knows" and "California Girls" – some of those are like obsessions in my head. I improvise on them.

Do you keep a songwriting schedule?

No, I don't keep a schedule. But I watch my piano regularly to see if there's something I can do. It's better not to keep a schedule, because you go to the piano when you're inspired.

Does all the praise you've gotten over the years weigh on you or make it more difficult to create?

I try to measure up to my best stuff, but sometimes I can't.

"Wouldn't It Be Nice" has that introduction that grabs you from the first note. You did that on "California Girls" too, where the intro is almost unrelated musically, but it sets up the song so beautifully.

The introduction to a song is very spiritual.

99

Is that something that you would usually write after the body of the song was written?

Yeah.

What were you listening to at the time of Pet Sounds *that influenced you?*

Spector, Motown, Burt Bacharach.

When you were influenced by a contemporary of yours like Bacharach, would you learn his songs to get inside them and figure out how they work?

Yeah, I would study his music and try to copy it in a way, like a copy job [laughs].

On "Here Today" there's that wonderful high melodic bass playing that McCartney said influenced his style from Sgt. Pepper *onwards. I've never heard you talk about how you got into that style of playing.*

I think it was Motown. Marvin Gaye's music inspired me quite a bit. James Jamerson's bass playing.

The blend of instruments on Pet Sounds *is really great – bass harmonicas, piccolos, banjos. Not having a formal music education, how did you get so familiar with the characteristics of the different instruments?*

By trial and error [laughs]. I'm a self-taught musician.

Would you get the players in the studio and tell them to play certain lines?

Yeah, I'd write chord charts.

In the beginning, when you were into the Four Freshmen, Phil Spector and Chuck Berry, did it occur to you that you were going to combine these things in a deliberate way?

It happened more organically. I just took it year by year, you know? Some years I would have some real good songs, some years I wouldn't.

I've read that "Surfer Girl" was inspired by the falsetto passage at the end of "When You Wish Upon A Star."

Yeah, I don't know how, but it did inspire the song [laughs]. I don't consider myself a very good songwriter, but with the voice, I consider myself to be as good as anybody else at voice.

But you don't consider yourself to be a great songwriter?

Not really.

One of my favorites of your early songs is "In My Room." I'd read where you said that Gary Usher, your collaborator on that song, taught you everything you knew about writing songs. What was it specifically that you learned from him?

He showed me how write around chords, play chords on the guitar and write songs. He was really up and it turned me on and I started writing songs on my own. But he had to teach me first about how to get that spirit going.

Was co-writing with Roger Christian on songs like "Little Deuce Coupe" or "Don't Worry Baby" different?

With Roger, it was like he would give me a finished lyric and I would go to my house and I'd write the song to the lyric. That's another thing, I usually write the music first then the lyrics. But with Roger it was the opposite. I would look at a line of the lyric and think about the rhythm, then I'd try to get a melody to that line. It took longer to do it that way, but oh boy, it turned out great!

Another favorite is "The Warmth Of The Sun." Do you remember much about writing that?

Yeah, that was done at my office on Sunset and Vine on the 11th floor. Mike Love and I went there the night that President Kennedy was shot and we wrote the song. We were just playing around and I came up with a very light chord thing, from C to Am7 to Eflat and Cm7, which I thought was a great new chord pattern.

When you embarked on a song as complex as "Good Vibrations," did you have much of a road map as to where it was going?

Yeah. I could see that whole song in my mind.

Did you write in a linear way?

No, it was done in sections.

Did it occur to you when you were making that song that it was like nothing that had ever been done in pop music?

Yeah. I thought of it as a record that people would like, even though it was complex.

If you're writing a song and you keep coming to a brick wall where the chorus should be, what helps you get through it?

Sometimes that will happen. I'll just constantly go back and rehash until I get it right.

If you feel yourself falling into a rut with your writing, what kinds of things help you get a new perspective?

Throughout my life, my whole career, I've been that way. I'll go to the piano and I'll go, " Damn it, I can't get anything written here." Keep trying and trying. Sometimes I will purposely write a song that isn't quite good enough. I call them simple songs.

How do you feel when your songs are used in commercials?

It's an honor that they would do that in the first place. Real honored by that.

Have you ever dreamed a song?

No.

Is songwriting something that's still fun for you?

Yeah, yeah, I have a hell of a lot of fun.

At this point in your life as a songwriter, what's the most challenging thing for you?

The most challenging thing for me is to be able to find the right key and to make a melody sound like it's more than just manufactured. Like "Hey Jude" is a very inspired melody.

Your songs have kept so many people in touch with their youth. Do they do the same for you?

Yeah, I get a very straight-ahead feeling from them.

Your work is definitely going to live on for centuries, but how would you most like to be remembered 50 years from now?

I think I would like to be remembered as a good songwriter.

What would you still like to accomplish as a songwriter?

I would like to write a song that imparts a love message.

Roger McGuinn

Eight Miles High ✦ Mr. Spaceman ✦ You Showed Me

Interview conducted in 1996

"When the Beatles came out, I learned their songs and I started using their beat with the folk songs I knew."

On June 5, 1965, when The Byrds' debut single, an electric version of Bob Dylan's "Mr. Tambourine Man," hit number one, the boundaries of popular music were expanding almost weekly. The best bands and writers of the day absorbed influences and rendered them into new shapes. Styles collided like atoms in a molecule, the resulting hybrids spawning new sounds never before heard. The Byrds were at the forefront of this musical experimentation.

Roger McGuinn, mastermind and guiding force of the band, once summed up The Byrds' style in six words: "It was Dylan meets The Beatles." While that went a long way toward describing their literate "folk-rock" style, they also incorporated elements of raga Indian styles, modern jazz, and country, increasing their wingspan on every album and single released during their 1965-68 heyday.

In their original incarnation, The Byrds boasted this stellar line-up: McGuinn (who then went by the first name of Jim), David Crosby, Gene Clark, Chris Hillman and Michael Clarke. While each brought strengths to the group – i.e., Crosby's inventive harmony lines – what set the group in flight was McGuinn's vision, nasally vocals and jangly 12-string Rickenbacker guitar.

While The Byrds covered Dylan and Pete Seeger for their earliest hits, McGuinn and Gene Clark soon blossomed as songwriters both individually and collectively. McGuinn and Clark co-wrote the classic "Eight Miles High" as well as standout tracks such as "Tomorrow Is A Long Way Away," "You Won't Have To Cry," "Please Let Me Love You," and "You Showed Me" (which the Turtles took into the Top 10 in 1969). McGuinn and Chris Hillman co-wrote "So You Want To Be A Rock'n'Roll Star," while McGuinn himself was responsible for "5D," "Mr. Spaceman," and later Byrds classics such as "The Ballad Of Easy Rider" (with a little uncredited help from Bob Dylan) and "Chestnut Mare."

Born July 13, 1942 in Chicago, McGuinn cut his teeth in the folk scene of his hometown. In the early 1960s, he toured with the Chad Mitchell Trio, and completed his musical apprenticeship working as a staff writer for Bobby Darin's music publishing company in New York's legendary Brill Building.

How did your stint as a Brill Building staff writer shape you?

It was a disciplinary thing. Prior to that, I would just play guitar, figure out a few chords and haphazardly write a song if I felt like it. At the Brill Building, you went to work every day and your job was to write songs, and your off-duty job was to listen to the radio and accumulate a knowledge of what was happening out there, and be able to custom gear a song to any specific genre. So it gave me an understanding behind the mechanics of it. And there's a certain satisfaction in knowing that you're creating something with the knowledge of what you're doing, as opposed to just doing it spontaneously. Now there's something to be said for the spontaneity of just writing a song off the top of your head; something that occurs to you in the shower. But going to work everyday and doing it, it's sort of a lost art. There aren't many people who do that, except maybe in Nashville. That may be the last bastion of that kind of songwriting.

In Nashville, there is a lot of cross-pollination with songwriters. Was it like that at the Brill Building?

No, that wasn't the case, although I did have partners who were part of the same publishing company I wrote with – Artie Resnick, Kenny Young and Bobby Darin. Even though Carole King and Burt Bacharach were in the same building, we didn't see each other. I didn't know who they were at that point, and they didn't know who I was. So there wasn't a lot of cross-pollination that I knew of. I would just show up at a little cubicle that was very small – probably 8 x 10 with a piano in it that took up most of the space, a couple of folding chairs and that was it. You'd get your cup of coffee in the Styrofoam cup, pop it up on the piano and go to work. I'd bring my guitar in there, and we'd sit there all day, knocking out songs. So it wasn't the kind of romantic thing you're thinking of. It was more of a sweatshop [laughs].

When you listened to songs on the radio for research, would you use them as models to write your own?

That was actually the assignment. Bobby told us to listen to the radio and write songs like the ones we heard. So if you hear a Frank Sinatra song, come up with a Frank Sinatra song. If you hear a Bobby Vinton song, come up with a Bobby Vinton song. The Beach Boys were popular at the time, so we came up with a surf song called "Beach Ball." It was our assignment to listen to the radio. I had three radios at my apartment, and I used to listen to them all at the same time. I had WABC, 1010 WINS and I forget the other one, but there were three Top 40 stations in New York, and I'd listen to them all. It was fun to hear overlapping things [laughs] and sometimes the same song would come on all three of them. Instead of crossing the dial, I had them all going as a scanner.

Did you learn the songs you were emulating?

I did. When The Beatles came out, I learned their songs and I started using their beat with the folk songs I knew. That's how the hybrid of rock and folk came together.

Do you think that's a valid way of learning how to write songs?

Absolutely. Imitation is the way you learn anything. A young child learns how to do things by watching his parents. You look at Bob Dylan, he started out imitating Woody Guthrie, and he lost it very quickly, became a self-contained singer/songwriter within a few years of that. But there was a definite Woody Guthrie influence if you listen to his early work. In fact, when I first saw Dylan, he was doing nothing but Woody Guthrie covers. He was playing at Folk City in

Greenwich Village and not doing a single original song at that point. We all start out imitating and then, if we have the inclination and talent, we go into our own style.

In The Byrds, how did the vocal arrangements come together?

We had one technique we used throughout. Gene Clark and I would sing unison on the melody, and Crosby would fly around between thirds, fourths and fifths on the harmony part. It was really two-part harmony. It sounded like three-part harmony to a lot of people because Crosby was popping around on different parts, but it was an almost Everly Brothers-type thing. Gene and I found that when we sang unison, we developed a distinctive voice. His was really mellow and low-ended, and I had a lot of high end, and the two of them together made a third voice that was really interesting.

When you wrote with Gene Clark, was there a certain role you played?

Writing with Gene Clark was a unique experience, because he was so self-contained. He was able to write solo very well. So what I would bring to the table would be more conceptual than melodic. For instance, on the song "Eight Miles High," it was my idea to do a song about an airplane ride, coming back from England and call it something "miles high." We started out with "Six Miles High," but it didn't sound right, so we changed it for poetic reasons. But basically my input on that song was the concept of it and what it should be about, then working out the poetry. Gene had the basic chord structure and the melody already. He was really a fine, talented songwriter.

Was the signature guitar lick on "Eight Miles High" part of the writing process?

No, it came later. He just had the three or four chord pattern. It could have been a country song actually, if you'd played it in that style. We were on the road in a motor home and the only music we had with us was John Coltrane and Ravi Shankar, which we listened to over and over and over again until it saturated our brains. So by the time we got back to L.A. to record it, that was what came out in the studio. Coltrane was doing his impression of Indian music on the saxophone, and that main line of "Eight Miles High" appears on

Coltrane's "India and Africa," and I copied that lick. Then he does a lot of quick flurries of notes, and I tried to get that too. So the guitar riff is a direct tribute to Coltrane.

In addition to Coltrane, I've heard you talk about Bach as an influence on your guitar playing. Were you ever aware of developing the "Roger McGuinn sound"?

I'm aware that what I play is distinctive, and I think it has a number of elements that came from my background. I play banjo, so a lot of my picking technique is banjo rolling style, as opposed to a guitar picking style. Then the obvious elements of folk music, Bach, jazz. I use a flatpick between the thumb and index finger, then on the third and ring fingers, I wear metal fingerpicks.

An earlier collaboration of yours and Gene Clark's, "You Showed Me," was an unreleased Byrds song that The Turtles later turned into a hit.

Terry Melcher, who was our first producer, had all the demos of the songs we'd written prior to recording the *Mr. Tambourine Man* album. And he just didn't think "You Showed Me" was strong enough to get on the album. The Turtles didn't hear the demo. Their road manager played the song for them on an old Farfisa organ that had a broken bellows, and because the bellows were broken, he couldn't play it at the right tempo. So that's why The Turtles interpretation of it came out at a slower tempo.

On the Byrds' first album, "He Was A Friend Of Mine" is credited to you and David Crosby.

I wrote that the night Kennedy was assassinated. I was in New York City, working at the Brill Building and I came home and my girl-friend told me that Kennedy had been assassinated, and I got really upset, really depressed. Both of us went over to a friend's house – it was Bob Carey from [the folk group] The Tarriers – and we were sitting around playing guitars, and I had heard the folk song "He Was A Friend Of Mine" that Dylan did. It's an old public domain song. I kind of rearranged it. I changed the melody and the words to fit the Kennedy assassination, then I didn't do anything with it for years, because I thought it would be inappropriate, like I was cashing in on it. So I kept it to myself until The Byrds.

On "So You Want To Be A Rock'N'Roll Star," you collaborated with Chris Hillman.

We were sitting up at his house for the purpose of writing songs, kind of like the Brill Building. We were going through one of those rock'n'roll teen magazines, and were amazed at the sort of turnover in the personnel. Every week or so, you'd see different people, and we thought it would be funny to do a riff on that, to write a tongue in cheek manual on how to become a rock'n'roll star. What you need is to have your pants tight, the right haircut, learn how to play the guitar a little bit [laughs].

The story is that your song "The Ballad Of Easy Rider" originated with Bob Dylan.

That was an assignment from Peter Fonda. He basically broke new ground in the film business by putting his record collection on the soundtrack. It was kind of a low budget film, so he was saving money since he didn't hire a guy to do the score, like everybody else did in Hollywood. But he wanted one song that was custom written for the movie, so he took the movie to New York, and he screened it for Dylan. And Dylan sat in the screening room, and he wasn't sure what this movie was going to be. He thought maybe it was just going to be a motorcycle movie like *Wild Angels* or something, and he wasn't sure about it. So he scribbled a couple of notes on a paper napkin and he gave it to Peter, and he said, "Here, give this to McGuinn [laughs]." So Peter flew back to L.A. and he gave me this little paper cocktail napkin, and it had pencil writing on it, and it said: "The river flows / it flows to the sea / Wherever that river goes / that's where I want to be / Flow, river, flow." And I took it, and got my 12-string out, made up a melody and finished off the words, and called it "The Ballad Of Easy Rider."

Did you ever talk shop with Dylan?

He never discussed his techniques or anything. We did sit down to write some songs at one point, but I didn't have any musical ideas at that moment, and we didn't write anything. He never talked much about his art. When I talked to Dylan, it was usually about something other than music.

More recently, you've collaborated with Tom Petty on "King Of The Hill."

It was a spontaneous thing. We were on tour in Europe and we had a day off. I came up to Tom's suite with my guitar and had that melody that I'd been kicking around for awhile. I showed it to him and he liked it. We'd both been reading a rock autobiography – it was *Papa John*, by John Phillips – and we both thought, "Gee, how decadent [laughs]." So we both thought that was good source material for a song, and we kicked it around until it became "King Of The Hill."

Petty seems like a guy who has a solid work ethic when it comes to writing.

Yes. He's a very hard worker and he's an extremely good songwriter. He has a lot of control over his imagination and his mind. I was watching him when we were writing "King Of The Hill," and I was kind of amazed how he would sort of fly up into the stratosphere, grab a line, then put it down on paper. Then he'd do it again. I got some lines in there too. It was really an amazing process.

Having written songs for so many years, do you ever try to change up your approach?

No, I figure if it works, don't fix it. It's basically the same technique I've always used, even at the Brill Building – you just work on it until you get it the way you like it. I've found that not going back is good – where you just write a song and that's it pretty much. If you don't get it in a few days, it's probably not going to develop that much. You shouldn't work on a song for ten years and hope it's going to work out. The thing is to write another one. It's sort of like a photographer in a photo session. They take lots of pictures. They don't just take one picture and try to doctor it up and make it look good. If you take a couple hundred pictures, you're going to get one or two that are really good.

Are there things that help you keep the channel open?

You just have to be open to it. It takes a certain leap of faith that you can do it. I think that's what writer's block is, is when you lose your confidence that you can do that. You just have to know that you're capable of doing it. Then it's just a lot of elbow grease. It's the old Edison quote of genius being one percent inspiration, 99 percent perspiration. It's hard work.

Nick Ashford and Valerie Simpson

Ain't No Mountain High Enough
✫ Ain't Nothing Like The Real Thing ✫ Solid

Interview conducted in 1995

"Whenever we write a song that's not so positive, people think it's about us and that we're breaking up."

When songwriting duo Nickolas Ashford and Valerie Simpson talk about their work, they often stress the importance of making a song "live." It's not just a pleasing arrangement of notes, chords and words they're after, but a living, breathing thing that bristles with energy and soulful emotion.

When you listen to their vast song catalog, from the classic Marvin Gaye & Tammi Terrell Motown hits of the 1960s ("Ain't No Mountain High Enough," "Your Precious Love," "Ain't Nothing Like The Real Thing," "You're All I Need to Get By") to the duo's own Top 40 successes as recording artists ("Found A Cure," "Solid"), you hear the undeniable lifeforce of their songs: pulsing loco-motive rhythms, heartbeat-thumping bass lines and melodies that soar with all the love and wonder of a human spirit in full-flight.

The duo met in 1964 at a Harlem gospel meeting, and became fast friends. Sharing a love of gospel music, they began to collaborate on songwriting, with Nick handling most of the lyrics and Valerie the music. They moved into the secular pop scene and scored their first hit in 1966 with Ray Charles'

"Let's Go Get Stoned." The duo then joined the staff of Scepter/Wand Records, where they penned hits for Maxine Brown and Chuck Jackson. In 1967, they moved to Tamla/Motown, where they became writers and producers known for their soft soul approach.

After they left Motown, they became a full-fledged recording act, releasing ten albums over the next decade. At the same time, they continued to lend their golden touch to artists such as The Fifth Dimension ("California Soul"), Diana Ross ("Surrender," "Remember Me," "The Boss"), and Chaka Khan ("I'm Every Woman").

In 1996, Nick and Valerie completed and released an ambitious album titled *Been Found*, a collaboration with the renowned poet Maya Angelou. Mixing their soulful writing and singing style with Angelou's spoken word gifts, the album was yet another milestone in the illustrious career of these two gifted singer/songwriters.

When you think back, was there a defining moment when you realized you were meant to be songwriters?

Ashford: I think for me, at maybe around 13 years old, I had a very inspirational feeling in the Baptist Church when I was just banging on the piano. I just had wings when I was singing and playing, so I knew something then, but I didn't think of it as a career or anything.

Simpson: For me, it was also in the churches. Because we were both writing gospel songs, the possibility of a career as a songwriter was introduced by someone who came to the church looking for talent to write love songs. I didn't think about people actually doing that for a living, but suddenly it became a possibility, and something that we had fun doing. So that really defined it for us.

When you first started writing songs together, did you settle into certain roles?

S: The process has stayed pretty much the same over the years. Nick writes all the lyrics basically, and I do the music, and we kind of collaborate on the melodies. There are many ways, and sometimes he'll have a prepared lyric. But most of the time, we like to try it spontaneously, just to see what's in the air and what we can feel naturally. We see where my playing might lead him. Some thought may come to him as a result of the color of the music, and that'll be the beginning of something. We don't labor too long over those things; we just kind of let them fall out. If they're good, we'll pick them up later.

Your first big hit was "Let's Go Get Stoned." Do you recall writing it?

A: That was a day we couldn't write a song. All that day, we couldn't come up with a thing. So one of us said, "Oh let's go get stoned." Of course, that meant go have a drink. So we went running down the steps, being silly and singing "Let's go get stoned." We had a couple drinks that night, then the next day when we went to see the publisher, he said, "You guys got anything for me?" And we said, "Yeah, we got a hit for you." I said, "Val what's that big hit we wrote yesterday when we were singing coming down the steps?" And Valerie jumped to the piano and sang, "Let's go get stoned." We were joking. We thought he was going to laugh and throw us out of the office, and instead, he got so excited and said, "My God, I hear this for Ray Charles." And we didn't even know what we had said. Then we really had to go and make something up [laughs].

How did the Motown approach and philosophy affect your songwriting?

S: We were fascinated with the Motown aura, and we were thrilled to be there. Coming from New York, we brought our own vibe and interestingly enough, we never lived in Detroit. We were always the visiting songwriters who would stay for a week or two, do our thing, then go back home and write some more. We were part of the family, and yet we had a distance, which was kind of good, because they always liked seeing us.

At the time, were you writing 9 to 5?

S: We had our own little office, but I don't think anyone paid that much attention to how long you were there as long as you came out with something eventually. I don't think it was all that regimented. There was a lot of good times and partying going on if you ask me. We did have a discipline that was self-imposed. There's no other way to get the work done but to do it. Sometimes you felt inspired and nothing was happening, so we wouldn't labor over it, we'd just try it the next day.

Were you aware that you were writing for specific artists, say Marvin Gaye and Tammi Terrell?

A: That was the great thing about Motown, the heavy competition. A song had to be the best, not only as a song, but also in production and everything. I don't know about Val, but I was intimidated a little bit because you'd walk by the rooms and you'd hear songs coming out and you'd think, "Hmmm, that sounds real good" [laughs]. It was very competitive, but I think that's what made Motown and all those writers there so good.

How did they decide which artists would cut which songs?

A: They had a system up there they called quality control. They had Berry Gordy and people like Billie Jean Brown that would sometimes pick songs for different artists . . .

S: But those things would also change. Halfway through production they'd take the song off one person and try it on someone else. Sometimes three or four artists would end up cutting a song and they'd choose the best one.

A: Berry and some other music people at Motown would sit and listen to each record. Also, the producers were in on it. Even the clerks and secretaries would come in and vote on the records.

How much freedom of interpretation did the artists have? How much different did a song like "Ain't Nothing Like The Real Thing" sound when Marvin and Tammi sang it versus when you wrote it?

A: The artists didn't have that much to do with the arrangement. The producers at Motown formed the song around the artist. The artist would sometimes just come in off the road and have to go into the studio.

S: It had a lot to do with what kind of interpreter the producer was. In our case, because we were singers, we could lay out a pretty well defined demo for Marvin or for Tammi, then because they were so special in their artistry, they could add that little extra something. Everything was pretty laid out, very clear and straight ahead. But it probably varied with other writers who were not singers, so it's hard to say how they worked.

Talk a little about the evolution of "Ain't No Mountain High Enough" from the first version to Diana Ross' symphonic version.

A: When we were new at Motown, we didn't produce the first version by Marvin and Tammi. That was produced by Harvey Fuqua and Johnny Bristol. That was also our first song at Motown. After we had some success and it was time for Diana Ross to bust out on her own, everyone wondered who was going to produce her first album? Lo and behold, Berry Gordy picked Ashford and Simpson [laughs]. We were like "What? Her first solo album; this can't be possible." So we were like little busy bees around here, and we started writing immediately, of course. Now at that time, Isaac Hayes and a few other artists had started coming out with long cuts, and that was the trend. We hadn't written anything with that kind of feeling. Knowing Diana Ross and her speaking voice and how sexy she was, we decided to take the existing "Ain't No Mountain High Enough" and rewrite some of it especially for her. We wanted to have something grand, long and sexy for her.

S: When we originally wrote that song, I remember that Nick came in with the chorus after walking down Central Park West. It was just at the point where you feel like you don't want the city to take you under and you're just telling yourself there's nothing anyone can do to stop me, and he came in with this dramatic statement, "ain't no mountain high." That was the easiest chorus for us to hook together, and it was clear that it was a hit. In fact, we even played it for Dusty Springfield before we took it to Motown, and she wanted it. But we couldn't give it away, because we knew we had to make a good impression when we went to Motown. Of course, Dusty would've killed it too [laughs].

What obstacles do you face being both husband and wife and a professional team?

A: There is an obstacle, but it's not an obstacle we have. It's a label people put on us. We're kind of known as a "love couple." So whenever we write a song that's not so positive, people think it's about us and that we're probably breaking up. They think everything is related to our relationship and it's not true. So that to me is a negative thing. I think the public's perception is sometimes limited. But you got to give them what they want [laughs].

What would you say is your favorite song that you've written?

A: I'd say "Ain't No Mountain High Enough" by Diana Ross. I still get goose pimples when I hear that. I won't be modest, I just think it's great.

S: I think "You're All I Need To Get By."

Tell me about the album with Maya Angelou.

S: We think it's kind of wonderful. It's twelve songs, six of which were written with Maya. She's also performing on those six songs with us. So it's kind of like a new genre, a song mixed with spoken word. Sometimes she's talking and we're interweaving with singing, sometimes we're singing and she's talking at the same time. But the songs really sound very interesting. The other six songs are just as exciting in their own right.

A: We think the album is so fresh and different for us, and since we had been out of the marketplace for awhile, we were looking for something new to come back with. And I think having one of the great poets in the world just made it magic. It wasn't a planned thing. We'd been invited down to her house for Thanksgiving. I was down in the basement, banging my heart out on the piano and yelling until finally they were lured down there. Valerie got on the piano, and I started moaning and Maya Angelou started talking poetically. Little known to them both, I had a tape recorder going on the floor [laughs]. Everything we did in that room was so natural and fabulous, all we had to do was put the pieces together.

After all you've done in your career, are there things you'd still like to accomplish?

S: Maybe just the freedom to jump off in any direction you want. I guess you feel like there's still room, and just a way to make things easier to jump off in other directions, whether it's Broadway or whatever. I think we'd both like to be able to try new and different things.

What advice would you give to a songwriter who wants to write hits?

A: As emotional as you may feel, if no one wants to hear it, then you have to step back. You have listen to the marketplace, you've got to be somewhere in the marketplace, unless you're new wave or something and don't care. Also, that depends on what is your definition of a hit. My definition of a hit is when the whole world is singing your song, not just segments who like this type of music or that type of music. My definition of a hit is a worldwide hit. I think you have to listen to all music, then put your heart in it and decide what you want to do, then just cry it out louder than anyone has ever said it. Make your own hit. Everybody's got their own feel and their own style.

S: I admire originality, I like people who try for their own thing, who are true to their own selves. As opposed to cloning the trend of the day. If you have a little streak, a little sound, a little nuance, you have to hold on to something that's really yours.

Barry Gibb

To Love Somebody
✷ How Can You Mend A Broken Heart? ✷ Stayin' Alive

Interview conducted in 1997

"The isolation of having nothing else to do and not even having television was very conducive to songwriting."

Barry Gibb of the Bee Gees has a vision of where song ideas originate. "There is an instinctive information vault that's indigenous to songwriters, a little box you can go to and all of your songs are in there," he says. "An imaginary barrel – that's what I always used to call it."

During an incredible career, now in its fourth decade, Barry, along with his brothers Robin and Maurice, have reached into this well-stocked barrel to pull out some of the most memorable songs of the pop-rock era. Consider an abbreviated list of the barrel's cargo: "To Love Somebody," "Massachusetts," "Words," "I Started A Joke," "Lonely Days," "How Can You Mend A Broken Heart," "Jive Talkin'," "You Should Be Dancing," "Nights On Broadway," "How Deep Is Your Love," "Stayin' Alive," "Night Fever," and "Tragedy."

Barry Gibb began writing songs when he was 12 years old. "The first song I wrote was 'Turtle Dove,'" he recalled in David Leaf's Bee Gees biography. "About four years after I started writing, Robin started. His songs developed along the same lines mine did, and eventually we both started writing together. The three of us are really one in that respect."

121

When the three brothers were signed by manager Robert Stigwood to Polydor Records in 1967, Barry was 20 years old, and Robin and Maurice were 17. They scored eight U.S. and 10 UK chart hits before the 1960s were over.

They also instantly became hot songwriters whose material was snapped up by other singers, from middle of the road artists such as Jose Feliciano and Vicki Carr to rock legends such as Elvis Presley (who recorded "Words") and Janis Joplin (who memorably performed "To Love Somebody").

But becoming famous at such a young age had its downside, as Barry attests: "That first fame thing will destroy you. You'll believe what people say about you, you'll start to believe that you're put on earth to give some great religious message to the masses and in fact, you're a young upstart making records. As you start to get older, a lot more logic creeps into your life. I guess they call it wisdom."

After breaking up in 1969, reconciling in 1971, and floundering commercially from 1972 through 1974, the Bee Gees adopted the R&B/ disco style and exploded beyond anyone's wildest expectations. They reeled off an amazing 13 hit singles from 1975-1979 and dominated the pop field. In addition to Bee Gees' hits, the brothers' songs also blanketed the radio courtesy of Olivia Newton John, Yvonne Elliman, Samantha Sang, Frankie Valli and their younger brother, Andy Gibb.

During the 1980s, with the Bee Gees' commercial fortunes declining, Barry turned to producing and writing hits for other artists, such as Barbra Streisand, Dionne Warwick, Kenny Rogers, and Diana Ross. A strong component of the Bee Gees renaissance in the 1990s was recognition of the brothers' extraordinary accomplishments as songwriters. They continued to be beckoned by the likes of Celine Dion, who recorded their "Immortality" on her *Let's Talk About Love* album.

After writing songs for almost 40 years, has it gotten easier for you?

I think you become more focused on what the core of a song really is – that's probably the only thing that comes easier. What songwriting has always been to me is basically like a flash. I have a flash of an idea or a flash of a chorus, or a flash of a song before it's actually constructed. That hasn't changed; it's continued right through my life. I'll get up in the middle of the night and put something on a dictaphone and go back to sleep. But I don't know that it's ever easier. I think it's always a challenge. At the same time, I think it has to be fun.

Are there things you do to keep the process fun?

Sometimes it's better not to write at all. The three of us don't spend time together when we're not working. That keeps our minds fresh and it also gives us a chance to absorb the culture, which is basically our standard answer if anyone says, "Where do your ideas come from?" You have to spend weeks or months just absorbing and then that becomes songs in a roundabout way. You don't just write a song based on something you see. It may be two months later.

Does it help you to have an image of a particular person in mind when you're writing?

Yes, the star of the movie, as it were. That's one of the first things we ask each other when we start. We've got our melody and we like our idea, or the core of the song, what it's about, and then we start asking questions like, "Well, who is the person? What's that person's environment? What's that person unhappy about? Why is the relationship breaking up? Why indeed are they falling in love?" So we'll look into that, and we will try to create a person. It gives the song a life of its own, a personality.

Can you describe the roles that each of you plays in the songwriting process?

My strengths have always been ideas and construction and lyric form. I started when I was about 8 or 9 years old, then Maurice and Robin sort of jumped on board when they became the same age. Then we all started writing together. I'd say Maurice is very creative in the area of keyboards and coming up with the magic chord when you're looking for one, or general ambience of a song, atmosphere. If I describe to Maurice the atmosphere that I want, he will give it to me, keyboard-wise. Robin is very good lyrically. Robin's a very good judge. In other words, I'm the person who will throw an awful lot of stuff out and Robin will be like an antenna and he will say, "I like that but I don't like this." He becomes the sounding board.

Do you do a lot of rewriting and last minute tinkering with songs?

No. We'll usually go with whatever we've done, pretty stubbornly. The song we wrote for Celine Dion, "Immortality," the demo is almost identical to her record. That's a perfect example of saying, "Well, here's the song, here's the demo and this makes the song shine, this brings out the personality of the person singing the song, that's it, it's a record." So they changed almost nothing, apart from Celine herself singing the song. That's when it works right.

I've heard that you often write away from the instruments. What do you feel are the advantages of that?

A total freedom. Emotional freedom, mental freedom, the freedom to bring the melody wherever you want it to go in your head without having to have a drum machine, guitar or a piano to establish chords. Sometimes it's nice to establish chords that you cannot name. Then you go find the chord you're thinking of somehow. I'd rather imagine something. To me, it's a bit like why I don't like videos because I'd rather imagine something when I hear a song than be told what to see.

When I interviewed Burt Bacharach he also talked of the importance of getting away from the instrument.

I can tell. I'm a big Bacharach fan. I think he's wonderful, and I think Bacharach & David are my idols, along with Rodgers & Hammerstein and Rodgers & Hart. I can believe that Burt Bacharach would have a melody, regardless of the beats per minute or bars, or whether it's 6/4 or 4/4, or whatever it is, where the changes are felt where the changes should be. When you're writing strictly with an instrument, it can be an obstruction.

A lot of songwriters I've interviewed say they feel that songs come through them from another source. Does it feel that way to you?

Yes. Without being able to explain it, because it does sound quite corny when you say that, but it's sort of like you've just been given a song. Somebody just gives you the core of it. I guess it might have something to do with what they call the collective consciousness, that all these things, all these wonderful film ideas and book ideas and song ideas are all actually out there anyway. And we somehow pick up on them. Or certain people pick up on them.

I'd like to mention some of your songs to get your reactions. "To Love Somebody"...

It was written for Otis Redding. It was written in 1967 at the Waldorf Astoria Hotel. I was on my own and Robert Stigwood had brought me to New York. I'd never been to New York before so it was a great thrill for me. I met Otis Redding early in the evening and Robert Stigwood had sort of suggested I write a song for Otis Redding, and I said I would try. I was inspired because I had just met him. The rest of the evening I was alone and I sort of concocted most of it in that time. Of course, he died about three months later in a plane crash, so he never recorded the song. But the song was then finished with Robin and Maurice.

Does it set your mind in a different direction, knowing you're writing for a voice other than your own.

Absolutely. It's also one of the reasons we always seize the chance to work with someone else that we really like. If we're always writing for ourselves, then I think we become bored with that. Your voice is constantly the instrument by which your song becomes heard. If you've got someone else's voice – the best example is Barbra Streisand – or someone who puts their personality into your song, it's the cream on the cake. That's what makes it happen. It stretches your songwriting. It makes you write songs that you would not write otherwise.

"Massachusetts"

The first time the group went to New York, we stayed at the St. Regis Hotel. While our luggage was being moved into the suite, we were writing "Massachusetts," sitting on a sofa, the three of us. It came from our first exposure to America, our first thoughts of writing a song about flower power, which the song is about. Or it's basically anti-flower power. Don't go to San Francisco; come home for Christ sakes [laughs]. We wanted to write the opposite of what it's like to lose somebody who went to San Francisco. The lights all went out in Massachusetts because you left.

How do you feel about the Odessa *album? Can you listen to it?*

No. My tendency is not to listen to too much of our old stuff. I don't know why. I guess I want to keep moving on and if I keep listening to things from the past, it might influence me in the wrong direction.

But *Odessa*, I guess I have strong personal feelings about that record because it was a time when the group was splitting up. We were in tremendous crisis with each other. Robert Stigwood wanted a double album and we didn't know why. I think it was basically a financial deal. So we were doing something that we weren't motivated to do. Everything was done for tax reasons, you know? You'd go to New York to record so you wouldn't have to pay taxes in England. We didn't even know these things. This was our management and record company. So the *Odessa* album to me was not a good experience. It was an album that was made over many many months, and we didn't really want to do it. A single album would've been perfect. A double album, it just seemed there was too much stuff that wasn't that good.

I would disagree. I love the way the album sustains a melancholy mood throughout.

You know, maybe it's because there was so much trouble and strife going on at the time the songs were written. I think there's probably a little bit of that in every song. Maybe that's why it's something you might appreciate. It probably goes deeper than I thought it did, and that was just my experience of it.

"Lonely Days"

It was the first of two songs that we wrote after we got back together. We'd been apart for nearly two years. Robin came to my place in Kensington and that afternoon we wrote "How Can You Mend A Broken Heart?" and that was obviously a link to us coming back together. We called Maurice, finished the song, and went to the studio with that and an idea for "Lonely Days." And those two songs were recorded that night.

"Jive Talkin'"

We were working with Arif Mardin on the *Main Course* album, trying to make a comeback. It was about 1975. We were sort of out of vogue at that time. Every night, we were going back and forth to Criteria Studios from living on Biscayne Bay, which is where I still live now. The bridge made a clickety sound, like [imitates rhythm of "Jive Talkin'" introduction]. It stayed in my head and one night, coming back from the studio, I just started singing this thing. Robin and Maurice picked up on it and I think we actually finished the song late at night and had it ready for recording in the next two days.

I've read about your initial reservations about singing falsetto. Since you've become so well known for that sound, have you felt trapped by having to use too much of it?

No. I do it when I love it and I don't do it when I don't feel like it. To tell you the truth, I've never had reservations about using it. The story is that during the recording of "Nights On Broadway," Arif asked me if any of us could go out there and scream some ad libs, sort of R & B style high screams. And I was the one who volunteered to go out there and in doing so, sort of discovered that this voice was hidden back there. Then I started developing it and started singing real songs with the falsetto instead of doing ad libs with it. It just developed from there. When I look back, it's actually something I ought to be proud of. Brian Wilson, Frankie Valli and even Prince – they don't make any bones about doing that. I think if you go back far enough, the first rock'n'roll record I ever heard was "Little Darlin'" by The Diamonds, and that was falsetto. So I think that falsetto in a way has been an integral part of rock'n'roll. I don't feel bad about it at all. I think it's nice to be one of those falsetto voices that's quite well known.

Do you have any memories about "How Deep Is Your Love"?

All of those songs [on *Saturday Night Fever*] were for our own album. They weren't for the movie at all. Robert just happened to hear those four or five songs and said he wanted them for the movie, and please don't make an album, this will be your new album. So we said okay. "How Deep Is Your Love," "Stayin' Alive," "More Than A Woman," "If I Can't Have You" – these things were all done in a chateau in France in really bad weather with nothing else to do. I guess the isolation of having nothing else to do and not even having television was actually very conducive to songwriting. It really worked well. There was no other form of entertainment so you literally had to go to work. We couldn't be lazy. So those songs came from those four or five weeks of horrible weather and not being anywhere near civilization.

Do you think a band today has a chance at a 35-year career?

I suppose anybody does. Anything could happen. I think someone like Oasis could, although they need to get past the obstacles they have at the moment. Hanson are a perfect example of what we might've been like when we were at that age. So I really like them and think they have a tremendous future if they keep their heads on. I feel very good about the business right now. The only negative side is that there are so many artists: thousands and thousands of groups, thousands and thousands of young individual singers that are all terrific. The great shame is that they won't all make it. And the business is now full of people who exploit. I guess they always were there, but there's more of those people too. There's far more deceit and corruption and decadence in the business now than there ever was.

What are some things you'd still like to do with the Bee Gees that you haven't done?

I think we'd like to have a really good song in a really good movie. I think that has never really happened to The Bee Gees, apart from *Fever*, and *Grease*, of course. But they were sort of novelty things in our minds. We've never had that serious shot at being nominated for an Academy Award for a song in a film and I think that that's one of our dreams. That would be wonderful. Apart from that, I really love doing the gigs. The isolated stage show here and there is where the fun is for me. Also, making records. I want us to go on making records. We're actually in our prime, believe it or not. I think vocally and mentally, we've managed to stay intact, somehow. We're very strong. I think if the Stones can drag themselves around the country one more time [laughs], then there's a few more albums in us. As long as you're having fun, that's the key. It's got to be fun. The moment it becomes a grind, it's over.

Dolly Parton

I Will Always Love You ✯ 9 To 5 ✯ Coat Of Many Colors

Interview conducted in 1996

"To be a true songwriter, I think you have to really allow yourself to feel and allow yourself the freedom to write it the way you want to."

"Without a doubt, songwriting is my greatest source of joy and the best outlet for my creativity," says Dolly Parton, who has written over 3,000 songs, including country classics such as "Joshua," "Jolene," "Coat Of Many Colors," "My Tennessee Mountain Home," "Touch Your Woman," "Just Because I'm A Woman," "The Last One To Touch Me," "Yellow Roses" and the most successful crossover single of the past two decades, "I Will Always Love You."

Yet for all this, in the public eye, Dolly the songwriter is usually eclipsed by the other facets of her persona: legend of country music, platinum recording artist, charismatic stage performer, wise-cracking comedienne, star of movies and television, tabloid queen, savvy entrepreneur, multi-millionairess, warm-hearted philanthropist, and cultural icon. In the 1980s, it was written that Dolly's image – the cascading blond wigs, the carefully applied make-up and the impossibly pulchritudinous figure – was the most universally recognized of any celebrity.

Her far-reaching accomplishments are incredible when you consider her beginnings. Dolly Rebecca Parton entered this world on January 19, 1946, in a one-room cabin in the mountains of East Tennessee, the fourth of 12 children born to poor sharecropper parents. While Dolly grew up without electricity, running water, a telephone or indoor plumbing, she was surrounded by a loving family who instilled in her a sense of humor, a good dose of common sense, and a passion for music.

At age 14, she made her first recording, a rockabilly number called "Puppy Love," which led to a one-shot appearance on the Grand Ole Opry and a songwriting deal with Tree Publishing. In her autobiography, *My Life And Other Unfinished Business*, Dolly writes of taking trips to Nashville with her Uncle Bill, also a tunesmith. The two of them lived in "an old junked-up car," writing songs, washing in gas station restrooms and meeting everyone they could.

On the day after she graduated from high school, Dolly grabbed a suitcase full of clothes, boarded a bus and headed for Nashville. What happened over the next 30 years is the story of the American Dream, the rags to riches transformation of a country bumpkin into Dolly Parton, one-woman industry. The clear sound of her lovely mountain tremolo voice and her hillbilly glam image have now become a permanent part of the tapestry of 20th century American popular culture.

Through all the records, concerts, TV specials, movies, magazine covers and business ventures, Dolly has always returned to her songwriting, which runs through the complexities of her life like a clear mountain stream. From that fount, she has brought forth countless memorable songs. There are her compelling story songs: "Coat Of Many Colors," a moving recollection of her childhood poverty; the chilling "Down From Dover," in which she plays a pregnant and abandoned young girl; and the idyllic "My Tennessee Mountain Home." There are the fun, upbeat tunes, such as "9 To 5," "White Limozeen" and "Romeo." There are the tender, lump-in-the-throat ballads such as "My Blue Tears" and "What A Heartache You Turned Out To Be." And of course, there is "I Will Always Love You."

That song was written as a goodbye to her singing partner Porter Wagoner. She first recorded it in 1973, and it reached number one on the country charts the following year. In 1982, she re-recorded it, and again it topped the charts, making Parton the first artist ever to reach # 1 twice with the same song. Then, in 1992, Whitney Houston recorded it for the soundtrack of *The Bodyguard*. It stayed at number one on the pop charts for 14 weeks and became one of the biggest singles in history.

There have been other significant cover versions of Parton's songs by Olivia Newton-John ("Jolene"), Emmylou Harris ("My Blue Tears"), Maria Muldaur ("My Tennessee Mountain Home") and Merle Haggard ("Kentucky Gambler," a #1 country hit).

You've been writing songs almost your whole life and I get the sense that it's something that comes naturally to you. Is that true?

It is true. In fact, everything I think or see is a song. I'm one of those crazy people that when I'm carrying on a conversation with somebody, I'll think, "Oh, that's a great idea for a song," or I'll say something to them and I'll think, "I need to write a song about that." It's just natural. I was born with the gift to rhyme. Ever since I was a little bitty kid, I could just rhyme everything. Every story was a rhyme. It was always fun and it just kind of carried on over the years. I love to write. That's my favorite thing of all. To me, I'd rather write than to sing. My biggest thrill is to write songs, then go in the studio and hear them back.

In your book, you talk about the importance of maintaining a wonder for life and learning new things. Are you always learning new things about writing?

I think that learning new things about life and people automatically gives me new things to write. But you know, I never was one of those writers . . . a lot of people write a formula. They write what's commercial. "You have to have this, you have to have that, you've got to have two verses and a chorus." That's what I was taught when I was young and started in Nashville. It was pretty much two verses and a chorus, but I never could get everything I wanted to say in two verses and a chorus [laughs]. So to me, some of the best songs I write just ramble on and on and on. They're more like stories. People say, "Oh, you shouldn't write a song more than three minutes long because they won't play it on the radio." But some of the songs I've written are like four and five minutes long. So I don't know if I'm really learning anything that I should learn, but I think I write better and better because I live more and more.

In the early stages of writing, do you like to have a title or a storyline?

It depends. That happens to me different ways. I do write titles all the time and song ideas, things that come. I'd love to be able to write them that second, sit down and write it, but I don't always have the time when a great title will fly into my mind. So I'm always writing titles down, and a lot of times when I do have the opportunity to sit down and write, I'll often look through my list of titles and pick one that's really outstanding, and I'll think, "Oh yeah, I remember, that was gonna be great," and I'll basically remember what I was thinking. So I'll use that. But, by the same token, sometimes when I'm not even thinking about writing at all, I'll just be walking through the house and I'll always have my guitars sitting around different places. Sometimes my hand just automatically reaches for my guitar and I'll pick it up and without thinking. I'll say "I'm just going to hit a lick here just to hear the sound of music." Sometimes it sounds really good and it'll hit a chord in me and I won't have anything in mind and it'll all come out at one time. I'll just start playing and I'll just start singing some words and all of a sudden, something will pop out, then before I know it, I've started a song.

One of my favorites of your more recent songs is "Yellow Roses." Did that start from the title?

Yeah, it did. There's some truth in that song too. In a way, it was kind of based on a true story about someone I knew that loved yellow roses and they had given me a yellow rose and the relationship had gone sour. That song is sad, ain't it? I'm one of those people that gets so involved in what I'm writing because I feel it. Everything is very personal to me and I write about everything I feel. Or sometimes I write about something I've seen other people go through, people that I care deeply about. So I feel their sorrow too. A lot of times when I write, boy, I'll just be sitting there with tears rolling down my face. I get caught up in the emotion of it myself. So sometimes things will just start coming, almost like it's just channeling through me, and it's almost like I'm watching the movie or hearing the song myself. And it hits me and oh, I'll just be writing and a-crying and a-singing [laughs]. There was another song I wrote called "There's No Good Way Of Saying Good-bye," and oh, I just slung snot all over that [laughs]. I love to write, because it's almost like going on an emotional journey every time I do it, whether I'm writing happy or sad. If I'm writing happy songs, I get really happy and really joyful with it, and if I'm writing a sad one, I just get down.

What surrounded the writing of "I Will Always Love You"?

I wrote it when I left Porter Wagoner [they'd been performing as a duo]. So it was full of every kind of emotion you could imagine. You know, seven years of fighting and creativity and our success and our relationship, it was just all those things. When you are able to write all those feelings, that's what I think truly makes the classic songs. But I remember exactly where I was sitting when I wrote it, I remember the time of day, I remember the fireplace. It was in my husband's and my first house, and we had a den that was part music room. The fireplace was right in front of the couch, and I always had my writing spot when I would write there. I always sat in the very corner of the couch. You remember those days when you really wrote something great. But I pretty much remember where I was and what I felt with every song I ever wrote. Even with the thousands of songs I've written, I almost remember what time of year it was, what time of day it was, if I was inside or outside, if I was on the porch, if I was in the car. You just remember those things when you allow yourself to feel that deeply. They leave an impression.

"I Will Always Love You" seems like it would be the hardest kind of song to write because it's so simply laid out and direct.

It depends. That one was easy because the times were so hard. And it was so hard for me to communicate with Porter. He wouldn't listen to nothing at that time because he was so angry and so spiteful and so mean about the whole thing that he wouldn't allow me a conversation to try to explain why I was doing what I was doing. I thought, "Well, the only way I'm going to be able to express it is to write it." Everybody can understand a song. There were so many things I wanted to say, there was so much emotion, feeling and heartache on his part and on my part. Once I started it, the song seemed to pour out.

What's the story about Elvis Presley wanting to record the song?

Elvis loved the song. I never met Elvis and there were many times I could have. I don't know why I didn't. I think I just wanted him to always be the way he was in my mind. I didn't want nothing to blow the image. So I just wouldn't meet him. He'd come to town lots of times and they'd send word. Felton Jarvis was producing him at the time, and Felton was a friend of mine. And so they would always let me know when he was in town, and I'd always make an excuse not to go down there to the recording studio. But at any rate, he had heard that song and he loved it. He wanted to do it, so they notified me and I was so excited. So, the next thing they said was, "But you know Elvis has to have half the publishing on the song. Everything he records, unless it's already a standard, he has to have half the publishing." I said, "Well, I'm really sorry, but I don't give my publishing to nobody. Not half of it, not ten percent of it, not any of it." I had just started my own publishing company, and I said, "If he loves the song then he'll record it anyway, and if he don't, well just say that I'm flattered with the thought." But I would not give up the publishing, and thank God I didn't, because that song made me more money than all of the others put together. If I'd given up half the publishing then I would've made half the money, plus I would've lost half the pride in it. The fact that I wrote the song by myself and published it myself just made the whole thing more special. It was not something you had to share. It wasn't the selfishness or the money, it was just that I was offended because the song was already out. I thought, "I'm not giving up the publishing." No lawyer told me not to do it. In fact, everybody else told me I was crazy. Elvis also loved "Coat Of Many Colors," but I wouldn't give up the publishing on that either.

I was watching Rhinestone *the other night and noticed when you were playing guitar it was open tuned. Do you write in open tunings?*

That depends. When I've got my fingernails on [shows her long candy red nails], I have to play in open tuning because I'm not willing to give up my fingernails. But as a serious songwriter, when I have the time to go on a writing binge, when I really have a week or two to write, I take these things off and I write regular with my other guitar. Then when I'm done writing, I get me a new set of nails [laughs]. But I can play in open tuning. I can fake it and get by with most things. But I can really seriously play guitar. I used to play the fire out of it before I got so sissy and thought I had to have these fingernails [laughs].

You've really mastered the story song. What would you say is the challenge of writing a song like "Coat Of Many Colors" where there's a lot of information?

That's my favorite style of writing. That's more natural for me, to tell a story. I can rhyme words really good, and to me, it's the same as writing a book. So I really enjoy it. Usually, I just start out writing and I think, "I'm going to write and I'm not going to think about how long it is or how many verses I got before I get to the chorus, or how many times I go back to the chorus. I'm just going to write what I think and what I feel, then if I have to tear it down and fix it up to make it commercial, then I'll do that." But it's much easier for me to write the story songs. Honestly, I can sit down and write a big long story song much easier than I can the more commercial, typical songs.

What about "Down From Dover"? That's a pretty unusual story.

I was on the bus one day with Porter and we were riding through Dover, Tennessee. I was sitting at the window of the bus, and what really made me write that song was that this cloud went across the sun and it swept a shadow across this field I was looking out at through the window. I just saw this crawling shadow across this field – it wasn't clover, but it rhymed with Dover and we were in Dover [laughs]. And I sang, "And the sun behind the cloud just cast a crawling shadow over the fields of clover." That was the first thought that came to my mind, and then I thought, "Time is running out for me and I wish that he would hurry down from Dover." It was like little word triggers. All of a sudden, I thought, "This is great and it's a pretty tune. What'll I write about? Who would live in Dover? Some simple girl would live in Dover, because it was like a simple, country town." And the next thing I knew I was writing about this pregnant girl. Everybody thought it was about Dover, England. People in England love that song because they think I wrote it about their Dover. Anyhow, it just came and boy, once I got into it, it was one line after another.

As somebody who didn't know much of your older material until recently, that song really surprised me because it was so dark.

Back then, most of the stuff I wrote was dark and sad. There were story songs like "Daddy Come And Get Me," "Jeanie's Afraid Of The Dark" and all those sad-ass songs. "Down From Dover" was so ahead of its time, but nowadays that would be very tame on the radio. We released that as a single and they wouldn't play it on the radio because it was so suggestive and it was about a pregnant girl and it was so against what country radio was about at that time.

Do you feel like those dark songs go against the grain of your image as Dolly Parton?

It goes against my image, but it don't go against who I am. There are many sides to me. But everything I ever wrote, I'm proud of. I was that girl. I didn't get pregnant, it wasn't a true story about me. But I had had numerous nieces and relatives that had gotten pregnant and their daddy wanted to kill the boy that done it. I was just trying to find a way to make it as sad and pitiful as I could. It's not against my nature at all. In fact, when I hurt, I hurt all over and I've been through some major sad things in my life. But I also have that other cheerful side and I try to show my best. This is my image. I'm a very positive person. In fact, I've often said that you have to work at being happy, just like you have to work at being miserable. And when I'm working on those sad songs, I'm working at being miserable [laughs], and I can do it. I've been to all them places in my emotions with broken hearts and feeling all those things.

I've heard you call songwriting "therapy." Does it keep you sane?

I think it does. I am so thankful that I can write, and I often thank God personally for giving me that gift because I think it has kept me sane. Because I think that so much you go through in life, or just if you're a sensitive person, as all writers are, you're so affected by everything on the news. I watch the news and I'm just tore apart by some of the stuff I see, some of it I can't bear to watch. I have to flip the channels around because I can't stand to see little starving kids or the idea that somebody beat up a kid or starved a kid or all the horrible things in the world. And I have to write those things too. And I just think, God if it wasn't for my ability to write and sing and express that . . . certainly to write, but when I get to sing it too, the whole vibration and just the feeling of having it come out, to be able to vocalize that, it kind of permeates every little cell in your body and somehow it kind of works it all out, and I don't feel near as bad after I've written it.

137

When you were first starting out, did you find it difficult to be a woman in the music business?

First of all, I never thought about whether I was a girl or a boy. I was a songwriter, I was a singer, and I think you get treated pretty much with the respect that you have for yourself. Being stupid, as I probably was, and country, I never thought about it. When men would flirt with me or all that stuff, I always took it as kind of a compliment. I also had all these brothers and my dad and all these uncles, so I had a great communication with men in general. So I just would walk right in with my songs or with my business ideas, and I never felt the effects of being a woman, or felt that I was kept down. I'm so lucky now, I see that, but I never had the problems that a lot of other people did. Then again, the certain type of woman I am, I guess they all thought I was a whore, 'cause I looked like it [laughs] and I was a good ole girl. I'd go in and I'd tell a joke as bad as they would. I kind of fit in and I was just one of the boys, so to speak, even though I was very feminine and all that too. It's a little different than if I would have been a very strict and straight-laced business woman. Anyhow, I didn't have those problems.

But songs like "Just Because I'm A Woman" and "Your Ole Handy Man" are pretty strong feminist songs.

They were at the time. But they weren't about women in general. I remember the reason I wrote "Just Because I'm A Woman." After my husband and I had been married for a year, he asked me if I'd ever been with anybody else, and I didn't feel like lying, and I had been. But he'd never asked me before, so I certainly wasn't gonna volunteer any information [laughs]. So I said yes, and he was really hurt, he was crushed with that, and he was in a terrible mood for two or three months over that. And I just felt terrible, so I wrote that from a very personal place. Not just about women in general or how they're treated. It was just about that relationship, that moment in time, like my mistakes are no worse than yours just because I'm a woman. So that came from a personal place. "Your Ole Handy Man" was not about me, period. I remember my Mom used to work like a dog and she'd sometimes say, "I'm getting tired of being the handy man around here." That's where that came from, but of course it fits so many people. But that's what you do when you're a songwriter. I'm surprised sometimes to hear all the ways that people interpret things.

How about "Eagle When She Flies"?

Male DJs on the radio would not play that song. They hated it. I wrote it for a theme for *Steel Magnolias*, which they didn't use. But I based it on my relationship with my mother and my sisters and both my grandmothers. Because it's about the strength of women and the stuff that they had gone through together. It had nothing to do with men. It was about me, like "being a sparrow when she's broken, but an eagle when she flies," meaning you're so sensitive, but yet when it's time to fly, when Dolly Parton has to be Dolly Parton, she has to go out there and shine and smile and do positive interviews and things that people ask. But when I hurt, and when I have my personal problems to deal with, they're hard to bear. My burdens are very hard to bear. So it was really about that. It was a very personal song.

What do you feel are your main responsibilities are as a star?

Living up to the image that I've created, for the sake of the fans. It's just that people don't want to hear all the sad, sappy shit. They do love to hear the gossip and the scandal and all the bizarre, sensational stories of how I was scarred for life in laser surgery [laughs], and all that stuff, or how her husband's leaving her because she has all these lovers. I wish I had as much fun as they said I did. But anyway, I think it's just being strong enough to tolerate all the different versions that people have of you. I think you have to have a great inner strength. I think you have to know who you are. Being Dolly Parton, I have to be strong to live up to that image that I have created and that other people have created of me. It brings me up to certain standards too. I need to live up to that. But by the same token, I'll sit right here and tell you how vulnerable I am and how tender-hearted, and how this and that. But just being true to myself, being true to Dolly Parton, and she is all those things. I've been guilty of most of the stuff that's been said about me to some degree. And if I ain't done it, I probably will [laughs]. Or I'm sorry I missed the chance.

If you were going to teach a workshop on songwriting, what kinds of things would you stress?

I wouldn't know how to teach somebody how to write a song. I think first of all, it has to be born of you to be a great songwriter. I think you have to have that gift and that burning desire. You can learn to write a song, as we were talking about, a formula song. But to be a true songwriter, I think you have to really allow yourself to feel and allow yourself the freedom to write it the way you want to. If people are just looking to be commercial, you can still be a great songwriter and still follow a form or a formula. But I think the best thing to do is be true to yourself.

Justin Hayward

Nights In White Satin ☆ Tuesday Afternoon
☆ Your Wildest Dreams

Interview conducted in 1995

"I had to write a song with the word 'afternoon' in it. I already had the opening two notes because I had a dog named Tuesday."

From their landmark 1967 album *Days Of Future Passed* to their mid-80s MTV hits to their current concerts with symphony orchestras, The Moody Blues have forged a reputation as one of the most innovative, respected groups in rock history.

When Justin Hayward joined the band in 1966 as a replacement for Denny Laine, The Moody Blues (Hayward, Ray Thomas, Graeme Edge, John Lodge and Mike Pinder) were transfored from an R & B-influenced band into an experimental outfit that delighted fans the world over with their heady concept albums and hit singles. Mixing romantic melodies, spoken word poetry, psychedelia, lush orchestral balladry, pounding rock rhythms, acoustic guitars and spacey sound effects, the Moodies created a style all their own, evident on albums such as *A Question of Balance*, *In Search of The Lost Chord*, *To Our Children's Children's Children*, *Every Good Boy Deserves Favour* and *Seventh Sojourn*.

Hayward has been responsible for writing many of the group's most famous songs, including "Tuesday Afternoon," "Nights In White Satin," "Question," "The Voice," "Your Wildest Dreams," and "I Know You're Out There Somewhere."

141

When people write about the Moody Blues, they often describe the songs as cosmic and truth-seeking.

I think they were. I was 19 when I wrote "Nights In White Satin" and there's a nice kind of naivete about it, but there's a lot of truth about it. We were very, very truthful about our feelings. We were a group of people who were seeking and searching for some kind of truth and something to believe in, and we were meeting a lot of people, particularly when we came to America, who were looking for answers. So we almost felt it our duty to go and find those, and to meet as many people as we could, to have the psychedelic experience, to do transcendental meditation and to have a lot of other self-realization courses and things like that. I certainly did all that, and a lot of it is reflected in the music. Also, there's a lot of artistic license, as there must be, for if you write a story, you don't actually have to have lived it. The mistake that a lot of fans make, and I do myself, is they think that every writer is writing about himself. It's just a song or story, but the story is what moves you, and it moves you so much that when you sing it, you do with complete sincerity.

I'd suspect that when you were 19, a song like "Nights In White Satin" was more true to life.

Yes, it was. It was the first song that I ever performed that really got right down to the bone. There was a kind of nakedness about it. It's also very risky. It's kind of borderline being good, but if you just go over the line a little bit, it would be really bad [laughs]. A lot of really good songs are like that, they tread that line. So I knew it was very powerful. The British and the French really went for it, but Americans didn't. FM radio was just beginning. "Tuesday Afternoon" was the record they released here. They said "Nights In White Satin" would never make it because it was four minutes long, and there's a long boring flute bit and you can't dance to it. But you know, a young girl interviewed me a few years ago, and I said that to her, and she said, "That's the biggest mistake they made." I asked her what she meant, and she said that at every dance she ever went to as a kid, they used to finish with "Nights In White Satin." Anybody can dance to it, you just sort of grope the person and shuffle around the floor [laughs]. They used to play it as the last dance. So actually, millions and millions of people have danced to it.

It's such an evocative title. Did you have it before you began?

No, I didn't. At the time, I didn't own many things in the world, but I did own something totally useless, which was a set of white satin sheets that this girlfriend of mine had given me. They looked quite nice, and they were quite romantic. It was really about that, about love, and the end of one big affair and the beginning of another. It was about real things that were happening in my life. I suppose I always thought that I would call it "Nights In White Satin." Now I think if I wrote it, I'd probably think of another title, probably go further into the song to look for a title. It wouldn't be an obvious choice now, but it was right for the time. It sort of had that double meaning, which was intentional, of sort of medieval knights as well.

When the band was writing the early records, did you all come in with songs, or was there discussion ahead of time about concepts and themes?

I've always been the conscientious one who did his homework. I would arrive with say four songs. We would sit around a table in the studio, and I'd usually play my songs and the other guys would get started. Some of the guys were very good with concept ideas and titles, and the album would be born from that. Usually, I'd do one of my songs as the opener, then that would start the ball rolling. The others might write at home or out of jam sessions in the studio. The concept and the storyline would evolve as we went along, and we'd all be kind of living that storyline for the length of the album.

It must have been an exciting time in the summer of 1967 when the Days Of Future Passed *came out. Did you have the sense that you were doing something new?*

Yes, we did have the sense that we were creating something really different, and we had the sense that we were creating something that no one was going to listen to [laughs]. We thought we were making a record – or I certainly did – for a minority audience, for a very small group. I thought that we'd get reviewed in *The Guardian* cultural page. That was exactly what I wanted, to mix with the arty crowd. The rock crowd was okay, but if you could cross over and include the arty people, that was it. That's the record I thought we were making, a limited appeal record. And it did hit that market. Right after that, we played with John McLaughlin, Ravi Shankar and a group called Indojazz Fusions, and for us, that was it, we'd made it [laughs]. We never got any money, but we were happy. I don't think we ever thought about it in sort of huge commercial terms.

Can you say that doing drugs helped your songwriting?

I think it did. I was never a marijuana smoker, but I certainly smoked hash for about 20 years. I think it did help, and I'm just being truthful about it. Everybody turned on. It was just part of the culture. It didn't really lead to anything serious. It just seemed an innocent kind of thing, just using sort of soft drugs. I think it helped me with a kind of dimension. It put an extra dose of taste in my lyrics and it helped me exclude the things that were a little bit uncool. It made me aware of what other people would think. Marijuana is no doubt very conducive to music. Cocaine, I've had a little dabble with that, and I found exactly the opposite. It's useless, not very nice at all.

What do you remember about writing "Tuesday Afternoon"?

We were writing for a stage show that we were doing. We decided that what we'd do is throw away our blue suits and the old stock rhythm and blues things we were doing, and just do our own material. We decided in our own pretentious way [laughs] to write this stage show that would start with a song our keyboard player had written called "Dawn Is A Feeling." That's how I wrote "Nights In White Satin," it was to be the end of this stage show. And somehow, I claimed the afternoon bit as well, and I had to write a song with the word afternoon in it. So I went back to my parents' home in the west of England, took my guitar, sat in a field and looked at the clouds and started writing this particular song. I already had the opening two notes because I had a dog named Tuesday. When I used to call her, it was like that [sings opening notes to song].

If you don't have a complete lyric to a song, will you sometimes write a dummy lyric, just to fill it in?

Yes, I will. I sometimes write by kind of mumbling. The words have sounded right but it hasn't made any sense. Sometimes the first idea you think of, you keep going with it and keep persevering with it, but in the end you realize the reason it's just not working totally is because it's just wrong. So you have to rethink it.

But won't you sometimes have one line that is just kind of insisting that it remain, even if you don't quite know why?

Yes, I know what you mean. I think "Your Wildest Dreams" was one of those where I had the whole sort of groove and a lot of dummy words, then I'd get to the end of it and sing "in your wildest dreams." I liked the way that it sang, but I had nothing else. It took me ages to get it, to really realize what it was about. I had to work backwards to make that phrase mean something. The key was getting the line, " I wonder if you ever think about me in your wildest dreams." That was it.

That song, for everyone who's ever seen the video, is intertwined with the story of meeting a first love after many years. Was that scenario in your head when you were writing the song?

Yes. That and the video after it, "I Know You're Out There Somewhere" were the only times I've ever persuaded a record company that the group should really script the video. So two of us did it with a friend of ours who was also the director. We had great success with it. Apart from those two videos, the rest have been rubbish because we've let go of control. I really believe that. A lot of people talk a great video but when it comes time to make it, they don't do it. But having said that, the story for "Your Wildest Dreams" is an idea that is common to so many people. Everybody would like to know what ever happened to first person they ever loved. Take it from me though. Don't find out [laughs]. Leave it as a nice memory. It's worth more that way.

You've been writing songs for a long time. Has it gotten easier?

I go in and out of modes. I'm constantly learning how to do it. Just at the moment, I've been very prolific. I'm just looking for someone to record them. At the moment I've got so many songs it's ridiculous, because the Moodies haven't recorded for years now. Where I live in France, in my little apartment, I've found it very conducive for some reason. Some places are very conducive to songwriting. Others are beautiful places and have all the ingredients but you don't write a song. I don't know why. I find it easier now to write bad songs. I find it a lot easier to write mediocre songs, and harder to write what I consider to be really good songs, whereas when I was young, I would go through a lot of pain for each and every song, believing that each and every song was good. Now I can write a song and almost throw it away. It's not so precious.

Steve Winwood

Gimme Some Lovin' ✸ Back In The High Life Again
✸ Higher Love

Interview conducted in 1996

"When I write a song, I don't like to have to explain it after- wards. It's like telling a joke, then having to explain it."

Think of Steve Winwood and various images come to mind: a pale, skinny 16-year old lad with the soul of an old bluesman shouting "Gimme Some Lovin'" with the Spencer Davis Group; the hirsute leader of the progressive rock group Traffic, hunched over his Hammond B3 organ, coaxing out the swirling, gritty chords of "The Low Spark Of High Heeled Boys"; the elegantly dressed super-star, sashaying and singing "Higher Love" on MTV.

Each of these images represents not only a decade in which Winwood has excelled as a singer, instru-mentalist, songwriter and producer, but also his incredible versatility in tackling every style under the sun: R&B, psychedelic, jazz, folk, progressive rock, pop, and dance.

By the time Steve was 16, he was fronting The Spen-cer Davis Group on the now classic songs he wrote such as "Gimme Some Lovin'" and "I'm A Man." With a record deal, TV appearances, hit singles on both sides of the ocean, and a tour supporting The Rolling Stones, the teen prodigy was getting his first taste of stardom. But music mattered more than fame to Winwood, and when he felt growing pains ("I got tired of just copying blues records"), he found solace in after-hours jam sessions with his friends Dave Mason, Chris Wood and Jim Capaldi.

147

The quartet soon formed the band Traffic. Their albums, including the rock classics *Mr. Fantasy*, *John Barleycorn Must Die*, and *The Low Spark Of High Heeled Boys* fused rock, jazz, blues and psychedelic into a style that, even today, sounds completely original. Living in the English countryside, the group avoided the trends and fads of the London club scene. "Traffic had a kind of rural lifestyle," Winwood says. "Which, in a strange way, was a driving force behind the music. Chris Wood opened us up to a number of different ideas. He would play us things like Chinese classical music and obscure British folk music. He also had a strong interest in geology, topography and birdwatching, and when we were all living together, we started to take an interest in these things. This opened up a new world for us, and we wanted to find a way to include this lifestyle in our music."

Following Traffic's dissolution, Winwood retired to his home in Gloucestershire, spending the next two years writing songs and tinkering in his home studio. He re-emerged as a solo artist in 1977, with the release of *Steve Winwood*. In the midst of the British punk explosion, the record was ignored. Things would go much differently for the follow-up. "With *Arc Of A Diver*," Winwood says, "I felt that my chance to bring into play everything I had learned throughout my career had finally come. I had regrouped, and I knew I had something to say. I felt as if I had definitely created a stamp to say exactly who Steve Winwood was, and what he would be doing in the 1980s."

What he did in that decade was dominate the pop music charts with multi-platinum, Grammy-winning albums and hits such as "While You See A Chance," "Valerie," "Talking Back To The Night," "Higher Love," "Freedom Overspill," "Back In The High Life Again," "The Finer Things," "Roll With It" and "Don't You Know What The Night Can Do?"

As he moved into the 1990s, Winwood once again followed his musical intuition and sense of adventure and reformed Traffic with Jim Capaldi. In 1993, they released *Far From Home*. "Traffic is a great vehicle in which to do things I can't do on the solo stuff," Winwood says. His 1994 album, *Junction 7*, co-produced by R & B guru Narada Michael Walden, found Steve back in the pop life again, singing an uplifting mix of dance songs and romantic ballads.

You've been writing songs for over 30 years. Has it gotten easier?

No, I don't think it ever gets easier. It certainly doesn't get any less interesting. It's just as mysterious as it ever was. It's still fascinating and there's still no easy solution with songwriting. It's a vast skill or craft or art or whatever it may be. I never think I know how to do it, so I keep a respect for the process of writing songs.

On Junction 7, *you wrote lyrics as well as music. Was that something new for you?*

Well, I wrote the lyrics to "Gimme Some Lovin'" and "Can't Find My Way Home" – that was 30 years ago, so it's not new. But I hadn't done much lyric writing as of late. And it's not that it comes less easily than music, but I'm more of a musician than a literary person. I'm more studied in music than I am in the written or spoken word. It's not that much more difficult to write lyrics, it's just that I've happened to work with lyricists more than with musicians.

If it's all right, I'd like to mention some of your songs from the past to get your reaction to them.

That's not my favorite thing to do, and I'll tell you why. When I write a song, I don't like to have to explain it afterwards. To me, it's like telling a joke, then having to explain it. The explanation doesn't add to the song at all.

Well, you don't have to explain them. Maybe just reflect on what the inspiration was or any memories connected to the recording of the songs. How about Traffic's "Paper Sun"?

When I started writing with Jim Capaldi, we came into songwriting as players and musicians, so our reason for writing songs was so that we had something to play. I think that's coming from a different direction than a lot of partnerships. I think it was only later that we began to develop our skills. In those early days, particularly with the Traffic songs, the song wasn't just a song, it was a performance whereas there are some songs that have a strength regardless of their performance. Part of the song itself was the performance. Later on, we thought about making songs stand on their own.

When you and Jim would write a song like "Low Spark Of High Heeled Boys," how complete would it be when you brought it to the band?

I'll tell you exactly how we used to write back then. What would happen is that Jim would jot some words down on a piece of paper – some lines maybe, and not too many, and certainly not arranged in a verse-chorus kind of way. He would just jot a few phrases or ideas down, and then we would go and jam. I would stand the piece of paper on top of the piano or organ, then during the jam when I felt it was right and appropriate, I'd sing what he'd written down and it always came out of a jam. All those early songs – "Paper Sun," "Dear Mr. Fantasy," "Low Spark Of High Heeled Boys" – they were jams. We were just playing together. It was born out of the fact that we were players rather than writers.

Is that still the way you and Jim write?

We can and do write like that, but I think that with the *Far From Home* Traffic album from 1993, and the couple of songs we wrote with Narada on *Junction 7*, we've learned to work differently. Jim has now learned to thread his lyrics into a melody rather than just starting out jotting down a few thoughts. He's learned the skills of writing, and obviously he's had successful songs with The Eagles and a few others. He's honed his skills.

Your next steady co-writer was Will Jennings. What do you recall about writing "While You See A Chance"?

That was the first song we ever did. The way I wrote songs with Will is that I always wrote the whole of the backing track and the melody, and he would just thread his lyric into that melody. A lot of the songs we did – "Talking Back To The Night" and "Back In The High Life" – were lyrics that he'd written beforehand. Interestingly enough, Rodney Crowell, who lives near me in Nashville and is a good friend, also works with Will Jennings. We were talking one day about Will, and I happened to mention that when we work together he doesn't really cross the border at all into music, and stays within the realm of the lyric. He doesn't try to influence the music or the melody at all. Rodney kind of looked at me sideways for a bit, then said that when he works with Will, Will only does the music and Rodney does all the lyrics. So Will is one of these people who can work with lots of different co-writers in different ways.

On a song like "Valerie," would the melody be suggesting a lyric to you before you gave it to Will?

It might, but I wouldn't necessarily tell him. I learned more about co-writing as I got older. When you're young, you tend to be more impetuous and more idealistic, and you tend to think you know exactly what the song should be about – every element, how it should be recorded, mixed, performed or whatever. But with the benefit of experience, I've learned to wait before I gave my thoughts on what someone else should be doing, to see exactly what they come up with. It can sometimes be completely different than what I had in mind. I learned that from Jim Capaldi. When he jotted down lyrics in the Traffic days, he'd have some idea what the melody or the groove or the rhythm was and I would come up with something completely different, and it would work. If it did work, he would be very pleased but he'd never say it didn't fit with what he'd had in mind. I think it's important to be open when you're working with co-writers. Because of that I sometimes try to keep quiet about my ideas regarding what they're doing. Only if it's going wrong will I speak up, but things don't go wrong that often with guys like Will Jennings.

What do you recall about working with Chaka Khan on "Higher Love"?

She came into the studio and knew exactly what she wanted to do, what the harmony parts were and where they should go. She required no direction at all. She was brilliant.

And James Taylor on "Back In The High Life"?

Same thing. He knew exactly what he wanted to do. Obviously he's a different sort of character, but in his quiet way he's got a wonderful strength about what he does. We felt there was no direction necessary with James. There again, it's the same thing with songwriting. You can use the same premise when you're producing. It's good to let people give their ideas first without any direction, because very often it's the best thing.

If you gave a workshop on songwriting, what would you say to your students?

I've spoken to people about doing several educational things and I am keen to help, and probably writing is the best thing for me to talk about because it's so vague and there really aren't any rules. I don't believe I can tell anybody how to write a song. Yes, there are elements to songs. For instance, I think there's a big difference between poetry and lyrics. Lyrics shouldn't be judged on their own, but rather on how they work in tandem with the music. The other thing I would say is that melody is very important. Melody is a very complex subject, and I've read books on it. There are techniques but I don't really know them [laughs]. I think with me it's more of a feel, in that I know how the melody should go and where it should go, but I don't know why it should go there [laughs]. So it might be hard to teach melody writing. I don't know if there's anything else to say about songwriting, except to make sure there's a lot of feeling in what you do.

Don McLean

Interview conducted in 1995

"The songs that were once the standards of another generation have almost become a touchstone to our poor, illiterate generation trying to find something that's beautiful that we can hold on to."

Don McLean is a passionate defender of what's become an unfashionable sentiment; namely that music and songwriting are art. While he says that it was always his intention to break new ground, he maintained a traditional ethic. He aimed to write more than ephemeral pop songs. He wanted to write standards that would last through the years. When you listen to the still potent blend of poetic lyrics, stirring melodies and deeply felt emotions of such songs as "Vincent," "And I Love You So" and the classic pop opus "American Pie," it's as obvious as the goosebumps on your arm that McLean succeeded more than once.

His first album, *Tapestry* (1970) included one of those standards, "And I Love You So," which three years later became a hit for Perry Como, and was also covered by Elvis Presley. Then in 1971, his career leapt into warp-drive with "American Pie" (which at 8:27, set a new record for the longest number one hit) and "Vincent," his haunting tribute to Van Gogh.

Subsequently, in addition to charting with his own compositions such as "Dreidel," "Castles In The Air," and "Wonderful Baby," McLean also recorded popular versions of Roy Orbison's "Crying" (a Top 10 in both the U.S. and UK in 1981) and the Skyliners' "Since I Don't Have You." His songs have continued to be covered by a variety of artists, from Julio Iglesias ("Vincent") to Harry Belafonte ("Empty Chairs") to Madonna ("American Pie").

Is songwriting something that's difficult for you?

Well, my creations, such as they are, are very personal and very uncommercial things, which happened in a few cases to become very popular. I do not repeat myself. That's sort of a cardinal rule of mine, which really flies in the face of commercial success. I always wanted to try to do something different, although it's mine and you can tell I did it, it's not the same as something else I did. So therefore, I never really had a musical writing style which clicked and then all I had to do was just turn this stuff out. So there was never any identifiable style where I did five similar songs.

When you were first learning to write songs, where did you turn for answers?

I turned inside myself right away, because my father died when I was 15, which was shortly after I started playing. Up until that point, my life was sort of idyllic. But it was completely shattered by that event, so I had plenty to write about and think about. I was quite convinced from the very beginning that I was very good, even though I had nothing to show for it. It was weird [laughs]. I was fortunate to be around some older musicians that I knew who encouraged me to look at all music as being beneficial. This was in the days of folk music, when people who were involved in it became quite arrogant about what was a good song, what was a bad song, what was a folk song, what wasn't a folk song and all that other stuff. I liked Nat King Cole, Benny Goodman, Frank Sinatra, but I also liked The Weavers and I also liked Elvis. I was wide open to musical influences from a very early age and I wasn't ashamed of it. I didn't really care what all those other people thought. I was really into using a wide variety of musical references, so that in the late 1960s, when I wrote "And I Love You So" I was trying to write a Jimmy Van Heusen song. Yet I was singing it in coffee houses. Talk about weird [laughs]. I couldn't explain it to anybody, but I didn't care. I knew exactly what I was doing.

Are you self-taught?

Yeah, I am. I can't read or write music, but I have a real good memory for it. My primary instrument is my voice. I'm a vocalist. That's really what I do as well or better than anybody in the world. My guitar playing is not all that great. But I think as a singer I'm as good as anybody.

Didn't Pete Seeger have something to do with you getting your first break?

Yes, he did. I met Lee Hayes, who used to be in The Weavers along with Pete. He was one of those people I mentioned who kept me aware that there were many different kinds of music out there. And he started becoming excited about my songwriting, such as it was back in 1965, and mentioned me to the Seegers quite a bit. I was quite a fan of Pete's. I finished college in 1968, and by that time the Seegers had me on a few of their festivals, and they were just beginning their Hudson River Sloop Program. By that time Pete and I had become friends. So in 1968, I joined a group of sort of ragtag musicians, and a bunch of us went around calling ourselves the Hudson River Sloop Singers, with Pete and all of his friends. We played all up and down the Hudson and the Atlantic Coast as we sailed our boat, The Clearwater, which had just been launched to New York City. We lived on the boat and sang. It was a wonderful experience, creatively and in every way. By that time, I'd gotten to know Pete and he was very helpful. He introduced me to his audience, brought me around everywhere, mentioned me, asked me to come sing with him, promoted me like crazy. He's done that with lots of artists that he's liked throughout the years. He even wrote letters to record labels to try to help me get a contract. He encouraged me with a lot of compliments and kind remarks about my songwriting. It was a good boost for me.

A lot has been written about the symbolism and the allusions in "American Pie." When you were writing the song, were you conscious of all of that?

I was conscious of the fact that I was trying to create a rock n' roll dream sequence. But it was more than rock n' roll, way more than rock n' roll. It was about an America that was coming apart at the seams. I was trying to create this American song which connected the parts of America that mattered to me, starting with Buddy Holly.

Buddy Holly didn't matter to anybody when I wrote this song, I have to tell you. He was long dead and forgotten. They didn't have oldies stations back in those days, so you didn't hear a lot of this stuff. What I wanted to do was write this anthem to close my show with, because I had all this other stuff – songs about other people, songs from *Tapestry*, songs like "Sister Fatima" and "Vincent" – and I wanted to close the show with this anthem that pulled together all the stuff that I'd been saying and singing about. And I wanted it to be about America. I wrote the opening part of the song remembering how it was the day I saw the newspaper, *The Standard Star*, and saw the article that said my favorite artist had been killed. Remembering that got me started. A while later, I wrote the chorus. It's a little about America, it's a little sexual, it's a little of that. Then I didn't do anything with it for awhile, I just sat with it. And then one day, in a blaze of glory, I just wrote the whole thing, and I tied together musical imagery of unspecified meaning with this story about America, but in a dream like context. So it was really funny to me that, after the song became famous, people started becoming so interested in the lyrics. I was trying to write about America, not Elvis. They were missing the point really by trying to say who's this and who's that in the song.

How far along were you before the title came?

When I did the chorus, I came up with the title, and I thought, oh what a great title. It's apple pie, and parts of the pie. We're always talking about the economic pie, and pie has sexual significance as well.

I've read that you didn't perform that song for years . . .

That's not true. I'm writing a book right now, and I'm going to explode a lot of these myths that were laid on me that were not true. I've always sung "American Pie." That story goes hand in hand with the idea that it was such a burden that I wouldn't sing it. It's never been a burden and I always sang it. But they created this idea of, well, since no one can follow this song up, and this guy can't follow it up, it must be a burden, so he won't sing it for awhile. It's not true. I'll tell you how these things got started. Back in the old days, when I was getting very famous – I was as big as Springsteen or any of these people – I used to be on the nightly news if I would sing in New York. That's as high as you can get. And there was an AP wire reporter at the Saratoga Performing Arts Center, and there were a couple of young ladies in the back of the room and I was feeling in a very comic and funny mood and I was kidding around with them. And one of them said, "Are you going to sing 'American Pie' tonight?" I mean I wouldn't even be there if it weren't for the song, right? [laughs] I said, "No, I'm not going to sing that again." And this fucking AP reporter wrote this article that Don McLean said he's not going to sing his song again, and it got all over the country. A little weasel. I couldn't believe it. Today I would've sued him. It was said in jest. So that's how it got started.

Now I did have a sort of nervous breakdown, an exhaustion period which lasted about six or eight months in 1974, around there. I didn't tour a lot during that time, then I came back and made the *Homeless Brother* album and started all over again. That's the only time that's ever happened, and that's because I was running like mad from 1968 to 1974, and I mean 365 days a year. So I just sort of went in a heap in the corner for awhile, but maybe those two things together created the impression that I didn't sing "American Pie." But I've always done it. Why have I always sung it? Because people pay money to hear it, and I would never disappoint people who come to hear me. That's the way I feel about the audience. I am not there on stage to satisfy myself. I'm there to satisfy them. That's the purpose of the whole exercise.

What do you recall most about writing "Vincent"?

I remember I was singing in a school system in the Berkshires in 1970. I'd gotten a job there and I was staying in a beautiful apartment that was part of a home owned the Sedgewick family, not too far away from Norman Rockwell's house in Stockbridge, Massachusetts. At the time I was reading this book about Van Gogh and I started to write the song.

When a song is first emerging for you, how much control do you maintain over where it's going?

That's a good question, and the answer is almost none. I let it be what it is, and I try to make it into something that is able to be sung by somebody else – that's the key to writing the kinds of songs I like. I want to try to write standards, if I can. Even though I'm trying to write songs that are uniquely my own, I want to try to write something that someone else can possibly sing, or enjoy, or pass to their children. So I will use a certain amount of craft to get the idea to come full circle and to make it be what it is. There's a song on the first album I made called "Three Flights Up," which I think is a wonderful idea. I've never heard anyone do anything like it. I hardly ever perform it anymore but it's a person looking at a building, and they're seeing three floors of a building and they see what's happening to these people. It's all interrelated. You can go pretty far out with a song like that, but I tried to keep it so that everything had a musical signature. There's three musical parts to it and some little beginnings and endings and things. A person could perform that song.

One of the problems I see today, as a songwriter, is that there are no standards being written. I mean really great songs. What you have is a complete pile of garbage over in the pop area with rap and heavy metal. It may be entertaining in a sort of perverse way, but there's nothing there that anybody can do anything with other than play the video. In country music, you have this sort of namby pamby kind of song that these guys write over and over again, which, when you compare it to Merle Haggard or Johnny Cash, it's no wonder that they like Merle Haggard so much, because he was writing about something real. So it's very depressing for me to look out on the landscape today and it's very inhospitable. There's nothing there that interests me. There used to be so much there that interested me when I was young. So many established acts who were truly great artists were doing great things and there were so many young acts that were coming up who were doing great things. Songwriters were doing things that were lasting. Every year there was a new wonderful song, maybe three or four. This is before even Dylan or The Beatles. There was this wonderful cornucopia of music right through to the early 1970s, then less and less until now we're in this situation.

Yet we always hear that a great song will break through . . .

But will a great songwriter be created in a society so perverse that he's afraid to write anything that's openly romantic? That's the problem. Society is the institution that creates what it thinks beauty is or what it thinks something important is. It's also the level of intelligence. We have an ever-decreasing level of education in our country; we have a total disinterest in the language, and so the songs that were once the bread and butter standards of another generation have become almost a touchstone to our poor, pathetic, illiterate generation trying to find something that's beautiful that we can hold on to for a second because we aren't producing them ourselves. It doesn't have to be that way. It shouldn't be that way, but the problem is that record companies and TV stations and the media are always looking for the lowest common denominator. They don't have someone in charge who's looking to enlighten and uplift the population by promoting artistry and setting tone. The tone and standard that's being set is, you know, let's go out and get a guy with as many tattoos as possible who takes his clothes off and spits on the audience, and then they'll pay attention to us. I don't know what that has to do with music.

There used to be places like Columbia Records with John Hammond, who would support great artists. They made the decision. We're going to support Mahalia Jackson. We're going to make her a presence felt in the music business, because we know she's great. We're going to support Bob Dylan because we know he's great, even though in 1962 everybody's laughing at him. So what's missing is a sense of media leading people in the right direction. Instead they're leading them in the wrong direction. There would be a lot of creative stuff that would happen if they'd change direction, but I don't know if it'll ever happen.

Todd Rundgren

Interview conducted in 1997

"Essentially what a songwriter does is packaging – taking the things that people are talking about and integrating them into a product that is consumable."

Todd Rundgren reached a crossroads on November 10, 1973, when his sentimental ballad, "Hello It's Me" rose to number 5 on the *Billboard* singles chart. One way pointed to superstardom. The other led to the shadowy land of cult status.

But for Rundgren, it wasn't a matter of choosing. While *Something/Anything*, the double album that spawned "Hello It's Me," was catching on a year after its release, it was a speck in the rearview mirror for Rundgren. He had already followed his muses into new experimental territory, releasing the ambitious *Wizard, A True Star*, an eclectic tour-de-force on which the 25-year old wunderkind wrote, arranged, engineered, produced and played every instrument. Though *Something/Anything* was chock full of potential hits, Rundgren refused to backtrack and allow anything else from the album to be released.

He did however concede to perform "Hello It's Me" on "The Midnight Special" TV show, a move that sealed his commercial fate. Fans who were seeing him for the first time were shocked. Sporting blue-orange hair, eyes painted with glitter teardrops, dark lipstick and a skimpy top made of iridescent feathers, Rundgren looked like a cross between a drag queen and the NBC peacock.

That incident typifies the erratic career choices that Rundgren would make over the next three decades and 30 albums, choices that would test the allegiance of even his most faithful followers. Looks, bands, labels, philosophies, styles – if it was a skin that could be shed, he would shed it.

The constant in this ever-evolving journey has been his masterful songwriting. Whether penning catchy pop hits such as "We Gotta Get You A Woman" and "I Saw The Light," beautiful ballads like "It Wouldn't Have Made Any Difference," prog-rock epics like "The Ikon," ferocious rockers like "Trapped," or party anthems such as "Bang The Drum All Day," he made it sound effortless. No amount of sonic grandstanding could hide his enormous gift for tuneful melodies and lyrics that addressed the human condition with an open mind and heart.

Rundgren formed The Nazz in 1967. Though the group had pop idol looks, stage presence and tunes right for the times (including the original recording of "Hello It's Me"), they failed to deliver on the promise of early comparisons to The Beatles. In 1969, after The Nazz split, Rundgren began a solo career with a series of brilliant albums such as *Runt*, *Something/Anything*, *Wizard, A True Star* and *Todd*. In four years, the prolific one-man band covered more stylistic ground than most artists do in a 20-year career. But still, Rundgren was restless.

In 1974, he formed Utopia, an ever-changing unit which became, over the next ten years, his vehicle for excursions into progressive rock, power pop, and political rock. At the same time, he continued to release solo albums such as *Hermit Of Mink Hollow* (which featured "Can We Still Be Friends," later covered by Robert Palmer) and *Healing*.

In the 1990s, Rundgren was a pioneer in the blending of music, media and new technology. In 1993, he established a new genre when he released the world's first interactive audio-only CD-ROM project, *No World Order*. 1995's *The Individualist* continued his forays into enhanced CDs, featuring multi-media accompaniment to the music. It was also one of the first CDs to be offered over the Internet, where subscribers could download the music before it was released in stores.

Can you name five records that most affected you as a songwriter?

One of those early Beatles records like "I Want To Hold Your Hand" probably had an influence on me in that I never even considered writing songs. After that, I think that there was Marvin Gaye's *What's Goin' On*. There was an album by Bill Evans called *Bill Evans & The Symphony Orchestra* that had a whole influence on the way I thought about music and a lot of the tonality found its way into my songwriting. *This Year's Model* by Elvis Costello. I think that at the time he set a new standard for consistently high quality in songwriting. Squeeze did something of the same thing. There were a lot of people making music, but not so many who knew what a song was. And there was a Yes album, *Close To The Edge*, that affected an entire phase of my writing, the early Utopia days, when we were writing these epic numbers almost like opera [laughs].

When you're writing now, with 30 years of songs behind you, are you influenced by things you've done in the past?

Well, certainly, in the same way that some psychological scar that you have when you're a child stays with you your entire life. Your earliest influences probably have a greater effect than things you experience later in life. The kinds of music that I like are still very much a product of the things that I heard when I was growing up. I definitely think that the kind of music you're exposed to affects your taste later in life, especially if you're a writer, in the kinds of things you gravitate towards. Sometimes it's a negative influence. Sometimes people associate the music they hear with some unpleasantness and they can never stand to hear that kind of music again [laughs].

I guess what I was getting at is, if you find yourself going to signature "Todd" chord changes, do you try to avoid that now?

I know that I have certain leanings when I write. It's difficult to know if you're doing it out of habit or whether you're exhibiting what people call a style. I don't know where that line is. It's such a subjective thing. If somebody listens to my music with great regularity, are they disturbed if I make any significant change in the way I write or are they disturbed if they notice that I write things the same way all the time [laughs]? It's hard to say. For me, I think that I go in long cycles of trying to absorb new influences and somehow integrating them into my personal style and hopefully expanding my range that way. Recently, I've been into a sort of reductionist phase, where I'm trying to understand something that came more naturally to me when I was doing records like *Wizard, A True Star* – which is the validity of almost any approach to music completely devoid of stylistic or even sonic precedence. In other words, I used to do a lot of experimenting with just pure sound, rather than thinking constantly in terms of songs. I believe that music, or at least a certain style of music, has evolved to that point, that being so-called techno music. Which is based around sound manipulation more than songwriting.

Does technology affect your songwriting directly?

I think it always has affected my songwriting in that once I had more or less free access to the studio, a lot of the process began to happen there rather than at home by the piano. Nowadays I rarely think of songwriting without thinking, "Okay, it's time to go into the studio." I do some amount of raw material development outside of the studio environment. I sit down at the piano and pick things out. But I find that as time goes on, it's more and more a mental process, in that I can develop an idea fairly well along without having ever played a note of it. I'm not exactly sure when that happened, but at one point I did have to develop a habit of being able to maintain these musical ideas in my head because I would get an idea for a song in some unlikely place, and not be able to get to a musical instrument. So I developed a discipline of remembering the songs I'm working on in my head, and not have to pick them out on an instrument.

When a song idea first emerges for you, whether in your head or at an instrument, do have the sense of following or leading?

It works both ways. Often you have specific goals you want to achieve and specific musical areas you'd like to travel through in order to get to that goal. And that's something that may require tinkering or engineering in order to get everything the way you want it. Then again, there are those instances where you simply dream a song or realize a song substantially whole. In a way, it's kind of preferable because your personal enjoyment of the song can be greater, in that you didn't slave over it. That's one reason why I think that the full realization of a song, something that your sub-conscious works out and then delivers to you complete, has some sort of mystical quality that to me is almost preferable to sweating it out. It reflects more directly what's going on in your mind.

Is it important for you to finish every song that you start?

I usually have a point at which I know how far the song is going to get. Rarely do I ever get to the point of writing lyrics if I don't have the intention of finishing a song. I usually flesh out a lot of the musical part of it before I ever get down to writing lyrics, unless I've already got some substantial lyric idea developed. And often, it's me just feeling around, trying to figure out what the implication is of the music I'm making, and then attaching some appropriate lyrical idea to it – which gets more difficult all the time because I've written so many songs. I suppose the thing that would be most disheartening would be to discover that I've run out of lyrical ideas, in which case I'd probably just commit myself to instrumental music or recontextualizing or revisiting music I like that had already been written. But I don't think I would start writing lyrics that were either trite or nonsensical simply because I felt I was obligated to put lyrics to every song.

Do you think the role of the songwriter will change in the next 30 years?

Not at all. The style of music may change, but the role of the songwriter is always to encapsulate an idea in either intellectual or emotional terms or both. Essentially what a songwriter is doing is packaging. They're taking the things that people are talking about, the musical wallpaper, if you will, to life and integrating them into a product, something that is consumable. Of course, there's always the songwriter who writes only for himself. To be honest, when I actually get down to the process, there's a huge element of that in there for me as well, in that I'm often looking to create something that I don't hear elsewhere. And not simply to be different, but for my own satisfaction. As far as songwriters are concerned, as long as there is something recognizable as a music market, in other words, if music doesn't suddenly become a free commodity [laughs], or government underwritten, or underwritten by patrons of some kind – as long as it's a consumer item, songwriters are always going to have to be aware of consumer tastes. And that's something that recording and duplication has done to the craft of songwriting. If the legacy of songwriting goes back to the wandering troubadour, who simply sang songs of political import and of the typical experiences that everyone had, but who had no greater expectation than to get a ducat or two at the point of performance, then you're talking about a more complete musician. You're talking about someone who not only writes but is obligated to perform what he writes [laughs], because nobody else is going to do it. Then when we got to the point where we could duplicate – the printing press allowed for transcribed music to be duplicated and sold, and that was the beginning of what we call the recording industry. Then you could actually transcribe the real sounds. That's when the two became separated, when the songwriter became separate from the performer. But public tastes, or economics, or anything else, may move things back in that direction.

What are some things that you haven't done as a songwriter that you'd like to?

I don't tend to plan that far ahead. I don't have a list of musical locations I'd like to visit. I try to stay open to my so-called muse and the opportunities available. I don't write songs for other people and I don't write songs without some idea of the way I'd like to have them performed. But this new idea of delivering online enables me to go back to a time when people wrote and recorded songs all the time rather than in specific chunks or time periods that related to the marketing of music. In other words, once the LP and the CD became a standard form factor, musicians spent less time creating new music and more time promoting old music, because your product cycles are two or three years apart. And if you've had any success, you're heavily invested in that, you spend three or six months writing and recording an album that you'll spend the next two years performing. So your periods of musical creativity become spaced further and further out. In some ways, success works against you, in that people like what you're doing so they want to hear you do it to death [laughs]. They're less interested in new stuff. They're interested in stuff you've done already. The whole idea of being able to deliver online or deliver electronically is that anytime I get a musical idea I can realize it and deliver it to people. So I may discover myself writing songs every couple of weeks rather than waiting two years to get into the studio, and bear down to create a dozen songs at once.

So online delivery could turn the clock back.

Back at least to the time when singles dominated and an album was a collection of singles. That's not to say that the grander concept doesn't have validity but the biggest problem for songwriters nowadays is that a form factor that used to hold 35 minutes of music, now holds an hour or more. Three minute songs? That's twenty at least. So the demand for music has gone up, but that doesn't mean you can create more music with the same quality. It's demanding that you create more music in the same amount of time, which any logical analysis would lead you to deduce that the quality is going down.

CDs that are 68 minutes long are wearying to me, because there's usually only about 28 minutes of prime stuff.

But if you bought a CD with only 28 minutes on it, you'd say, "Hey, where did the rest of my money go?" The whole thing has put the squeeze on songwriters, but I'm looking for online direct delivery to at least put me in a situation where I only released the material I was inspired to write, not that I was forced to write. Although I've never been in the same situation as a lot of performing songwriters, having to meet some prior expectations. I have a certain freedom to do what I want on a record and do it when I want. But I find myself, just because of the nature of the process, in the same situation as every other songwriter, in that you're faced with this 60 minutes of real estate to fill up and you tend to try to do it all in one go.

Billy Joel

Just The Way You Are ✮ Piano Man
✮ We Didn't Start The Fire

Interview conducted in 1995

"I don't write because of record company schedules or because I need money or because I want to be more famous. I write purely out of a compulsion to write."

"Ain't it wonderful to be alive when the rock'n'roll plays," sang Billy Joel in his 1985 hit "Keeping The Faith." For over 25 years, this living legend has been returning to the altar of pop, rock and soul music, soaking up inspiration. His work reflects his deep love of everything that has proven to be lasting and true musically: George Gershwin, Ray Charles, Brill Building pop, The Beatles and The Rolling Stones, to name a few.

Joel's songs, diverse as they may be stylistically – he's equally adept as a crooning balladeer or a soul screamer – all share common threads: unforgettable melodies, well-tuned lyrics and a high sense of craftsmanship. With a list of pop classics which includes "Just The Way You Are," "Piano Man," "Say Goodbye To Hollywood," "New York State Of Mind," "Scenes From An Italian Restaurant," "Only The Good Die Young," "She's Always A Woman," "My Life," "You May Be Right," "It's Still Rock And Roll To Me," "Allentown," "Honesty," "Uptown Girl," "Tell Her About It," "Leave A Tender Moment Alone," "We Didn't Start The Fire" and "River Of Dreams," Billy Joel has kept the faith as one of the finest American songwriters of the past three decades.

171

It seems that you kind of started out more folky and then became a rocker.

I got into this whole singer/songwriter thing in a strange way. I had all these songs written and I wanted other people to do them. Then I was advised by other people in the music business that, "If you want your songs heard, you should make your own recording." This was 1970-71, it was the era of the singer/songwriter. James Taylor, Joni Mitchell, Paul Simon, Judy Collins, Jackson Browne, Jimmy Webb – all these singer/songwriters were coming into the forefront. So I made a recording and I ended up being a "rock star." Which I still think to this day is very funny. I look in the mirror every morning and go, "You're a rock star, ha ha ha, pretty funny." I set out to be a writer. Don't get me wrong, it's a great gig, but it really wasn't what I had in mind [laughs].

When you recorded the Piano Man *album did you have a strong sense of where you wanted to go musically?*

No. I really don't know when I start an album where it's going to end up. The process usually works like this. I always try to come up with some kind of concept so I'm motivated to sit down and begin this huge process. It never goes the way I plan it to go, never. I try to organize things, I try to direct where it's going to go. I can't control the muse. I write one song and then my musical instinct is to write some kind of variation away from that type of music. If I wrote a slow song, I'll write something fast. If I wrote something really loud and hard, I'll write something soft. If I wrote something in one key, I'll write something in a completely different key, an unrelated key. Purely for variation. I love variation. I can't stand monotony. It drives me nuts. So the next song reacts to the first song, then the next song that comes after that is written in response to the song that came before that. So a lot of times, what you hear on an album is the actual sequence of the writing. I don't have to mess around a lot with sequencing. I write one song, I write another and it seems to spin itself out like a novel. There's a beginning, a middle and an end. There's a reason for everything getting written and they're all interconnected and they all live with each other.

Do you have a problem then with singles being taken out of the storyline of an album?

Yes, but I must admit I owe a great deal of my perceived success to having had hit singles. But a hit single is taken out of context of the album. It's cut out and repasted somewhere else. So you take a song like "Tell Her About It," which was a hit single. To me, that sounds awful on its own. It sounds like Tony Orlando and Dawn. I hate that single. But in the context of the album it makes sense, because the *Innocent Man* album was sort of a tribute to old rock n' roll influences. One of those influences was Motown. And there I am doing The Supremes. But if you take it out of context, it sounds like Tony Orlando and Dawn. But if you put it next to the song that came before, which sounds like The Platters or Wilson Pickett, then it makes sense.

I assume the same holds true for "Uptown Girl."

"Uptown Girl" is a joke song. It's a tribute to Frankie Valli and The Four Seasons. I did it in that style. I even tried to sing like Frankie Valli, in that strained falsetto. It's a joke, but if you listen to it in the context of the album, you get it. The Four Seasons were a hugely influential group in my youth. But like I said, taken out of context, it's like "What kind of pop silliness is this?" So I don't set out to write a hit single. I write songs in response to other songs I wrote. Then when I get to about the tenth song, if I'm lucky, I'm pretty much tapped out. I've had it. The little guys in the brain close up shop. And if I ever mentally let the shop close, it's so hard for me to start writing again.

Has that happened?

On the *River of Dreams* album, I'd written what I thought were enough songs and I mentally closed up shop. And then I recorded. I thought one song was going to be the last song on the album, but it wouldn't work. So, there I was, shop's closed. And I couldn't write. I had this incredible block.

What did you do?

I think a lot of writers always have extra stuff floating around. Or they just write more. I know a guy like Bruce Springsteen will have way more than enough songs for an album and he'll cull through his material. I don't write like that. I write an album from A to Z. If there's ten songs, I write 1 through 10, that's it. If I die tomorrow, there's no basement tapes. So I had to write another song and it took me weeks and weeks of banging my head against the wall. And the last song I wrote was "Famous Last Words," which was very apropos

because it's really the last words I have to say. It was kind of pro-
phetic because really that's the last complete song with lyrics that I
wrote. That was 1993.

*Your melody writing has always been so consistently strong. If a
songwriter wanted to improve his melody writing, do you think that
going to the classics is a good thing to do?*

I don't think you can really beat classical music, especially the
romantic era, for melodic composition. For the use of chords in
conjunction with melody, I think composition reached its height.
Now I'm not going to advise people to listen to classical music so
that it'll help your songwriting. I don't think it can hurt, although
some people may not find it inspiring. My theory about classical
music is that it – especially the melodic, ultra-romantic music of
the 19th century – evolved into the popular music of the 50s, 60s,
70s, and 80s. I don't know how much of it is left in the 90s. Not
necessarily the blues-based hard rock, but melodic songwriting.
Even before the 50s, with composers like Richard Rodgers, all
the way back to Gershwin, Cole Porter. I feel that classical music
became popular songs. Take a song like "I Will Always Love You,"
by Dolly Parton. If you play it as a classical music piece, it could
be something by Schumann.

*You've always kind of played down the importance of lyrics in pop
music, even calling your own lyrics "coloring" to the melodies.*

But that's how I hear popular music. I remember my first exposure to
popular music was probably at a beach listening to a portable radio,
or at a party listening to somebody's little dinky record player where
they played the 45s where the speaker was about two or three inches
big and you really couldn't hear lyrics. What you heard was a melody,
some chords, a rhythm. The drums were always prevalent in
rock'n'roll and pop music. You heard the sound of the singer's voice
and you heard the production of the recording. One of the last things
you ever heard was what the hell they were saying.

How about when you were in a band learning covers?

Well, how do you learn the lyrics? You had to listen to the 45 and
you had to stop the record or lift the needle off to try to get the
words. Mick Jagger was trying to sing like a black guy and he was

an English guy, so to a white kid from Levittown, this was like double jeopardy [laughs]. What is he saying? We never really knew. Does anybody know the lyrics to "Louie, Louie"? I don't think even The Kingsmen know the lyrics. So my exposure to popular rock'n'roll was that lyrics were one of the last things you ever got to. So I write music first. Actually I wrote music when I was a little kid. I made up my own operas, made up my own compositions. I didn't need words. Then I got into a band and we started to write songs and they looked to me to be the lyricist. And I said, "What are you looking at me for?" "Well, you read a lot of books." So I ended up with the task of writing words for these songs. But I did it backwards.

Once you have a melody, how do you go about setting words to it?

It's this tortured process of having a melodic phrase with a pentameter to it, with a definite conclusion on each phrase where an actual rhyme would have to go. I hate the tyranny of rhyme. But if you're going to be musical and you're going to make something work, nine times out of ten you have to rhyme because it would be as if you ended a musical phrase in a different key with no relation to anything else that had happened before. It needs to have a harmony. So I have this tortured process of here's the mold, it's all shaped already and I have to look through my vocabulary, my pitiful words and jam them on to this musical phrase and make it match the emotional feeling that the music has. How does that make me feel? What was I thinking when I wrote that? What was going through my mind? Why did that music get written? So there's something encoded in the music and I have to figure out what that is and then drop the right words in. It's like trying to put together a jigsaw puzzle and the pieces aren't pre-made. You have to cut them yourself. Sometimes you have to smush the board a little bit and bend the frame and make up your rules as you're going along. It's a tortured process.

I'd like to ask about a few of the more famous songs from The Stranger. *"Just The Way You Are"*

"Just The Way You Are" is kind of a real standard-y ballad, kind of syrupy, lovey-dovey, mushy, People who heard that who didn't like that kind of music could have written Billy Joel off altogether. I almost didn't put that song on the album. I didn't like it very much. It just goes to show you what musicians know really about what's going to be a hit or not. I tend to like the really obscure stuff that nobody ever hears. We were in the studio listening back to it and I was not even going to put it on the album, and then Linda Ronstadt and Phoebe Snow showed up at the studio and they said, "You've got to put that on the album!" So I'm going to listen to what women say. I put it on the album.

"Scenes From An Italian Restaurant"

It was actually three different songs that I sewed together. One song was called "The Italian Restaurant Song," because I wrote "Bottle of white, bottle of red," and from there I went "perhaps a bottle of rose instead." So obviously, it's in an Italian restaurant, there's a couple talking, there's some kind of reminiscing going on, it's a little slice of life. The "things are okay with me these days" section was actually another song I wrote, a little piece of a thing called "Things Are Okay In Oyster Bay." I was living in Oyster Bay and it was one of the first apartments I ever had. It was like a hippie crash pad, but I really dug it. It was one of these dopey little songs. So I said, "Ah it's just this cutey pie little tune, it's not worth anything." So then I needed to get from the instrumental section and I recognized we're going somewhere with this. You know where we're going? We're going to Brenda and Eddie. That's what they're reminiscing about. That was another song called "The Ballad Of Brenda And Eddie." It was sort of my ode to the king and the queen of the high school – the legendary popular couple in school, which I think is a universal concept. The story just told itself to me as I was going along. I didn't sit down and have this whole organized chart.

Did you have a lot of problems with the Catholic Church on "Only The Good Die Young"?

I didn't have a problem with the Catholic Church; the Catholic Church had a problem with me [laughs]. The song came out on the album and it was no big deal, and then Columbia decided to put it out as a single. A radio station in New Jersey banned it. Then it was banned by the archdiocese of St. Louis. And then it got banned in Boston. All these archdiocese areas started putting pressure on radio stations to ban it. And the record as a single had been out a short amount of time and it wasn't doing that well. The minute they banned it, the album starting shooting up the charts [laughs], because there's nothing that sells a record like a ban or a boycott. As soon as the kids found out that there was some authority that didn't want them to hear it, they went out and bought it in droves and it became this big hit. Then I did it on "Saturday Night Live" and everybody was all freaked out about it, saying you can't do that on TV. I think some people took offense at it, but there were all these novels written about Jewish guilt, so why not a song about Catholic guilt? Every Catholic I know is still recovering from this incredibly guilty upbringing they had. It was supposed to be lighthearted. It was taken out of context with the rest of the album.

I think my favorite album of yours is The Nylon Curtain. *You were in a very Beatlesque mode and writing more abstractly than usual with songs like "Scandanavian Skies."*

I like that album a lot. That would probably be the album I'm most proud of making, as a labor of love. What I realized after I made it, which was just after John Lennon was killed, was that I found myself singing like John Lennon. I didn't realize I was doing it and I was writing these songs that I pictured John Lennon singing. Like "Scandinavian Skies." I remember Phil Ramone, who was the producer at the time, saying, "You're really singing it like John Lennon too much" and I didn't realize it. Then when I came back and listened to it, it was weird. And then I said, "Okay, I'll try to sing it more like whoever Billy Joel is." I'm still not sure what he sings like. And it didn't work. I had to sing it as it was written, as it was conceived to be sung.

You made the comment about not knowing what Billy Joel sings like. I've always liked the different sort of characters you get into when you sing.

I don't think of myself as a singer really. I think of myself as a writer and I'm able to write all over the place, so I'll change my voice depending on the mood of the music. I'm not a stylist, I never have been, as a singer. I always wanted to sound like a black man from Georgia. I always wanted to sing like Ray Charles or Wilson Pickett. Or when I was singing a ballad I thought of McCartney, or I thought of Nilsson, or John Lennon. A lot of different voices. So I'm not really sure what my voice is, but it doesn't bother me, I don't really care. I think with certain journalists, they have a problem with that though, because they think that I live in a stylistic no man's land, that I'm some kind of a Zelig. But I'm not doing it consciously, I'm just doing it as an extension of the writer. I never really took myself seriously as a singer. You want to hear a singer, listen to Ray Charles, there's a singer. Pavarotti, there's a singer. Annie Lennox, there's a singer. I'm not a singer. I'm a writer.

I beg to differ. I think you're a great singer.

Yeah, people think that but it always surprises me. I don't think so and it's not false humility. It's just my opinion. I tend to approach production more as a composer than as a recording artist. A recording artist is supposed to sing and project and sell that record, you know, and give the record company something they can get on the radio. He's supposed to be a rock star. People are supposed to hear you and go, "That's Billy Joel, the rock star." Well, I don't think like that. I go in and I do a couple takes, and after the second take I go, "Yeah, that's close enough, let's not beat it to death. I still like this thing." You know, you do more than three vocals, you start hating the damn thing.

I love the song on River of Dreams *that you wrote for your daughter, "Lullabye (Goodnight My Angel)."*

Thank you, I like that song too. I wrote it originally as a classical piano piece. It had no lyric. I actually wrote it when I knew that Christie [Brinkley] and I were going to split up. My daughter did ask me what happens when you die? So that was part of it. But the other part of the song was mommy and I are going to leave each other, but I'm never going to leave you. I had a hard time recording that one. To sing it was like, my throat was starting to close up. We'd have to stop and start it again. But that means it's a good song.

While you were married to Christie, was it frustrating to know that a lot of people were listening to your songs looking for clues rather than listening to the songs?

Sure, but I did that too. I remember when The Beatles were writing music, I'd try to find who their girlfriends at the time were. Oh, that's about Jane Asher. Or with Mick Jagger, oh, that's about Marianne

Faithfull. I think we all play those games. I'm not going to deny that she was the muse for a great deal of the music I wrote during the time I was with her. She was what I epitomized, what I loved about women. She was the woman I married. That was my muse. She was my inspiration. But to assume that everything I wrote had something to do with our relationship isn't true. I mean I had another life. I had a family before that, I had friends before that, I have my opinions about things.

Have you been approached by a lot of companies to turn your songs into commercials?

Yeah. I haven't done it, not because I'm a snob and not because I think my music is somehow sacrosanct, but just because I thought it was kind of cheesy and I didn't like the whole idea. I didn't want my music to be perceived as a huckster for somebody's product. If I believed in something and I thought that it was a compatible campaign, and they paid me gazillions of dollars [laughs], I'd consider it, absolutely. But if they come to me with deodorant for "A Matter Of Trust" and "She's Always A Woman" for feminine hygiene spray, I got a problem with that. Now I'm fortunate – let me be clear about this – I'm fortunate that I can afford my conscience. A lot of people can't. I can afford to sit and judge, I don't want to do this, I don't want to do that. Most people can't. So I don't want to appear like I think I'm so great because I haven't done that. And I'm also, again in the press, somewhat typed as somebody who's commercial. There's that whole image of me as well, he's had so many hits, he's sold out. Look, I didn't make 'em hits, I just wrote the songs and recorded them. You made them hits, not me. So why shouldn't I sell my songs, if I'm going to be perceived as a sell-out anyway, what the hell do I care? Frankly, I really don't care what somebody thinks of me. All I care is what I think of me.

You've been writing songs for over thirty years. Has it gotten any easier?

No. I think because once you achieve a certain level, which is purely your own criteria, you have something to measure yourself against that you can no longer fall under. You can't ever let yourself slide because you know what you're capable of. So you're constantly pulling yourself up higher, you're constantly trying to achieve a new plateau. So it never gets easier.

You've always said that the prospect of writing scares you.

The factor that has changed is the fear factor, because whenever I start a writing project, there's a great deal of trepidation. Where I used to approach it with absolute white knuckle terror, now I just have the everyday ordinary jitters. So I must be extremely compelled to write because I find it to be a difficult process, excruciating sometimes.

Do you write everyday?

No. I'm what they call a cold start guy. Some people, to keep themselves in the flow, will write a song every day. Stevie Wonder does. Or he used to. And he told me that when I met him. I love Stevie Wonder. I admire him tremendously, but at the time he said that I thought, "Well goody goody for you, but I bet you out of 365 days, there's 300 days we're definitely never gonna hear." So everybody's got their own way of doing it. I do it by not writing for a long time. Like a novelist. I write when I feel like I have something to write. I don't write because of record company schedules or because I need money or because I want to be more famous. I write purely out of a compulsion to write.

What do you do musically during the down times?

When I'm not writing, I'm not necessarily doing anything actively, but passively, all kinds of things are going on. I know I dream music almost every night, because when I wake up in the morning I'm either humming or whistling something that was programmed in my dream. Either someone else's song or a song I wrote in my head. That's how I feel the writing process begins to work itself out for me; it starts to get written while I'm sleeping. I think there's a great deal of input that comes in. Emotional input, visual input, technological input – whether I'm aware of it or not.

Do you listen to other people's songs?

I don't even listen to songs so much anymore. I only hear pop music accidentally or incidentally. What I listen to now almost exclusively is classical music, and it's been like that for the last three to five years, maybe longer. I've rediscovered my love of classical music and I've learned to pick out a good amount of the symphonies on the piano by ear. I'm learning a lot by doing that, learning a lot about theory, learning a lot about playing, learning a lot about composition. What it's also made me realize is that I was always writing classical music, even the popular songs I wrote. I recognize a lot of them as being classical piano pieces, and that's how I started composing when I was a little kid.

What advice would you give to songwriters who are looking for their own original sound?

I have a theory that the only original things we do are mistakes. The only things that we can really attribute to ourselves that are purely original are our screw-ups. Because you can be taught to do everything the right way, but only you can exquisitely fuck something up in your own unique way. That goes along with the theory of painting yourself into a corner. Okay, well you got yourself in there, now get yourself out. That's where ingenuity comes in. Everything that I think I've ever done that was good was done purely by accident, purely by total serendipity. I recognized it to be something good after I did it. That takes talent to do. But to screw up I don't think takes that much talent. It takes humanity to do that. It's good to be a human being.

181

Phil Collins

Against All Odds (Take A Look At Me Now)
☆ In The Air Tonight ☆ Sussudio

Interview conducted in 1996

"I'd love to be more obtuse like Peter Gabriel, but I write the way I write, so there's no point in me trying to be anything else."

Phil Collins is the Spencer Tracy of pop music. He's the regular Joe who became a star. The supporting actor who rose to leading man status, not on flash or matinee idol looks, but on talent and an honest everyman quality. Equally adept in his songs at gripping drama and light comedy, Collins can play it quiet and intimate, or when a dash of theatrics is required, deliver the goods with a brassy bravado. Remembering Tracy's famous advice to actors – "Know your lines and don't bump into the furniture" – you might say that Collins' musical credo has been "Know your heart and don't bump into the microphone."

Philip David Charles Collins was born January 31, 1951 in Hounslow, a suburb of London. He showed a flair for music immediately and was pounding his first drum set at age five, but the theatre beckoned the young lad. His acting career reached a peak when at 14, he played the Artful Dodger in a West End production of *Oliver!* Around the same time, Collins appeared briefly as a fan in the Scala Theatre scene of The Beatles' *A Hard Day's Night*. The thrill of rubbing shoulders with the Fab Four influenced Collins to drop acting in favor of rock'n'roll.

After gigging with various bands, Collins responded to an advertisement seeking a "drummer sensitive to acoustic music," and landed a job behind the kit in a fledgling group called Genesis. Led by Peter Gabriel, a flamboyant singer who would sometimes prance the stage in fox heads, scarlet gowns, flower masks and other show-stopping costumes, the band offered a challenging mix of pop, folk and classical – what later became known as progressive rock.

On the strength of visually stunning live shows and albums such as *Foxtrot*, *Selling England By The Pound* and their swan song with Gabriel, the dense, weird masterpiece, *The Lamb Lies Down On Broadway*, Genesis built a small, but intensely loyal following. In 1975, after Gabriel quit to pursue his solo career, Phil Collins stepped out from behind his drum kit into the spotlight. Genesis evolved and hit their stride with a leaner sound. The lengthy suites and obscure Lewis Carroll-esque poetry were replaced by more concise melodic pop songcraft. As a result, their audience broadened.

With hit albums such as *...And Then There Were Three* and *Duke*, Genesis became more popular than ever, but Collins' personal life was in turmoil. Out of the bitterness of a divorce from his first wife, he documented his battered emotions in a dozen songs. Initially, he had no intention of releasing them, but emboldened by the positive feedback from his manager and producer, he made those demos into his first solo album, *Face Value*. Both the album and its singles ("I Missed Again" and "In The Air Tonight") gained more commercial attention than anything Genesis had previously done.

In the 1980s, Phil Collins was simply everywhere. With Genesis, he scaled the charts with hits such as "Misunderstanding," "That's All," "Invisible Touch," "Land Of Confusion," "Throwing It All Away," "Tonight, Tonight, Tonight," and "In Too Deep." As a solo artist, Collins racked up best-selling albums such as *Hello, I Must Be Going*, *No Jacket Required* and *But Seriously . . .* and seven #1 singles, including "Against All Odds (Take A Look At Me Now)," "One More Night," "Sussudio," "Another Day In Paradise," and "Two Hearts" (the latter co-written with Motown legend Lamont Dozier).

In the 1990s, Collins left Genesis to concentrate on his solo career. He released the albums *Dance Into The Light* and *Both Sides*, and in 1999, he wrote the score for Disney's massively successful animated version of *Tarzan*, which featured the hit "You'll Be In My Heart."

Reading through past interviews you've done, I get the sense that you may feel underappreciated as a songwriter.

Not by other songwriters or not by the general public. But by critics, I do, yes. I think I'm a little underrated in the artistic sense. But that's my lot. Some people are destined for that and it's fine. I've sort of grown to accept it. With my last album, *Both Sides*, I thought those were some of my best-ever songs. And it's such a low-key album. They're all my demos – as all my albums are – but they were more obviously my demos. When it didn't do well, my manager said, "This is your *Nebraska* after *Born In The U.S.A.*" But I thought even if the public didn't get it, maybe this will be the album that critics say, "Well, he's gone against the grain and he's done something that is actually not immediately accessible." Some critics did get it. *Q* Magazine in England listed it as one of my best albums. And I thought, "Wow, they got it." At least they got the idea that it was not a bad album because it was unsuccessful commercially. It wasn't unsuccessful in this country, but in a global sense, yes.

Did the sales of Both Sides *make you second-guess yourself?*

When you do your best work and people, apart from your avid fans, don't get it, then you start to wonder, "Well, what is it about me that they want?" You always assume your fans like you for the right reasons. Hopefully they think your music is good for the same reasons you do. But when they don't go along with it, you think maybe all they want from me is "You Can't Hurry Love," "Two Hearts," "Sussudio." I'm proud of those other songs, they're great fun, but if I go deeper, maybe they don't want to hear that from me. If they want to hear that, they'll go and buy a Neil Young album, not a Phil Collins album, thank you very much. Get back to where you belong, don't you know your place? So it's kind of weird.

I was trying to trace your songwriting back through the years because it always amazed me that when Face Value *came out in 1981, you emerged as this fully-formed writer. Were you writing in the early days of Genesis?*

I wrote "For Absent Friends" on *Nursery Cryme*, that was me and Steve Hackett. "More Fool Me" from *Selling England*, I did the words and Mike Rutherford did the music. "Lilywhite Lilith" on *The Lamb Lies Down On Broadway*, that was Peter's lyric and my music. On . . . *And Then There Were Three*, I started to write. And obviously there were group tracks that we all contributed to. "Follow You, Follow Me" was all three of our names, but that was because it came out of a jam. There were other songs where I brought a bit in that fitted with one of Mike's bits or Tony's bits. But at that time, I'd never finished a complete song. After . . . *And Then There Were Three*, when my marriage broke up, I was going to leave the band and just live in Canada. But the guys said, "Listen, you're not leaving the band. Just do what you have to do, we'll get on with something else. We'll do our solo albums." When I came back two months later, they were only just beginning their solo albums, so I had a lot of time on my hands before the next Genesis project. During which time I started to write at home, because I had this 8-track machine, a desk, a drum machine and some keyboards. I was just trying to work out how to use the machine, trying to see the meters move, trying to learn how to record. And in doing that, I recorded everything I did, bits here, bits there. Some of these songs were "You Know What I Mean," "Against All Odds" – musically that was written at that time, lyrically it changed for the movie – and "In The Air Tonight."

Did the songs surprise you?

My strength, I thought, was really in arranging other people's ideas. I thought "That's my gig. I'm good at envisioning other people's songs." Then suddenly I was writing songs. I remember "Misunderstanding" being the very first song I finished. And of course, it was our first hit in America. But when I started writing songs, it wasn't for an album, it was just writing, learning how to operate the machinery, this is a message for the ex-wife, when she hears this, she'll know how I feel, blah, blah, blah. And they were, not therapeutic really, but messages that ended up being complete songs. When Tony Smith, my manager, heard the tapes, he said, "This is an album." So I took the demos, met up with Hugh Padgham, who'd I'd just worked with on Peter Gabriel's record, and he said, "We'll use the demos." So we copied my demos onto the 24-track, did some drums, got my friends in to do some bits and pieces, and put it out. And that set the pattern not only of me writing about my personal life and not getting embarrassed by it with albums to come, but also the fact that my demos, with every album except *But Seriously* . . ., have formed the backing track of all my stuff. So basically it's home recording.

What do you recall about writing "In The Air Tonight"?

It was completely improvised. I opened my mouth, and those lyrics came out, except for one line. The entire song came out, and I wrote it down so I wouldn't forget it. So if someone says to me, "Was it about this?" I say, "I know how it was written, and I don't know what it's about." Obviously, you can make up your own stories. Maybe that's why people like the song, because it can be whatever you want it to be.

Are there often things that come out where you don't know quite what they mean?

Oh yeah. "Sussudio" was like that. That's an obvious one in terms of, what does "Sussudio" mean? I don't know. Actually, it just scanned perfectly with the rhythm, da-da-dabio. So then you go back and say, "This is crap, this is a rubbish word, a nonsense word. What word works?" And after scratching me head for a couple of days, nothing worked, so I thought, "Okay, let's now make Sussudio make sense." It's the name of something. In my song it was a person.

How about "Against All Odds"?

It was originally called "How Can You Sit There?" There was one ballad too many on the first album, and that was my least favorite. I loved "You Know What I Mean" and I loved "If Leaving Me Is Easy," but that was a song I left off. So when Taylor Hackford called, he'd done this film and he wanted me to write a song. I was in Chicago where we were playing, so I said, "I don't write on the road." But if you need a song, I actually have a song. So I sent him the demo, which was basically the melody, and he loved it. Then he sent me a rough cut of the film and I wrote the lyrics to suit the film. Then he said, "When are you going to record it?" I said, "I can't record it until we finish the tour." So I then decided to give it to someone else to produce, which was a big thing for me. My solo career has always been like "This is mine!" I want to see all the photographs, I want to see all the press releases, everything, because people see this stuff and think that it's you. So to hand over production of a song like this, I thought, "Okay, it's a song for a film. It was never one of my favorite songs anyway."

So I got Arif Mardin, who I always really admired and at that point didn't really know. I got him to produce it, and we went to New York, the RCA studios, and got a piano player. Ever since I wrote it, I've never really been able to play it. I tried playing it at Live Aid twice, and fucked it up both times [laughs]. So somebody else played it, and we had the orchestra in there, and I did the drums in L.A., then Arif sent me a mix, and I said, "A bit less of this, a bit more of that." Really it was his production, and it was my first number one record.

When I hear that song, I get goosebumps. Do you give yourself goosebumps when you're writing?

I suppose when you're writing, you think, "Someone out there is going to love this." I get that with "Take Me Home," even when we play it. We always end the show with it, but in 1990, on the *Serious* tour we had the carousel and it closed at the end of the set, leaving me outside it with the band inside. So it was just a naked moment with me and the audience. The house lights were on and everyone was singing, and it was the most moving moment. Invariably, I'd get tears in my eyes, because I'd been there for two and a half-hours doing my best, and they were responding to me. It was very emotional. But as a song, it still does that to me, when I sing it or if I hear it.

Do you see any parallels between your development and Peter Gabriel's? Do you look up to him as a songwriter?

Oh yeah, I do. But I'm sure he doesn't look up to me. I think I'm much more direct than he is. I don't mean simple, but more direct, whereas I'm sure that sometimes maybe he'd like to be more direct. But his upbringing – public school upbringing in England fucks you up. Emotionally and mentally, you go through some very weird times. And my upbringing, I was listening to *Younger Than Yesterday* and *Sgt. Pepper* while I was studying for my exams in the classroom with the teacher there. I mean, totally precocious. This was a drama school, where we got away with murder. All the guys in Genesis pretty much were like that, which is why I was a good balance in the band because I was kind of the joker. But Peter and I are both drummers, and I was there with him at the beginning. I see lots of differences. He's far more intellectual than I am as a person. He's far more painstaking, which can be frustrating. But if he asked me to be his drummer tomorrow, I'd probably pack everything up and do it. I love what he does. We were always soul brothers in the band. I was always the guy who related to what he was saying, although his best friend was Tony Banks. They were like oil and water, though, always at each other's throats. The closest and the farthest apart. Whereas him and I used to work really closely together.

It was with Gabriel that you developed the famous Phil Collins drum sound.

I remember people saying that was the Peter Gabriel drum sound, but I was the guy who played that stuff on the third album, "Intruder" and all that. It was as much mine, because with that kind of sound thing with the drums, you're composing [sings drum beat from "Intruder"]. That was me, you know? I came up with that. So don't tell me it's a Peter Gabriel drum sound. That's me! I'm as entitled to use it as anybody else. But I do admire Peter tremendously as a songwriter. He writes songs that I wish I'd written, which is always a good sign.

Tell me about how the Tarzan *project came about.*

It was kind of strange for me, because when you think of Disney stuff, you think they'll want you to write a song like "When You Wish Upon A Star" or "Under The Sea." Initially I said, "I don't know if I'm capable of doing this. I don't think I can write like Alan Menken." And they said, "No, we don't want you to be Alan Menken, we want you to be Phil Collins." They want you to be you, but fulfill the same job. They told me that [on *The Lion King*] Tim Rice was at the end of a fax machine everyday changing the lyrics as the film gathered momentum. I said, "I don't know if I'll be able to do that. If I'm on tour and someone says 'Hey you've got to change the lyrics,' I might not be able to do that." These are all the things that went through my mind at the beginning.

How was their initial reaction to your work?

Well, the first thing I sent them lyrically was a broad piece, a celebration after Tarzan's done something to try to ingratiate himself into the crew of monkeys. He's trying to become one of them. They loved it. It was an interesting moment because Chris Montan, who coordinates these projects for Disney, said, "Michael Eisner called me. This could be our first hit that isn't a ballad." Then I met with the directors and they said, "Yeah, we love it, but we don't know how it's going to fit into the movie yet." That made me realize that we're not talking about hit songs [mimics the crack of a whip], we're talking about what's right for the film [whip crack]. I know Elton wanted to write a ballad for a film like this, and he wrote what he thought was a great ballad. And when he saw the movie, it had been cut out. And he said, "This is a fucking disaster, what's happening?" Of course, the song was cut out because it didn't fit into the movie anymore. So it just changes all the time. Apart from that side of things, as a discipline for a songwriter, it's great. You can't be too long. A few minutes tops. You can't repeat the chorus lyrically, because it has to move the story forward all the time. So as a songwriter, it's very interesting.

If you were teaching a workshop on songwriting, what kinds of things would you stress?

If I had a class of songwriters out there, some of who might be much better than me, I'd feel like a klutz. I would say don't ever feel that a song has to be lyrically complicated or musically complicated. There's something in a song, like a little spiritual zap, that will reach a listener, and that's what you've got to go for. That's what you've got to try to get, rather than something that's very, very clever. That's what reaches people when they hear a song. That's why I guess some people like what I do. I'd love to be more obtuse like Peter Gabriel, but I write the way I write, so there's no point in me trying to be anything else. But the reason people relate to it is because they can hear it, understand it, and it's just what they feel. So there's something that zaps out and connects with them.

190

John Mellencamp

Pink Houses ✶ Jack And Diane ✶ Small Town

Interview conducted in 1997

"I never did like 'Jack And Diane.' The guys in the band made me put it on the record."

These days, the term "roots rock" is liberally slapped on any American band whose sound is revved up with rough guitars and gravelly vocals. But when the stylistic term's currency was stronger, it was associated with three names only: Bruce Springsteen, Bob Seger, and most accurately, John Cougar Mellencamp.

"Roots" described not only the basic music and fashion ethic of these artists – garage band spirit, blue jeans and T-shirts – but also their attachment to their home turf. Springsteen had the Jersey Shore. Seger mined the soul of Detroit. And Mellencamp's stomping ground was Seymour, Indiana, a place as middle as middle America can get, the aorta of the heartland.

While the career trajectories of Springsteen and Seger distanced them from their roots, Mellencamp, despite significant musical growth, has remained firmly planted in his midwestern soil. He still lives in Indiana, not far from where he grew up. A good part of his band consists of high school friends who made the long journey to success with him. And his best songs still find their lyrical power in small town characters and attitudes.

Those attitudes are evident in a long string of heartland rock classics, such as "Hurts So Good," "Jack And Diane," "Crumblin' Down," "Pink Houses,"

"Authority Song," "Lonely Ol' Night," "Small Town," "R.O.C.K. In The U.S.A.," "Rain On The Scarecrow," "Paper In Fire," "Cherry Bomb," and "Check It Out." Beyond the radio hits, his albums *Scarecrow* and *The Lonesome Jubilee* are considered among the best rock albums of the 1980s.

How has living in the same neck of the woods, in Indiana, for most of your life affected your outlook as a songwriter?

People get the idea that I live in a farmhouse in Indiana and I never leave. That's not true. I'm in South Carolina right now, looking at the ocean as we speak. So I'm very fortunate that I move around and do what I want to do in a very quiet way, and have never allowed having musical success stop me from living a pretty normal, down to earth lifestyle.

You're often associated, because of a few specific songs, with small town life in the Midwest. Are you comfortable with that?

I never really saw myself that way. I wrote one song about small towns [laughs], and all of a sudden I became keeper of the small town. I wrote one song, "Rain On The Scarecrow," and I did Farm Aid, and all of a sudden I was the keeper of the farmland. When I started doing this I was in a fucking rock band. I had tattoos and pierced ears and rode motorcycles and I was there for the girls. That's how I always saw myself up until I kind of became an adult a few years ago. It was always laughable to me. I never took myself very seriously. In the mid-80s when all this stuff was happening, I was at my immature highest [laughs]. So I never really saw myself that way.

When you were writing your first songs, what kind of expectations did you have?

Well, I had a record deal before I wrote my first song [laughs]. When I first started making records, the idea of writing songs never really occurred to me, because I was in a bar band in Indiana and I was a singer. We did other people's material, so when I got a record deal, it was like, "Oh, you have to write your own songs? I don't know how to do that." Consequently, that's why my first four or five records are pretty rough. I was still learning how to write songs. Literally, the first song I wrote, which was probably "Chestnut Street

Incident," ended up on my first record. All that early stuff was just Woody Guthrie and Bob Dylan. Everybody thought it was Springsteen, but it was really me doing Guthrie and Dylan.

Was there a milestone you passed when you felt like you had a grasp on how to do it?

I think I thought that for a little bit in the late 80s. I think after *Scarecrow*, I started thinking, "Hey, I kind of have a handle on what I should be doing." But that faded pretty quickly. I think of those records now as being almost country music. *Scarecrow* is what country music is today. It was called rock back then, but if you put it out today it would fit in country.

Have you recently made any new discoveries about your songwriting?

I don't know that I made any new discoveries. I just keep doing what I do and try not to repeat myself. Bob Dylan told me one time that we all write the same five songs a million times, and I think he's right. So it's just trying to write songs that are not so similar to something else I've already done. I'll kill songs in the writing, no matter how inspired they may be, if it's too close to another song I've done. I think, "What's the use in finishing this, I already wrote it"

The reason I asked is because I've read how much importance you put on the idea of re-inventing your sound.

Well, I think that comes automatically, or it should, with songwriting, just because your point of view in life is always changing. Your perspective of what you think at 21 and 31 and 41 are quite different in terms of what's important to you. So I think just that alone is change enough. I don't think, to be cliched, you need to throw the baby out with the bath water. You can't just go someplace that is very foreign to you and expect to come out with very much.

Will you sometimes start with an intent of what a song will be about?

Never [laughs]. Maybe on "Rain On The Scarecrow," George Green and I sat down and talked about what we wanted to say. But very rarely do I sit down and say, "Gosh, I think I'll write a song about a small town." That just doesn't happen.

How does your collaboration with George Green work?

George and I went to pre-school together, so we've known each other our entire lives. Our songwriting can come from table talk, just sitting around talking – then one of us will go away and write a song about what we discussed – to faxing lyrics back and forth. It can be very personal; it can be very impersonal.

The lyrics to some of the songs you've written with George, like "Key West Intermezzo" and "Human Wheels" could almost stand alone as poetry.

Both of those songs were primarily lyrically all George's stuff. You can identify his stuff from mine real easily I think. "Human Wheels" was a speech that he gave at the funeral of his grandfather. George read it to me and he said, "This is what I'm going to say," and I said, "Great, after you're done I want to use it as a song [laughs]." I'll go in and I'll change the meter of lines or change a phrase here and there. But three-quarters of the songs we write together, particularly those two, are lyrics that George has written and sent to me and said, "What do you think about this?" When George writes something inspired, it's great. Those two songs were great. But his math is not very good. It's the same way for me. When things are inspired, they're beautiful. But when they're math, they're terrible. But you know, math songs are the biggest hits in the country right now. Turn on the fucking radio and that's all you hear is math.

What's the best way for a young songwriter to find their voice and avoid being, as you put it, a mathematician?

I think it's very important for young people to try to avoid – and I know I was guilty of it when I was young – this idea that, because something's popular, you need to sound that way. I've been recently listening to demos of young bands and so many of them sound derivative. They sound like Pearl Jam or they sound like this band or that band. They're missing it. You have to sound like yourself. Go for that, whatever that is. There's always that fear, "Well, nobody wants to hear what I really sound like." And the record companies of course promote that; they don't really promote individuality. As a matter of fact, they don't like it when they get a record that's too individual. I remember when I delivered *Lonesome Jubilee*, they didn't know what the fuck to do with that. "What is this,

194

accordions and violins – how are we supposed to sell this?" Which is their only interest in records at all. Record companies are really a terrible place to distribute your music, but it's the only way to do it right now.

I'd like to mention some of your songs to get your reactions. "Jack And Diane"

I never did like "Jack And Diane." Even when I wrote it, I didn't particularly like it. The guys in the band made me put it on the record. But, over the last 20 years, it's changed. I love the song now, because I see how much people like it. Have you ever had a friend who you didn't really particularly like, but he liked you so much that you started liking him on that basis? That's kind of how that song is. I never liked the song much, but it liked me so much that I started liking it. Now, it's one of my favorite songs to play live. I've played it a gazillion times. The audience loves it so much, how could I not like it?

"Pink Houses"

I almost feel obliged to play that song live. I wouldn't play it if I didn't feel that way. I'm very sensitive when I play live to the fact that people who are in the audience have come to hear that song, and would be very disappointed if I didn't play it. So I play it against my better judgment. I'm glad I wrote that song. That song was very important, I think, for its time. It preceded all that U.S.A. shit that happened later on.

"R.O.C.K. In The U.S.A."

That's a math song. Strictly math, but the audience, once again, loves that song.

"Paper In Fire"

I like that song. I still think that's a legitimate song, an inspired song and I was glad it was a hit. I was surprised actually, back in the 80s, that you could put a song like that out and have a hit record. It wasn't at the time, and still isn't, the type of song that generally gets played on the radio. Once a song like that gets played enough and it becomes recognizable to people, then I really feel successful.

"Just Another Day"

Well, I've always been interested in people who were able to live a kind of freeform lifestyle. I always thought that I would live that way, but of course I don't. But I sometimes vacation on these islands, and you see these guys sitting at the tiki hut everyday and you wonder, "How in the world do they get by doing this?" They don't have any jobs and they just sit in the tiki hut drinking and smoking. They appear to be living the life of Riley. Who really knows what's going on underneath, but the appearance is that these guys have it made. Then I look at my own life and it's kind of like, I'm on the phone everyday doing this music business stuff. Sometimes you feel like, "Well, maybe I did miss the boat here. Perhaps what they said is true, that less is more."

There's kind of a Simon & Garfunkel sound to that song.

You're talking about the arrangement. For me, those are two big, distinct, different things – the arrangement of the song and the song itself. Because all my songs are folk songs in the beginning. In the writing of the song there was never any thought of Simon & Garfunkel, but in the arrangement, there was. When we did the *Mr. Happy Go Lucky* record, *Bookends* was a big influence. We listened to it a lot during the physical arranging of the material, because it's such a brilliantly arranged record. Particularly when you consider it was 1968 when the record came out. I know Paul and I asked him, "Did you do all that?" He said, "Oh yeah." To meet Paul Simon and to talk to him, you just can't believe that this guy could come up with this, because he doesn't appear that way to me. He's so unassuming.

After writing for so many years, are there things about the process that still mystify you?

Yes. I don't know how you can write so many terrible songs, then all of a sudden you get one good one. When that happens, you're very aware of it. But as we know, today the quality of the song really doesn't matter much. It doesn't matter if it's a good song or not. I don't know if it ever did. It only matters if it's a hit song. That's all people care about.

What kind of feeling do you get when that one out of a hundred comes through?

Very humble. I'm very humbled by the experience, because it's kind of an out of body type of feeling, like, "Wow, where did that come from?" You've got to just look up and go, "Thanks."

I didn't know until recently that you painted. How is that different from songwriting?

Painting is much more powerful than songwriting for one thing. I've been painting for years. I started in maybe '85, then I seriously started painting in '88, where I would spend 14 or 15 hours straight in front of the canvas. I haven't painted in the last three or four months, because I've been too busy doing music business junk. I can't paint and try to write songs at the same time, because if I do, the painting always wins out. The truth of the matter is that I'm more akin to painting that I am songwriting. That doesn't mean I'm a better painter than I am a songwriter [laughs], it just means that I feel more in-spired by paintings than songs.

Do you feel that both disciplines come through you from other sources?

I think the desire to create is kind of that way. Some people just don't have that. I think they do have it, but they just don't know how to tap into it, and if they have tapped into it they've kind of ignored it. The desire to create is what makes life bearable. Not even the creation itself. It's the desire to create. The end result has little or no impact on anything. If a song is good it doesn't matter. If a paint-ing is good it doesn't matter. But it's the desire and the actual activ-ity of creating that makes life livable. I really don't understand how people can live and not do that.

Nick Lowe

Cruel To Be Kind ✶ The Beast In Me
✶ (What's So Funny 'Bout) Peace, Love And Understanding

Interview conducted in 1992

"You hear so much piffle now. It's sort of a lost art, writing songs."

Webster's defines "Renaissance Man" as a "person who is expert in several areas." It might as well have accompanied the entry with an illustration of Nick Lowe. For nearly 25 years, Lowe has been wearing an impressive array of musical hats, and doing so with style and flair.

As a songwriter, he's penned an impressive catalog of enduring and respected pop-rock gems, including solo hits such as "Cruel To Be Kind," (a top 20 US/UK hit in 1979), "I Love The Sound Of Breaking Glass," (top 20 in the UK in 1978), plus FM radio staples such as "So It Goes," "Raging Eyes," "Half A Boy And Half A Man" and "I Knew The Bride (When She Used To Rock 'N' Roll)." He's written successfully for other artists: "(What's So Funny 'Bout) Peace, Love and Understanding" was recorded by Elvis Costello on *Armed Forces*, and by Curtis Stigers on the multi-platinum soundtrack to *The Bodyguard*. "Love Is A Battlefield" has been recorded by both Diana Ross and Nanci Griffith. "The Beast In Me" was featured on Johnny Cash's Grammy-winning *American Recordings* album. "I Need You," a 1982 collaboration with Paul Carrack, became a Top 40 hit for Carrack and was later covered by Linda Ronstadt. Lowe's songs have also been covered by Tom Petty & The Heartbreakers, Carlene Carter, and The Fabulous Thunderbirds.

199

Lowe has also served as a producer for Elvis Costello, The Pretenders, The Mavericks, Graham Parker, John Hiatt and others. In addition to recording nine critically-acclaimed albums of his own, he was a founding member of pub-rock pioneers Brinsley Schwarz, the seminal roots-rock outfit Rockpile, and the 1990s supergroup Little Village (with John Hiatt, Ry Cooder and Jim Keltner).

Despite his accomplishments, Lowe remains almost overly modest. With his dry wit and an easy-going charm, Lowe strikes you as a combination of British comic Peter Cook and singer Ricky Nelson.

How did you get started in music?

Initially it wasn't really anything much to do with music that got me interested. It was more being a guy with a guitar on, being perceived as that. I thought it was a really fantastic way to make a living – loads of girls and everything [laughs]. My mom taught me a few chords. She could play the guitar a little bit. When I was a kid, she played me lots of show tunes, Les Paul and Mary Ford, Danny Kaye, and things like that – very early 50s kind of pop music.

Was there much rock'n'roll in England then?

We had a guy in England called Lonnie Donegan, who was about the nearest thing to a homegrown rock'n'roll singer. He had a very distinctive voice, sort of whiny, and he used to sing Leadbelly songs, sort of Negro spirituals. And he was wild, especially for England at that time, which was post-war, very austere, gray. Donegan started the skiffle craze. It had real easy rhythm, but frantic. I still love that stuff.

Do you remember writing your first song?

Sort of. I think the first song I wrote was a copy of a Lonnie Donegan-style thing. With the first songs I wrote, it was very obvious where I got them from. My influences were very much on my sleeve. Over the years I've tried to find my own style and explore all sorts of little avenues, but it's funny how much of the stuff that I liked when I first started is in the music I do now.

Do you consider yourself a disciplined songwriter?

No, absolutely not. I know some people who are. John Hiatt is, for instance. He goes to work everyday, to an office which has got his piano and his guitars and sets about doing it. I'm much more of the when-inspiration-strikes type. I'll carry around some things in my head for years. I had a song on my *Party Of One* album called "What's Shakin' On The Hill?" I had the first verse of that for about seven or eight years and I couldn't see any further than that. So sometimes that happens. Then other times, the whole picture comes. You see it really clearly in your head. It's a complete mystery to me how it works, why it works. Sometimes I think anyone could do this. Then other times I think, "This is sheer genius; what a gifted guy you are" [laughs]. When I've tried to encourage the process, it goes away. I can't dial it up. It either comes to me or it doesn't. And I used to panic about it, thinking, "Shit, I've got to do a record and I can't think of any songs. What am I gonna do?" But the older I've gotten, I tend not to worry about it as much and instead keep a relaxed attitude.

Do you prefer to start with a title or a concept, or can you just pick up a guitar and bump into an idea?

Well, all of the above, really. Sometimes just walking along, you get a little rhythm and some words suggest themselves to the rhythm you hear in your head. You know, Hiatt's got a great concept about this. He says that people perceive songwriters quite different to how they really are. He thinks that people believe that a lot of songwriters think much more carefully about their lyrics and how their songs go than they actually do. The only reason you have lyrics is you've got to have something to say in your tune. And you're very constrained by the number of bars, so you really can't afford to think about it too carefully. It's just how lucky you are, really. It's much more hit or miss than a lot of people think.

How would you define a great song?

I think stuff like "I've Grown Accustomed To Her Face" and "Get Me To The Church On Time" are really great songs, and that is just completely beyond me. That seems to be real music. The stuff I do doesn't seem like real music. It's just sort of like jingles really and it's sort of naive. But I like it, and it's what I do. It's just not very schooled. Nothing wrong with that at all. But I like Cole Porter and Hoagy Carmichael, those are who I think are really great songwriters. They were writing for common people, yet the lyrics

201

are so sophisticated and so sexy and just wonderful. It doesn't sound like they're talking down to anybody. You hear so much piffle now. It's sort of a lost art, writing songs.

You said before that songwriting is mystery. Do you see songs coming from some kind of greater power, or do you believe in muses?

It's a very direct question, and one I've never been asked before [laughs]. I've got to be awfully careful here, because you can sound really precocious and awful. Yes, I sort of do believe in that, because when the thing comes on me, whatever it is, I'm a complete slave to it. There is nothing else more important. The house could burn down, and I'm ashamed to say, family and all that sort of thing doesn't matter. I can't help it; I really can't help it. It's not something I'm particularly proud of. I'm so helpless in its grip. I hope I didn't sound too precious.

Do you have a favorite song that you've written?

Well, I like "What's Shakin' On The Hill" because it's quite sophisticated musically and its story is very plain. I've written quite a lot of songs where I've got a tune going and the words sort of sound like something, but it's not about anything. And that's always kind of frustrating. The best stuff is plain in its meaning. That's why I like old country, because there's no doubt what it's about. That's what I try to do as much as I can - just really get to the core of the feeling I want to express.

Is there a story behind "Half A Boy And Half A Man"?

No, that's one of those that's purely a tune with an interesting title. It's waffle, but it sounds all right. It's very unfocused, but it cheers people up. Another one like that is "The Rose Of England," which sounds like there's something going on. It's got a great tune and a great title, which sounds very traditional and rather folky, but it's just lots of little phrases joined together. It's not really about anything. Yet it's evocative of a mood.

On the Little Village record, the songs are attributed to all four of you collectively. Tell me about that writing process.

The only sort of unspoken rule was that no one was allowed to actually bring in a song. None of this, "Here's my song, we're gonna do this today and we'll do yours tomorrow." We had to make it up from scratch, which I didn't actually believe could be done. I've written songs with other people before, but only if I've been very drunk, or we've both been very drunk. I find it very hard to communicate with another person about songwriting. I can do it if someone's got a bit of a verse or a little bit of a lyric, I can get them to sing it into a tape recorder and I'll take it away and come back with something else. But I find it difficult to sit in a room with someone. Maybe I feel kind of awkward or shy about it, I don't know. With four of us doing it, I thought, "This is going to be impossible." But strangely enough, it wasn't.

We recorded the record in the shed at the end of Ry's garden. We'd just sit in the shed and start playing, recording it on a walkman or something, When we'd finish, someone might say, "I'll tell you what, we got into something about five minutes ago, just wind the tape back." Then we'd have some titles that we'd logged. Like "Don't Think About Her When You Drive" – one of Ry's friends said that to him. And "She Runs Hot," a girlfriend of his supplied that. So we'd put it together with the title and one of us would flesh out the lyrics. For instance, I did words and tune for "Take Another Look," which was one of Jim's wild things. So there was a random element to the writing, but I think it was the better for that.

What advice would you give to someone who wants to write songs professionally?

Well, I don't know really, because I suppose I write songs professionally but I don't think I'm a professional songwriter. Someone like Diane Warren, that's who I think of as a professional, where all the songs are sort of [singing dramatically] "Tonight..." [laughs]. "Tonight" figures very heavily in those songs. "Streets" are very big. You've got to have that [laughs]. And the big power chords. That sort of thing is very easy to do, I think. You just listen to the radio a lot and imitate. Maybe that sounds a little crass, saying it's easy to do, rather snobby. I don't mean that. It's just that you don't need much inspiration to do that. Whereas the thing I do, I can't tap into it. Old Diane can probably go to work each day and trim out three or four of those babies. That's a skill. I'm not taking anything away from it, it's just that I don't happen to be moved by that sort of stuff. But I can recognize it as a talent and a skill. I suppose that you could acquire that skill by listening to the radio a lot and copying those licks. But I would say, just listen to yourself, like yourself, and believe what you write.

Glenn Tilbrook

Tempted ✷ Hourglass ✷ Black Coffee In Bed

Interview conducted in 1993 and 2001

"I think a lot of songs work on a purely intuitive basis, both for whoever wrote them and for whoever listens to them."

Strong songwriting has always been the lifeblood of the band Squeeze, ever since they rode in on the crest of the late 1970s new wave movement with early hits like "Up The Junction," "Cool For Cats," "Pulling Mussels (From The Shell)" and "If I Didn't Love You." While most of the bands of that period vanished into pop oblivion, Squeeze, thanks to the prolific pens of Glenn Tilbrook (music) and Chris Difford (lyrics), remained vital and fresh.

It wasn't always an easy road. The 1980s saw the band break up, reform, and go through numerous personnel changes, but nevertheless produce some of their finest work. For pure pop perfection, check out the Elvis Costello-produced *East Side Story*. "In Quintessence," "Someone Else's Heart," "Woman's World," "Is That Love?" and "Vanity Fair" are the kind of three-minute miracles that rightfully earned Difford and Tilbrook comparisons to Lennon and McCartney. The album's single, "Tempted," with its soulful melody and detailed lyric, went on to become an FM radio staple over the next decade. Almost as potent was the follow-up LP *Sweets From A Stranger*, an exploration of the dark side of relationships, with standout songs like "Black Coffee In Bed" and "I've Returned."

Although Squeeze never quite equaled the high water mark of *East Side Story*, there were some commercial highlights over the next decade and half, including the Top 15 hit "Hourglass" in 1987, and their well-received musical revue, *Labelled With Love*, which ran in London. Difford and Tilbrook's songs have been covered by Marti Jones, Patti Austin, Joe Cocker, Tim Curry, Rockpile, Rita Coolidge, and others.

What made you want to write your own songs?

The way I initially started writing was, we used to have these record songbooks at home in the 1960s with just lyrics in them. I used to learn songs from there, but only if I knew the tunes. The songs I didn't know tunes for, I'd just make up my own. I was about ten and it was very rudimentary [laughs], but that's how I began.

Who most influenced you as an aspiring songwriter?

The influences that I had in those formative years, up to about age 15, is the stuff that stays with me a lot, that's still evident in my writing. It was 1960s pop music, like The Beatles, The Monkees and The Hollies. Jimi Hendrix, too. I really admired him. Aside from being the best guitarist ever, he was a very imaginative songwriter. He was a big influence on my melody writing

What makes a great melody? Does it have to have unexpected jumps and rhythms?

No, I don't think so. Because some of the greatest songs seem so very obvious, and that's part of their charm. The thing about writing melodies is that they touch all sorts of different emotions. It's a very intuitive process. I think a lot of songs work on a purely intuitive basis, both for whoever wrote them and for whoever listens to them. A good example is a song like "I Just Called To Say I Love You," by Stevie Wonder. Now that is a really, really simple song and I didn't like it when I first heard it, but after a couple hearings, I changed my mind. It's expressing a wonderfully simple sentiment in a very simple way, which is a difficult thing to do. And I think on an emotional basis, it really works.

Are you the kind of writer who keeps a schedule?

In order to write, one has to be quite disciplined about the way that one works. I always work regular hours and I try to do something even if I'm having no success.

So are you and Chris always at it?

With us, it always works out that we have a period of time when we say, "'Okay, we're going to work on a new record." We'll sit down and start writing, and at that point, I probably haven't written anything for a year or so. Getting started is the most difficult thing. As time goes on, one gathers momentum, and things get easier and easier. And this has always been the case for some reason. It's like turning on a tap that hasn't been used for awhile. It ends up that half the songs are written in the last two weeks of a four-month writing period.

So you guys have to write a bunch of songs to get one you're happy with?

Yeah, but it does vary. I'm loath to judge anything too quickly. "Some Fantastic Place" was one that actually just tumbled out. It was one of those very rare occasions where it took ten minutes. It was lovely. That's the song I'm proudest of, of all that we've written. But that's the exception to the rule.

Can you describe how you go about setting music to one of Chris's lyrics?

I like to not read the lyric until I'm going to sit down and do something with it, so I have a first impression at that time. Sometimes I've read through a bunch and picked out the ones I like the best, but I find that tends to be less satisfactory than just working on one at a time, and then seeing what happens next. After reading it, I'll see if I feel something that suggests a tune, then if I get something straight away, I'll go with it and that'll form the basis for the song.

When you're working on a melody like that, do you write on an instrument or away from one?

I always work with an instrument. The way I've always worked has been the same. With my first royalty check, I bought a four-track and I've used that same tape recorder, my lucky four-track [laughs], for years. When writing I'll alternate between piano and guitar, switching every half-hour or so, just for the change of perspective it gives me. Very rarely will I write away from an instrument, say with just a drum machine, but I have done it. Sometimes I just leave the recorder running and improvise, then go back and fashion the good bits.

207

You and Chris actually sat down together to write for the Some Fantastic Place *album – not your usual private collaboration. Was that a big adjustment?*

We started out writing in the usual way. But we decided to try again to sit down in the same room and see what happened. We'd done it before, on "Hourglass," but that was an isolated incident. This time it felt more comfortable for some reason. I think everyone who collaborates and actually works with somebody must know the good feeling of bouncing ideas off of each other. It set off a whole train of things for us that wouldn't have happened. For instance, the song "Cold Shoulder." That was really the work of us sitting together, beginning with just a fragment. The melody was something we both contributed to, and we're very proud of it. The whole thing felt like being in a new partnership, which is very lucky after 20 years together.

Have there been Squeeze songs that went through different musical settings before you found the right one?

"Tempted" is an example of that. The tune for that was actually very difficult to write. It didn't flow at all. It took about a week of deciding where to go. I had the opening line and that felt great, but all the places I went to after that were wrong. It was like being stuck in the middle of this maze you couldn't find your way out of. It took a lot of time working on it to get to a place where it felt right. It wasn't a fun song to write. Then when we first recorded it, it was a version with the completely wrong feel. It sounded like ELO or something. So that song took a while to get right.

I like the way you write against the grain of a lyric, with an almost contradictory musical mood. "Up The Junction" is a great example, where it's kind of a sad story with an upbeat melody. Is that deliberate?

When I wrote that, I wasn't really thinking about that [laughs]. That's the honest truth. You know, one area we haven't really touched on, which is important, is the way that a song is arranged, and I'm going to answer your question within that. Again to refer to "Some Fantastic Place," I said that took ten minutes to write and that's right. Everything in the song was there when it was written. The approach to the song was vastly different than the one we ended up with on the record. It was written as a very slow ballad. Everything about it was the same except the tempo and the feel of it. Indeed we started playing it that way at some dates and it just felt wrong. And actually, the way we arranged it was more upbeat and uplifting like a gospel thing. Something really joyful. But the arrangement is a very big part of the song's success.

Let me mention a few songs to get your reactions . . . "Pulling Mussels (From A Shell)"

It was quite a lot slower when I wrote it musically, and it was influenced by the way I was feeling at the time. The chorus is influenced by The Tubes song "White Punks On Dope." They had these sort of grand chord changes, and I wanted to get a sense of that. The chorus to "Pulling Mussels" is my response to that.

"Labelled With Love"

It was a song that I thought we'd never use because of its style. It didn't seem like a Squeeze song, but Elvis Costello said we should record it, so we did. And I'm glad he said that.

When you were working with Elvis Costello, knowing that he's obviously such a great songwriter, how did that affect the dynamic for you and Chris?

I thought Elvis was great, and still think he is. I think Chris was sort of intimidated by him. I never thought he should be, because on his day, he was his equal. But I don't think Chris had the confidence to feel that, which was a shame.

"Vanity Fair"

I'm very proud of that. It's very musical, and I like that. I'm never a man to have one chord if I can have five [laughs], which has sometimes been my downfall as well. I think it was influenced by Kate Bush and The Beatles.

When you got that lyric, did you immediately go to that musical mood?

I think that all the writing I like best is about putting yourself into a place where you don't even think really. It's just about tuning into the mood of whatever you're working with. If you're working with a lyric, trying to get inside that or just finding some music that makes you feel good.

209

"Black Coffee In Bed"

I think it was a great song, but I think we made a real mess of the recording. I don't like it all. I think it's a horrible vocal. I know I can't say that because people like it, but I don't. I do like the song. I wish we'd recorded it better. What happened is that we were in a weird place. It wasn't a happy time for the band. We'd been into the studio with Gus Dudgeon, who'd produced Elton John, to do a version of it. I came across it recently. He worked us very hard and then he edited three different takes together, and I don't think our pride was having that. We wanted to record it all in one, so we said we didn't want to work with him. When I came across the version he did, I think, had we finished it, it would've been a better version than the one we ended up with. The real reason I hate it is because of the vocal. I like my voice, and I like it on most things I've done, but on that song, I think it's a dreadful vocal [laughs]. I just want to slap myself.

"Hourglass"

That was written as a total sort of dance song. I love the way the band recorded it. It was a brilliant sort of response to the record we'd made before, in that we went in and played it all together. When I say dance music, I mean like Prince. That song especially was Prince-ish, I thought. I'm really proud of that.

David Byrne

Once In A Lifetime ✶ Burning Down The House
✶ Wild Wild Life

Interview conducted in 2001

"Even when

you write

through a

character,

you are

revealing part

of yourself."

In Zen meditation, there is a principle called "beginner's mind." It's the attitude that includes both doubt and possibility; the ability to see things always as fresh and new. For over 25 years, David Byrne has been applying beginner's mind to his art, combining a naivete with a keen sense of composition and design. Like other multi-media savvy musicians – David Bowie, Todd Rundgren, Pete Townshend – Byrne has let his ventures into film, video, books, painting, and photography feed his songwriting, keeping it vital and full of surprises.

David Byrne was born in Dumbarton, Scotland on May 14, 1952. His parents moved the family to Canada, then Baltimore, Maryland. While enjoying a fairly typical childhood, Byrne began performing solo and in bands in junior high school. "I'd perform at school dances and local college coffee shops. My dad helped me with primitive electronic effects and recording technology. I made tape collages and multi-tracked feedback pieces and a version of The Turtles' 'Happy Together' using Tupperware tubs for drums. My passion for music stayed with me."

After high school, he went to the Rhode Island School of Design, where he met fellow freshmen Chris Frantz and Tina Weymouth. Though he was exposed to numerous artists – from John Coltrane to Andy Warhol to Marcel Duchamp – who would influence his work, Byrne didn't like art school – he stayed only one year – later calling it "a racket." In 1974, Byrne, Frantz and Weymouth formed a band called The Artistics. When they moved to New York the next year, they changed the band's name to Talking Heads and began performing at downtown hot spots such as CBGB's. Along with Blondie, Television and The Ramones, they would lead the charge of the American New Wave movement of the late 1970s.

Their debut, *Talking Heads 77*, introduced a curious sound, like a more delicate Velvet Underground. On songs such as "Building On Fire" and "Psycho Killer," Byrne's wavering, herky-jerky voice balanced like a blindfolded tightrope walker above the net of clean guitar, bass and drums. 1978's *More Songs About Buildings And Food* brought keyboardist Jerry Harrison into the fold and gave the band its first hit, a cover of Al Green's "Take Me To The River." It also marked the beginning of their collaboration with producer Brian Eno, who would become Byrne's foil in all kinds of sonic adventures over the next few years.

Each successive Talking Heads record channeled new influences – from the African rhythms on *Fear Of Music* to the dense sound collage of *Remain In Light*. Even amidst arty experiments, Byrne displayed a continuing knack for conjuring up songs with commercial pop appeal, such as "Life During Wartime," "Once In A Lifetime," "Burning Down The House," "Wild Wild Life," and "And She Was."

But even as he led the group to greater success, Byrne kept himself busy with outside projects, from a collaboration with modern dance choreographer Twyla Tharp on *The Catherine Wheel* to directing a feature film, *True Stories*, which picked up the thread of cinema verite ideas he'd begun in art school a decade before. You got the feeling that even the famous big suit he wore in the Talking Heads' concert film *Stop Making Sense* couldn't contain his rapidly growing ambition.

In 1990, Talking Heads split up over creative differences. Byrne added the title "impresario" to his resume by starting his own record label, Luaka Bop, which showcased his love of world music. The label's first release, *Beleza Tropical*, a compilation of Brazilian music, sold a quarter of a million copies. His solo albums have encompassed exotic sounds like Cuban salsa and Brazilian samba. As Byrne wrote in a much-reprinted essay on world music for *The New York Times*, "To restrict your listening to English-language pop is like deciding to eat the same meal for the rest of your life."

Byrne's 2001 album, *Look Into The Eyeball*, continued his exploration of new sounds and textures. He says, "I had been wondering if there might be a way to include the warm, lyrical, beautiful, emotional sounds and association of strings and orchestral parts with groove music and beats for the body. I want to move people to dance and cry at the same time."

There's a line in your song "The Accident" that says, "It takes all these wild and wonderful things to set me free." Are there things that set you free in your songwriting?

Yes. Probably half the time, I'm starting with the guitar and some kind of chord progression that I think is nice, and I just start singing melodies over it without words. The other half, I start by programming or looping rhythms. You can get lost enough in just playing along with the rhythm that it frees you up. I often try to do something that I'm not very good at, like put myself at a disadvantage so I have to invent something, so I won't fall back on tried and true things that I know how to do. For instance, I'll program a rhythm, then I'll do a two-finger keyboard poking thing of trying to come up with a string part for it. Then if I get something I like, I can move it to a computer, copy it, edit it, and sequence it and do all that sort of thing. It means that I'll come up with something I'd never come up with on guitar. Not only texturally, but harmonically as well.

You've mentioned that you had an inspiration CD of other artists' material. Did that affect your writing process?

It was in the back of my mind while I was writing. I put a bunch of artists on there, some old, some new, some American, some foreign. From Serge Gainsbourg to Isaac Hayes to Bjork. When I started putting that together it was just a little research to say, "Well, if I'm going to work with this musical palette of drums and bass and strings, which somehow emotionally felt like what I wanted to do, then let's see who's done this before and what they've done with it." I ended up with such a variety of things. Things that were total commercial formula stuff, things that were very innovative and creative, and things that were accessible in the sense that they were easy to listen to but not necessarily radio singles. It made me feel that I wouldn't be limiting myself to one sort of thing.

You once said that you had to become a different person to write lyrics. How do you usually approach writing a lyric to a finished piece of music?

I do something to distract myself. I'll go for a walk, or go jogging, or drive a car, and carry a micro-cassette player. I'll hum bits of the melody I'm working on over and over again, and I'll just say whatever word comes into my head. I'll try not to censor myself, even if it's something I consider too cliched or too stupid. Anything goes. I'll fill up tapes that way, then come back and transcribe them in an orderly way, so that all the phrases that match the meter of a verse will be on one page, and the chorus on another page. So I get these pages filled with random phrases. Then I'll look at those, and occasionally, four lines might emerge as being the key into the song. Those lines play against the melody and the groove in exactly the right way, and all the rest of the stuff on the page is expendable [laughs]. So I'll use those four lines as something to concentrate on, a direction of where the song is going. Then it becomes more of a craft, rather than just spewing out of whatever. Sometimes I find little tricks that are useful. If all the lyrics are looking at one subject from the same point of view, then I find that for a last line or chorus, I have to kind of invert it and look at the same subject from a different point of view. From a bird's eye view, from another person's point of view, from the opposite point of view, from a more metaphorical point of view. I have to put a spin on it in some way.

There's a Portuguese word, "saudade," that is the basis for a lot of the emotional pull in the lyrics of Bossa Nova music. The idea of happiness tempered by a sadness and longing. I picked up on that in the songs on Look Into The Eyeball.

I like that in a lot of music I listen to. Whether it's Jobim or another Brazilian, I like when the lyric is going against what you'd expect from the melody. Sometimes the lyric and the melody can become borderline melancholy, but the rhythm can be really up. I think I do that fairly often where the melody or the words are melancholy or angst-ridden, but the rhythm is really up. If one asked the question "How do we survive and how do we get through this?" the groove says, "Like this."

The song "UB Jesus" seems to explore a lot of words like "skin," "blood" and "fire" that can be interpreted sexually or religiously.

That's real common in gospel R&B. Obviously, I'm a long time fan of Al Green and Marvin Gaye. Those guys were always straddling that fence. Is the ecstatic experience sacred or is it profane? It's very confusing to be able to tell the difference. You use some of the same words to describe it. You get the most tension out of it when you do straddle that line.

What inspired "Neighborhood"?

I was messing around with a chord change, and right away felt that it was reminiscent of the chord changes from those Gamble-Huff songs from Philadelphia in the 70s: O'Jays, Spinners, that stuff. Originally I had programmed this real pounding tom-tom tribal beat to go with it, very un-Philadelphia. It was kind of cool, but the beat ended up kind of overpowering everything, so I took the same rhythm and calmed it down. I tried to write something that had that positive, celebratory feel that a lot of those songs from the Gamble and Huff song factory had. I enjoyed it, and when I played the demos for friends, they really liked it. But I felt a little self-conscious about it because I thought, I'm really consciously following someone else's model here. I've done that many, many times in the past, but usually, without being immodest, I've missed by a mile [laughs]. But maybe I'm getting a little bit better, so I'm getting closer to the target than I used to be able to get. Which is not always a good thing [laughs]. You might betray your sources. But on "Neighborhood," I thought I should go all the way with it, and somehow track down Thom Bell and see if he'd be interested in arranging it.

Do you feel like people can know you through your songs?

Yes and no. On lots of songs I've written, I'm writing through a character, so that's obviously not me. But people know that it takes a certain kind of mindset to empathize with a certain kind of character and to make the decision to write from a certain character's point of view. That betrays some of my interests as well. Even when you write through a character, you are revealing part of yourself. Not necessarily that you are the character, but somewhere in some of the decisions you've made, you're in there.

Have you been approached about using your songs in television commercials?

Yeah. I haven't done it. I sometimes feel like I'm foolish for holding on to some supposed principles. Nobody cares about his principles anymore [laughs]. That's a lot of the current attitude. If you can make some money at it, go ahead and do it. On the other hand, when a song that you would like to think was written from the heart and was written about a relationship or something that the writer is really passionate about gets reimagined as being about a car or a tampon or a breakfast cereal, then that's what you think of when you hear the song. You don't think of it as having a personal meaning, you think of a software company or something. Then it's lost some of its value. Maybe the trade was worth it, maybe not, but definitely there is something that's being sold and can't be bought back. On the other hand, in many cases, artists sold a song to a commercial and that's what kicked off their record, brought the album to an audience. The album was tanking, going down the tubes, then got revitalized by being licensed or sampled by someone else. Think of that Dido record. It was around for years, and now she's in the top ten. It's unbelievable.

If you were to teach a workshop on songwriting, what would you tell your students?

I would probably tell them to do what I've done [laughs]. Get songbooks by other people, even people you don't like, even if you hate their voice or hate their band or whatever. They may be the worst lyricist in the world, but maybe in the way they put their song together, there might be something you can get from it. I've found that by looking at songbooks, you start to internalize what a good song is. And it can be old songs from an anthology of folk music or whatever, or really complex art songs. You start to internalize what a song is, and how it fits together. It becomes part of your grammar.

Andy Partridge

Dear God ✶ The Mayor Of Simpleton
✶ Senses Working Overtime

Interview conducted in 1999

"There is sometimes an element of Dr. Frankenstein – you're hammering the limbs of one unfinished song onto the torso of another."

"I'm a ludicrous optimist," says Andy Partridge. "I'm in front of the firing squad and I've got the clown's makeup on and I'm telling gags to get them to sort of wobble and put their aim off." The XTC frontman has relied on this irreverent attitude to survive the trials and tribulations he and his band have been through over the years.

XTC began in 1976 as Swindon, England's entry into the then burgeoning punk movement. Except they weren't punk. They were too smart, quirky and melodic, though they definitely had the required manic energy. Two early singles, "Making Plans For Nigel" and "Life Begins At The Hop," charted in the U.K., while albums such as *White Music*, *Drums And Wires* and *Black Sea* were popular at college and underground radio in the U.S.

Following 1982's *English Settlement*, which included a British Top 10 hit, "Senses Working Overtime," the band's touring career came to a dramatic end. While onstage in Paris, Andy Partridge collapsed from exhaustion. This led to an increasing sense of stage fright. Like the Beatles and Steely Dan before them, XTC became essentially a studio band.

While *Mummer* (1983) and *The Big Express* (1984) strengthened their cult status, it was the exquisite

Skylarking in 1986 that brought XTC to the brink of huge commercial success. Produced by Todd Rundgren, the album is a psychedelic song cycle about love and the changing of the seasons, with unforgettable tracks such as "Grass," "(That's Really Super) Supergirl" and "Earn Enough For Us" flowing seamlessly into each other. It also gave the band their first sizable U.S. hit with the controversial "Dear God." In 1989, their *Oranges And Lemons* album and its single, Partridge's "The Mayor Of Simpleton," went to #1 on the alternative charts.

Even though "The Ballad Of Peter Pumpkinhead" also reached #1 on the Modern Rock charts, 1992's *Nonsuch* suffered from a lukewarm reception at Virgin Records. The label wouldn't release the band's follow-up, deeming it uncommercial. At the same time, they refused to let the band out of their contract. During this period, Partridge also went through a messy divorce and suffered health setbacks, including a severe middle ear infection, which left him deaf for nearly a month. Bassist Colin Moulding's wife became very ill, and he effectively retired from playing and writing for a few years. Disenchanted by the frozen state of affairs, guitarist Dave Gregory quit the group. Prospects looked bleak.

Then, in 1998, Virgin wearied of their prisoners, and XTC was finally set free. In 1999, two CDs of all-new material, *Apple Venus Vol. 1* and *Wasp Star*, were released.

"Despite all the shit I was wading through in the last six years, I had faith that the material I was working on was some of my best stuff ever," says Partridge. "I knew that one day we would get out of the legal hell and we would get another record deal, and then we could work on these songs. So that was a little Bunsen Burner of hope."

Partridge says his hopes for XTC's future are modest. "I'd just like to make more records, to write more songs, and just to keep living and do all this because I've got lots more inside me. I feel I've only just got started really. I'm starting to get half-good at this now."

Do you prefer to write from a place of turmoil, like you were in for much of the 1990s?

People say that the best material, the best art, is made either from extreme joy or extreme misery. I think that's probably true. I've been through enormous dollops of both of those over the last six years, going through divorce, going through a lot of illness, going through a lot of turmoil in my personal life and business life. Not being allowed to work, and also finding the strongest love of my life and getting together with her. I've been through real incredible lows and incredible highs, so I'd say that whoever said that was probably right. Extreme misery or extreme joy are great engines.

When it came time to choose material for Apple Venus, Vol. 1, *were you actually reviewing six years of material or did you tend to go for songs you'd written over the past year?*

I really wanted to work with material that had sort of orchestral textures and acoustic backbone to it. All of the stuff that I wrote between '92 and '94 had that feel to it. I thought, "Well this would be great to put all this together on one record." I really wanted to work in that direction. Then after a couple of years of working that material out, I honestly thought to myself, "I've got that out of my system now, where's the old electric guitar? Where's that volume control?" And the material that was written from '94 to '96 was all much more simple, much more immediate, electric guitar stuff. So *Apple Venus, Vol. 1* is the record that should've been made had our world not been turned upside down in 1993.

When you're in writing mode, do you keep a schedule?

I don't go into the shed everyday. When I'm in a kind of writing space, it's almost guaranteed that if I go into my shed and stare at a piece of paper that nothing's going to come out. At the same time, it's also guaranteed that if I go around the shops or go for a walk or go on the telephone or whatever, an idea pops into my brain. I've been known to run home from walks or ring myself up and sing my idea to the answering machine. It's kind of like when you tune your brain to nothingness, when you don't have anything pressing to think about. I'm very bad at business, so if I have anything business-wise to think about, I can't create.

I've talked to a lot of songwriters who like to keep a few songs in the oven at once. Are you like that?

I have bits and pieces of songs where some of them remain around for years. Because you never know when it will fit something else and you find just the piece you want. You'll think, "Well, this chorus is great, but that verse is crappy, but I've got another song that has the same feel and I never finished it off, and that could become the verse of this," and so on and so forth. There is sometimes an element of Dr. Frankenstein – you're hammering the limbs of one unfinished song onto the torso of another. That can happen. Sometimes you finish a song very quickly; sometimes it almost comes in an hour or less. Then other times you can be fiddling with it for months, or sometimes years. There's no set pattern.

You mentioned staring at the blank page and how that sometimes makes you freeze up.

I have a few tricks for sort of unfreezing myself. One of them is to turn my brain to like an insanity or nonsense switch and just write any words that come into my head, whatever they are. And inevitably, after a half of page of writing, they start rhyming with the previous line almost unconsciously. Then I go back a few days or a week later and find that page and look at it, and see stuff and think, "Christ, where did that come from? That would've never come out if I were in sensible mode. That line is great, or those two lines are great, or that word is wonderful, and it rhymes with that word." If you can spew out this gibberish, what you're doing is getting in touch with your subconscious store cupboard. All sorts of stuff comes out.

I've read where you will sometimes use songs by other artists as spring-boards for your own.

Oh sure. Sometimes it's fun. You'll be playing around with something and that will unwittingly unlock a little cupboard somewhere and this idea will fall out, just because you were messing around. A good example of that is I was messing around and I wanted to know what the chords to "I Get Around" were. I always liked that as a kid, but I never worked that out. I started to mess around with it and I found a change and I thought, "Wow, I know that change. They've gone from a G to E7 with an Aflat on the bottom. That's just the change I want for this song!" It was a change I'd used before, but just reflecting back, it made me sort of happy that it was the change in that Beach Boys song. Odd little things can come out. Another thing was messing around trying to play "Blackbird." "Knights In Shining Karma," [its descending melody line], came out of just dicking around and getting "Blackbird" wrong. You're not stealing other people's ideas. You're using them as little springboards to get up to a higher place. I've never knowingly stolen anything before. I'm not interested. It's much more of a kick if I can think of it myself.

What was the inspiration for "Knights In Shining Karma"?

I was going through real hell with the divorce thing, the whole cuck-olded husband thing. I felt really betrayed and let down, and I was deserted and was momentarily looking after my kids on my own. When they weren't here or at school, I'd be moping around the house in a real bad state. I'd be making myself a cup of tea or washing up, and just crying in the sink like a real wreck, a real emotional mess. I think I wanted to write something that strengthened me, almost spiritually strengthened me, gave me some kind of armor. It's like the spirit of me was removed and it stood next to me, and it's guarding me. I wanted to write something to armor myself up against all this depression, almost sort of father myself and say, "There, there, you're a good person, you'll pull through."

A lot of songwriters I've talked to say that when they write, it almost feels like the song is coming through them from an outside source. Does it feel that way to you?

It's more like there's something very deep inside me that is miles down inside my guts. It's like you're momentarily turning yourself inside out to empty this out. Because what I feel comes out is me, but I don't know normally how to reach this stuff, this expression, these thoughts, or this voodoo. It's almost like you feel nauseous artistically, and suddenly you're pulling yourself inside out. Then something comes out and you think, "Wow, where did that come from?" And it's patently you, but how you find it and how you do this turning inside out process, I don't know.

How far will you let yourself get into a song and still not know what it's about?

Oh, all the way to completing it. Say for example the song "Rook" on *Nonsuch*. I had no concept of what it was about. I only know it frightened the shirt off of me and every time I tried to complete writing it, I'd burst into tears. I still don't know what it's about and I still don't know why it frightens me. But it deeply affected me so it is obviously about something that is very important to me, but I can't grasp it yet because I'm not far away enough from it. I might see it in a few more years.

There are moments on Apple Venus *where I could very easily hear you making the leap to musicals.*

I'd love to. I'd love to do an old-style, real cheeseburger kind of family musical. Colin bought me the soundtrack of *Oliver!* for Christmas and it's wonderful stuff, it's great. And this is from a man, Lionel Bart, who couldn't even play an instrument. He would sit with a piano player and say, "Play me a chord. No, no, don't like that one, play me another. Yeah, that one's good. Now, la-la-la-la-la, play me another chord. No, don't like that. Another one. That's a good one." He would sit with people and just sing stuff and they'd have to play and he'd pick the best bits they stumbled on. He sort of played piano by proxy. That's somebody with a real drive and ability. I like musicals, especially the really beautifully put together ones like *West Side Story* and *My Fair Lady*. The really good ones are just massive, really wonderful. I would also love to write an opera. I don't know how I would start. I detest the form of opera, but there's something inside me that says because I detest it I have to conquer it, if you know what I mean. You have to hate your mountain before you can climb it.

If you were to teach a workshop on songwriting, what would you impart to your students?

You have to learn to be selfish. Not personally selfish. But with your art, you have to learn to become selfish. You have to have it your way. If it's not going to be the way that you really, really hear it then it's not going to be your song. You end up, if you're not careful, with music by committee. Selfishness is good in the arts. Also, lots is good, because the more coal you shovel, the more chances you have of finding the diamond. If you only write four or five songs, you may not find it. If you write four hundred songs, you may find one or two real killers in there. But you really have to shovel. Don't expect to sit down with a pencil in hand and find it in the first half dozen, because you won't. Also, if you like bands, try to figure out what makes them tick, song-wise. Sit down with your Beatles records and say, "Okay, what's going on here?" There is a formula. There's a Bacharach formula, there was a Beatles formula, it was usually half a chorus and you're straight in to the verse. No spare flesh, no bars of hanging around waiting for someone to step up to the microphone. Two middle eights, you can bet your bottom dollar on that. Find out what makes your favorite bands tick, analyze them, listen to all their recordings and say, "Is there a system here that I can see that they might not even be aware of themselves?" Just play whoever it is you like, The Byrds, Smokey Robinson, find out what makes them tick, because it's only notes and sounds and stuff and you can unravel this knitting. You have to play surgeon to find out what makes your favorites tick I think, then it will help you up to a higher place.

What are you hopes for XTC's albums now?

I just hope that enough people respond to the music or enough radio stations play it to enable us to keep our heads above water and carrying on doing it. Even when I didn't have a record deal and even when things were looking as black as black for me, I couldn't stop writing. It's a disease. It's a condition that once you catch it, you can't stop. But it's good to get this stuff out. If I didn't have a record deal I would still write. If it just enables me to keep my head above water then fine. If it makes me money on top of that, that's jam.

Marshall Crenshaw

Someday, Someway ✸ Whenever You're On My Mind
✸ Til I Hear It From You

Interview conducted in 1994 and 2000

"Songwriting

is just a

means to an

end for me. I

want to play

guitar and

sing."

Marshall Crenshaw once played John Lennon in the Broadway musical *Beatlemania*. It was perfect casting. Crenshaw has shown time and again that he, like Lennon, has the rare gift for writing seamlessly perfect three-minute pop songs with instantly memorable melodies and conversational lyrics. Upon the release of his self-titled debut in 1982, *Rolling Stone* said, "Every song here sounds like a classic."

His first single, "Someday, Someway" crashed the Top 40 charts, while "Cynical Girl," "Rockin' Around In NYC" and "Whenever You're On My Mind" (from his second album *Field Day*) all became favorites at album-oriented rock stations. "You're My Favorite Waste Of Time," a B-side from this period, would turn out to be not only a fan favorite, but also a Crenshaw perennial, being covered by both Bette Midler and Owen Paul (who took it to #3 on the UK charts in 1986).

But consistently applying his love of classic songwriting to his trade has been both a blessing and a curse for Crenshaw. While he's delighted fans with some brilliant records (a standout is 1991's

Life's Too Short, which featured the should-have-been hit "Fantastic Planet Of Love"), he's never fit into modern radio formats. This, combined with his aversion to making videos, his mild-mannered appearance, and some bad luck in business, has kept him from the big-time success he deserves.

His songs have been covered by Marti Jones, Lou Ann Barton, Robert Gordon, and Ronnie Spector. In 1995, he co-wrote The Gin Blossoms' "Til I Hear It From You," which was featured on the soundtrack of the film *Empire Records* and became a monster hit. In recent years, he's done solo acoustic tours throughout the Northeast and Midwest U.S. "I'm kind of like a regional act," Crenshaw says. "Like Don Ho – which doesn't bother me a bit. I mean, Don Ho never really made it anywhere but Hawaii, and he's probably pretty happy."

Are you the kind of songwriter who's always at it?

No. I'd say I've only written songs sporadically throughout my career. My output isn't consistent. If I don't have anything much invested in a song, then I can finish it no problem. But if it's a song for me, sometimes I just can't get to that place.

Do you play a lot around the house?

Yeah, I'm always doing something constructive in music, so it doesn't prey on my mind much if I'm not writing. It's never been my raison d'être anyway. Songwriting is just a means to an end for me. I want to play guitar and sing.

Who were your influences?

Brian Wilson, Burt Bacharach. I love the kind of chord changes you find in their songs, lots of minor and major 7ths, suspended chords. Those chords have a heartbreaking quality. I really dig those kind of songs. Those guys were going for beauty in their songs. Lyrically, I like really straight ahead blues poetry kind of stuff. Motown, 1970s Philly soul, blues also. I'm really a romantic pop songwriter at heart.

How did you learn how to write songs?

By doing it, I guess. A friend of mine once taught me a formula where you can use a song as a kind of blueprint for one of your own. Say using "When You Walk In The Room" by Jackie DeShannon. It starts with a guitar riff, then the verse imitates that guitar riff, then the verse ends with the title. I used to write that way back in the late 70s.

How do you like to work now?

I always come up with the structure and the melody first. The lyrics come way after the fact. I like to decide on a good groove first, then take it from there. "Someday, Someway" has a beat you hear on a lot of 50s rock songs, like "Party Doll" by Buddy Knox and "Lotta Lovin'" by Gene Vincent, which are two of my favorite records. I'm mumbling and muttering words. That's my favorite part of songwriting, because I can work really fast in that mode. I don't indulge in a lot of second-guessing at that stage. I get more bogged down in the latter stages of deciding what the song is going to be about.

Tell me about writing "Someday, Someway."

It was 1979. I was in Boston with *Beatlemania*, and I was getting ready to leave the show for various reasons. I was starting to become preoccupied with other ambitions I had besides being a fake Beatle. I had a few songs that I felt really confident about and proud of. I was on a roll and I wanted to keep it going. I figured that was going to lead me to the next phase of my life. Every night I'd walk home from the theater to my hotel room, and I'd stop at this deli on Copley Square. I'd go in there and I'd get two coffees and a chocolate brownie. This is ten o'clock at night. I figure, I'll drink the coffees, eat the brownie, and I'll write a song no matter how long it takes, even if I have to stay up until six in the morning. So I'd ingest all this caffeine, I'd start to write, and I'd have a song in about 20 minutes. Then I'd be up the rest of the night, just watching TV or something. But anyway, "Someday, Someway" was just a caffeine-fueled burst of inspiration. I just picked up my guitar and started playing these major chords. The lyrics just came out in a flood. I didn't really even think about what they were saying. I was just trying to make sounds that fit the melody. But I had lyrics in no time, which is rare for me. It was a real pivotal moment in my life.

How about "Cynical Girl"?

The way I did that is the best way for me to write songs, which is to just start doing it, without any forethought. I literally picked up my Vox 12-string, started banging on it and singing before I had time to think about what I was doing. I beat it out in about ten minutes. That's the best feeling there is, when something comes to you that way.

"You're My Favorite Waste Of Time"

That dates from the *Beatlemania* period too. I was in the Stanley Theater in Pittsburgh. It was the day before the show opened, and I was just kind of cooling my heels in Pittsburgh, hanging around the theater, watching them set up the production, sitting around playing this Gibson J-160 that I used in the show. The title somehow popped into my head. I was thinking about my courtship years with my wife, thinking about the things we used to do when I'd go over to her house. We'd just kind of kill time waiting for her parents to go to bed, basically [laughs]. Anyway, I just started coming up with these humorous, tongue-in-cheek lyrics, and it all just came together in my mind really fast. That was amazing, because it was only about 20 minutes of work. It wasn't even work. It was just this joyful process, just knowing I had a song. I was on a roll during that time, bursting with inspiration.

"Whenever You're On My Mind"

As I said, it's sort of a rewrite of Jackie DeShannon's "When You Walk In The Room." I really loved that record. I really connected with it emotionally, with the performance and the atmosphere of the record. The lyrics were written by this guy named Bill Teeley, who's a friend of mine. He was really in love with somebody right when he wrote the words, so it's real. When you're first falling in love, it's almost like you're in an altered state, because you're constantly obsessed with this person.

"Blues Is King"

That's one of my failed songs. I never liked it. It was a difficult time for me and for my writing. I had to really beat myself up to write that one. It's about being depressed. Lyrically, that is. I wrote the music and I thought it was really gorgeous, but then I couldn't think of any words. For a long time, I had really bad writer's block, and I couldn't get myself to write any lyrics. With that one, I actually booked the studio time to record it before I had the song written, just to make myself write it. So that's what came out. Unfortunately, there's a lot of my songs I wish I could take back. Everybody's written songs where you get a little distance from them and you think, "No, that didn't quite hit the bullseye." I love the song, but I don't like the lyrics or the title. It just didn't work the way I wanted it to.

"Fantastic Planet Of Love"

I was listening to a lot of sort of Vegas lounge music – Freddie Bell & The Bellboys, Louis Prima – so "Fantastic Planet" was me trying to write a 50s rock song with jazz chord changes. I really didn't know any formula, so I just bluffed my way through that. The lyrics are about a guy who's really cranky and feels disenfranchised, but then he says, "It's only when I'm next to you that I ever dream of a fantastic planet of love." It's a love song for cranky people [laughs]. During the 80s, even when I was feeling down, I'd still try to come up with these poppy songs, but some kind of dark-spirited vibe would creep into it.

"Til I Hear It From You"

Jesse Valenzuela from the Gin Blossoms called up Premier Talent, who were booking me at the time. He was looking for me because they were fans of mine. He already had the title and some of the chord changes, so the song was underway before I got involved in it. We worked on it, and I had a few suggestions. I put the verse melody together, then that was it. The singer [Robin Wilson] wrote the lyrics. It was pretty darn stress-free for me. It turned out to be a big hit, and that was a good thing for my sense of self-worth. It came pretty far after the fact of me having whatever success I'd had with my own records. I had actually spent a couple of years floundering at that point. It was a real nice boost for me, and put me back on track in a lot of ways.

What's the best advice you've ever received about songwriting?

When I met Doc Pomus, I hadn't been writing songs for very long, and I hadn't written anything in a while. I didn't understand the process at all, and he just basically said, "There's no limit to what your mind can come up with if you'll just be patient with yourself." All the advice that I've benefited from has had to do with writer's block. That was something that plagued me for a long time. I just couldn't understand why I couldn't write all the time. In the 80s, I struggled with a lot of pressures from being in the record business, and it affected my writing. Now, I know I can write if I can find the time and the isolation. It just takes time to realize songs. You have to rest your brain sometimes. You've got to pace yourself, take breaks. You've got to gather information and strength and inspiration.

Neil Finn

Don't Dream It's Over ✶ Something So Strong
✶ Weather With You

Interview conducted in 1991 and 2000

"I think pop has come to mean an appreciation of simple, elegant melodies over interesting chords. I'm very pleased to be a pop musician."

In the songwriting community, Neil Finn is revered. As longtime fan Shawn Colvin says, "I just can't imagine a world without Neil Finn songs in it, that's how deep they go for me – like The Beatles or *West Side Story* or something."

Finn's best songs, both with Crowded House and on his own, match lyrics full of emotional personal experience with some of the most beguiling melodies since Lennon and McCartney. There is always one pivotal moment, usually involving an unexpected chord change, when the mood alters in a dramatic way, and the words and melody lift you right out of your seat. Think of the gorgeous minor-to-major shift from verse to chorus in "Four Seasons In One Day" or how the solo section in "Nails In My Feet" seasons the hymn-like song with a sudden exotic Arabic flavor.

"One of the first things I ever understood was that idea that a chord change can change the mood," Finn says. "That's the deciding point as to whether you've got a song or not."

Finn formed Crowded House with Nick Seymour and Paul Hester in 1985. The group's debut, featuring "Don't Dream It's Over" (which soared to #2 on the charts) and "Something So Strong,"(#7)

231

became the sleeper hit of 1987, and Crowded House, with their Beatles-influenced style, emerged as saviors of pop music. Although it received a lukewarm reception at the time, their second album, *Temple Of Low Men* stands as a masterpiece of moody pop. With songs like the near-hit "Better Be Home Soon" and the spine-tingling "Into Temptation" Finn sounded like Paul McCartney meets Hieronymous Bosch. "We'd had a very happy time making the record, but the sentiment in a lot of the songs gave people the idea that I was going through a trouble period," he recalls.

Despite having no hit singles, their third album, 1991's *Woodface*, is considered by many to be their strongest, most cohesive record. Neil's brother, Tim Finn, formerly of Split Enz, joined the lineup and co-wrote half the material with Neil. The album's unforgettable songs such as "It's Only Natural," "Fall At Your Feet," "Chocolate Cake," "Four Seasons In One Day" and "Weather With You" picked up airplay on radio formats as diverse as Adult Contemporary and Modern Rock, solidifying Neil Finn's reputation as a consummate pop craftsman.

Do you remember writing your first song?

Yeah, I actually took the lyrics off the back of a Donovan record [laughs]. He had this little poem and I wrote some music for that, because I couldn't conceive of writing a lyric at that time. I was 12. Then when I was about 14 or 15, my brother asked me to support Split Enz, acoustically, on their New Zealand tour, so I wrote three songs for that, and they were the first real songs I wrote. There was a friend of mine who helped me with some of the lyrics. And some of them were incredibly weird for a 15-year-old to be writing. There was one called "Late In Rome," about a dancer looking back on his life, a really old man looking back on how great and how tragic the whole thing was. In those days, I was definitely imagining myself in a character, because I guess I hadn't gotten accustomed to the idea of writing from personal experience.

Do you feel like your songs have to be grounded in some kind of real-life experience?

There has to be something real about them, but they don't have to be from my experience. The greatest compliment in a way is if people think I'm writing a diary. But it's also frustrating in another sense, in that they read too much into the songs. I think it's important that a song is rooted in reality in terms of expressing emotions or notions that people feel. I'm not into creating a fantasy world with my songs, but I allow myself a fair amount of license in terms of expanding on what my experience is or exaggerating it. Also, I'm not at all hung up by being literal, that is, making sense in the literal fashion. The best lines I've ever had have been totally stream of consciousness. They don't always make sense, but they always mean more to me than things I labor over in an intellectual way. I tend to trust the ideas that present themselves.

How long does it take you to finish a song?

It varies. Sometimes they come all at once, words and music. Sometimes I get just a verse and a couple of lines, and the verse can sit there dormant for like five, ten years. Then I'll find another bit that I'm looking for a verse for and voila! So there are no real rules.

What advice would you give to someone aspiring to be a professional songwriter?

Have a rigid sense of self-criticism in terms of what you accept as a good song. It's very easy for people to get the idea that you're an average songwriter if you allow your average songs to emerge. And also, look for something that is inherently yours and distinctive. Whenever it seems obvious that you should put a certain chord in, if it's begging for a chord to resolve, don't resolve, choose another chord. I don't know, these are things I do. There's no textbook for songwriting. More important, believe that you can do it. Half of writing a song is believing you can do it.

Let me mention a few specific songs..."Fall At Your Feet"

It was a chorus. I had a different verse for it originally, but we weren't entirely happy with that. Eventually, our producer, Mitchell Froom, kept hammering me about finishing it. Then when we were in the studio, he heard me playing another piece which I'd had around for years and years, and it became the verse. He said, "That's it!" And I went off and finished the lyrics in about an hour. We recorded it that day.

"Four Seasons In One Day"

That was an instrumental up until Tim and I did all our writing together. One day I just started playing it, with Tim vibing along and I kind of wrote the lyrics in one go. It describes Melbourne, where the weather is changeable on an hourly basis. It's also about mood swings.

Let's talk about how you collaborate with your brother Tim. What are his strengths in the collaboration?

I think Tim is usually very good for titles and a starting point. He often has a notion for a good, hooky chorus line, a la "Weather With You." He's good at organizing words on the page. What I often find is that I'm throwing quite lateral thoughts down, or singing them, and Tim will be writing them down and organizing. We have started in many instances with nothing. I'll be playing a chord sequence, and he'll be coming up with a melody, or vice versa. It's just a matter of recognition when you've got somebody you trust in the room with you, you have the confidence to go beyond the point of embarrassment and you also have somebody who can spot the winner, who can go, "That's great, let's focus on that."

How do you feel about the constant comparison of Crowded House to The Beatles?

I sort of try to ignore it. I can't relate to it really, though I can understand that certain things about the way I sing remind people of the way that McCartney and Lennon sing. It's not something that I'm that conscious of, but it's something that people say so often that I realize it must be the case. And I grew up listening to their music, but it's probably just the tone of my voice – which I can't do much about [laughs]. Musically, I guess I'm writing three-minute songs that are traditional in the sense of having discernible chord changes, and a melody that you can hum along to. So I guess in that sense it's traditional, and the Beatles were the most obvious exponents of that sort of music.

There now seems to be a burgeoning pop underground, courtesy of Internet sites, fanzines, etc, that's becoming a refuge for classic pop songwriters. Do you feel part of that?

I suppose in the sense that we're not in the mainstream, it does put us in the underground. But it's quite an odd thing, isn't it, because

234

the definition of pop music is "popular." But I think that pop has come to mean an appreciation of simple, elegant melodies over interesting chords. It has a non-rock aesthetic. No posturing or feet on the wedges or leather pants. No macho edge to it. In that sense, I'm very pleased to be a pop musician. I think there are a lot of people out there who appreciate pop. In L.A., there's a community that I've come in contact with via the venue The Largo. Jon Brion, Grant Lee Phillips, Elliot Smith all have a strong appreciation for pop music. Jon Brion in particular is a virtual sponge. He's absorbed every piece of pop music of the past 20 years and can play them all. There's a power in a good song, and people are in awe of it still. They're in short supply. I think that when you look at the songs that become hits on the charts, there's something else going on. There are a few good pop songs in there, but something else is becoming successful, and that's the extremely sophisticated marketing campaigns in proliferation. It's a combination of image and flash production married with pretty faces of boys and girls. It's always been there to some extent, but it seems extremely prolific at the moment. Pop charts are dominated by listeners from ten to 14. Perhaps it used to be from 12 to 18.

I'm hoping that the trend passes.

Well, I wouldn't bet on it [laughs]. The music industry has never been, in my impression, a more unfriendly place for what I term loosely as "career artists" – people who are writing good material over a long period of time. Record companies are loathe to see anything but a profit by the end of the year in terms of what they're signing. Because of that, we've been marginalized to some degree, and people are thinking of alternatives. The Internet is still in its early stages for that to make any real impact, but there is the murmur of a revolution in the wind.

Ben Watt and Tracey Thorn

Missing ✯ Apron Strings ✯ Driving

Interview conducted in 1992 and 1994

"All I really want to be as a songwriter is a reflection of you the listener."

Ben Watt and Tracey Thorn met in 1982, two teenagers in post-punk London, each pursuing their own musical careers (their solo albums, *North Marine Drive and A Distant Shore*, respectively, are now collector's items). Sharing a love of moody jazz and incisive songwriting, the pair teamed up as Everything But The Girl, taking their quirky name from a second-hand furniture store. Their debut single, the infectious, Latin-flavored "Each And Every One," became a European hit, and set the standard for other jazzy pop acts coming out of Britain such as Sade, Swing Out Sister and The Style Council.

While sophisticated chord changes and seductive rhythms would remain at the core of the EBTG sound, the duo stretched stylistically, exploring jangly Smiths-like pop ("When All's Well"), Bacharach-esque orchestral drama ("Come On Home"), confessional ballads ("Apron Strings"), slick, West Coast R&B ("Driving"), and electronic dance ("Missing").

But the pivotal event in the duo's lives and career occurred in 1992, when Watt contracted Churg-Strauss Syndrome, a rare auto-immune disorder that ravages the internal organs. After six

237

months in the hospital and four life-saving operations, the formerly cherubic musician emerged 45 pounds lighter and minus most of his digestive system.

"The certainties that had started to appear in our lyrics were all blown out of the water, and a whole set of worries and angst replaced them," he said. "There are a lot more open-ended cries and questions since 1992 than in the work before."

The result of this embracing of the chaos of life was their masterpiece, 1994's *Amplified Heart*. The album title was inspired by a medical condition known as "amplified emotions," in which the patient's feelings and reactions become anywhere from ten to 100 times more intense than normal. On brilliant songs such as "Troubled Mind," "Rollercoaster," "Get Me" and "Two Star," Watt and Thorn amplify those little moments of mystery and misunderstanding between lovers in a way that's heart-stopping. Thorn's "I Don't Understand Anything" may be one of the most moving songs ever written about the inarticulate yearnings of the heart.

The mix of acoustic guitar with scratchy loops on *Amplified Heart* would later be co-opted successfully by artists such as Beth Orton, Lisa Loeb, Shawn Mullins and David Gray. Ironically, the album's brilliant single, "Missing," in its original acoustic incarnation, failed to chart and Everything But The Girl was dropped from their major label deal. A year later, remixer Todd Terry put a dance-floor groove beneath the song and it went to #1 on charts from America to Italy to Japan.

Do the two of you sit down together to write?

Watt: No, never. We've known each other and worked with each other for years, and we very rarely stand around the piano hammering it out like Leiber and Stoller or something. The creative input from both of us is usually done in isolation, and then we come together. At least the sort of key creative moments in the lyric and the music are done in separate moments, separate days. And then we'll mesh the two together, and perhaps there will be a degree of editing that will go on. You know, the odd line will be changed or the structure might be changed a little bit.

What's the difference between your styles of writing?

W: She gets quite frustrated because I'm far more prolific than she is. I tend to just write all the time. It means a large percentage of what I do is ditched, but at least I'm active. She tends to keep things bottled up for a while, then she'll have a little purple patch where she'll write.

Thorn: I don't know the rules of songwriting as well as Ben does, and I think for that reason I tend to write in my own little way, really. I'm not a good guitar player or piano player, which Ben is. I mean, he can sit down and if he hears a song in a certain style, he can usually master it, and perhaps absorb it in some way and it might come out in his own stuff. I don't really have that amount of skill. I don't really have the skill to choose what I write. What comes out is all there is.

Do you remember writing your first song?

W: I started writing at about 13 or 14. The first songs were terrible, probably pretty maudlin and introspective. I was trying to copy a lot of things I was hearing. I remember I picked up on Stevie Wonder from the radio. That was one of the first records I bought. I've got older brothers and they were really into the singer-songwriters of the early 1970s – people like Paul Simon, Carole King, James Taylor. They were quite influential on me at that time.

T: I think the first songs I started to write were very much influenced by the more sort of poppy side of punk songs I was listening to. I liked Elvis Costello's songwriting as soon as I heard it, and I liked The Buzzcocks, who seemed to write quite straightforward three or four chord love songs. And at that age, about 16, it was quite easy to write those songs because all you had to do was copy out a page from your diary [laughs]. That seemed to make up a song. So I don't think my influences were very sophisticated or complicated. And I never really thought particularly about people as songwriters until I started to get older. At that time, I just thought, I like that record or I like that group. But I wasn't really aware of there being a tradition, if you like, of people who had been influenced by everyone from Dylan through Bacharach, and all of those classic people.

What's your ideal situation to write?

T: I think the best songs I write tend to be literally when I'm away from an instrument. I'm just walking around and a song will just come from nowhere. And I will have the melody and the words. Then I go back home and try to find the chords which work for it. Sometimes it's quite frustrating for me because I can hear the way the chords should go and how it should work, but it takes me a long time to then find where they are on the guitar. I mean, in that sense, I'm really quite an amateur songwriter.

W: I go through various moods of writing. Sometimes I try and write things really, really quickly and force myself to keep them, at least for a while, before changing them. Even if I'm sure that at least 60 percent of it might get changed later. Other times I can spend days or weeks on things, just moving around the same eight bars and being very methodical about it. Sometimes I just go in the coffee shop with a notebook. I'll sit all afternoon and just watch people go by and think of ideas for songs. I'll see characters who might appear in songs. That's a good way to get inspired.

How do you know when a song is finished?

W: In the end, I think for the good stuff that anybody writes, one third of it is untrue, one third of it is completely true, and one third of it is half-true. That's how it works out. The untrue bits are often some sort of detail, some fabrication of time and place or just a separate atmosphere from perhaps other songs where you've covered similar territory in terms of emotional themes. I allow myself the freedom to do that. You kind of know when you've finished whether it rings true or not. There usually have to be a couple of key lines in there or a couple of key moments which really do ring true, which you really do feel very strongly about, for you to believe in it yourself. Otherwise you won't end up recording it because you don't believe it yourself.

Where do you think songs come from?

T: It's unanswerable really, isn't it? When you hear songs of other people's, when you hear them completed and finished, they seem perfect, they seem like they just dropped from heaven, as if they were just given to this person. But I think when you write songs yourself, and you work on them and you know how much you change them and edit them along the way, then you realize that they come partly from an original idea, which is sort of intangible, and partly they just come from work and thinking about them in quite a rational way. Whereas the original idea might've been an emotional one, then the work you have to do on them can be quite cold-blooded. So in that sense they come from somewhere quite ordinary.

When you're writing, do you let yourself be influenced by other people's records?

W: That's often like a kick-off point for me. Maybe the tempo of a song or maybe the first few chord changes of a tune of somebody else's. Just recently I've been writing new stuff and I've been listening to Springsteen's *Tunnel Of Love*. There's a track on there called "One Step Up" which has this sort of cyclical chord sequence and a sort of cross stick mid-tempo rhythm going through it. And I just played it a lot for quite a while. Sometimes you just program the same rhythm on a drum machine and start messing around with it; even using the same kind of chords. Sometimes things come like that. I tend to write much plainer things on the guitar, because of the nature of the instrument. When you pick up an acoustic guitar, you tend to lean towards those sort of classic big, open sounding chords right down at the neck's end, like the open G. When I write on keyboards, I tend to write in a slightly more soul-oriented way.

Let me ask you about a few of your songs. "Apron Strings"

T: That was written for a John Hughes film called *She's Having A Baby*. He got in touch with us, and all he told us was the title of the film and a simple basic plot idea. It's a young couple. She gets pregnant, and it's about what they feel like during this period of change in their lives. It was quite good because it set me off thinking about something that I hadn't thought of writing a song about before: the idea of whether or not it's good to have a baby and how you feel about it. It was the first time I'd ever written a song for anything specific that wasn't just my own idea to start with. But once I got started on the song, I realized that it was something that was in my own mind as well.

"Imagining America"

W: I got the idea from the story that I learned about my grandfather. Somewhere early in the century, he got married to a young wife and they lived in Glasgow, Scotland. And he vowed to make his fortune for her. So he left her behind and set sail for America on a big ship. And the plan was that he would arrive in the land of promise and plenty that America still represents to a lot of people, and come back a rich and successful man. The fact is that he lasted about three days and came home [laughs], but that was beside the point. Then basically I made the link between that and the trip that we made to go and record *The Language Of Life*. I just got the bug, the feeling, the spirit of crossing the Atlantic and maybe making our fortune, going to California to record an album.

"One Place"

T: I was walking around the streets where we live here, and it was a really nice summer evening. The opening lines of the song were all things that I'd heard walking past people's houses. We'd just come back from a tour and I just felt very much that there was a whole kind of stable home life going on around me that I wasn't part of at all. When you're traveling, life can seem a lot more rootless. It's quite hard to settle down in a house with babies and pets and things, because you have to leave them. That's what started the idea off. And the song just goes on to sort of muse on the idea of whether it's better to be stable in one place or in the end if you get more out of life by moving around and keeping things open. I don't think it really comes to any kind of conclusion.

"Twin Cities"

W: I liked the title of that. It came first. There's a band called The Go-Betweens. Robert [Foster] from that band wrote a song called "Twin Layers Of Lightning." We're actually pretty good friends with Robert, and he wrote that song about him and his girlfriend, being twin layers of lightning. It's a brilliant song. I wanted to write a song about that feeling of travel, of taking your spirit with you, of not feeling homesick. A nomadic life can be a good life. You don't necessarily have to put down roots. I felt that very strongly as we were traveling across America playing songs that year. The fact that you can see your spirit reflected in the landscape around you, the towns you pass through, the railroads. There's a quality of life in those images which is worth cherishing. And also the fact that we were traveling as Ben and Tracey, as Everything But The Girl, as a partnership. Just that idea of fluidity of life. You know, one river, twin cities just traveling through life.

Do you have a favorite of your own songs?

T: No. I think "Driving" is a really good song that Ben wrote [laughs], but I can't take any credit for that at all. But I've always thought that has a kind of perfection about it, which pleases me every time we sing it. I still enjoy singing "Fascination." That's one of my favorites too.

W: "Frozen River" is one of my favorite songs that I've done. The inspiration behind it comes from the two characters in the opening line, Joni and Jane, who are Joni Mitchell and Jane Siberry. The two tracks of theirs in particular were "River" from Joni's *Blue* album and a song called "Hockey" by Jane, which talks about playing hockey on a frozen river. And that was the image that set the song spinning off. The idea of skating away, that you could get away from life, the idea that love itself is that very image, that you can skate away through winter trees, away from what binds you, what gets you down. It's just a love song really.

Ben, what discoveries did you make about songwriting during your long convalescence?

W: That if I wasn't careful, I was all too adept at writing something that was formulaic and generic [laughs]. I think during the initial phase of coming out of the hospital, I was eager to be writing again, having been deprived of it for so long. I was writing almost anything, and it really took a couple of people around me to point out that this really was fairly average stuff. I knew how to do it, because I know how songs go, but I really wasn't saying anything fresh or real. That was kind of shocking at the time, because I genuinely thought it was pretty good stuff. So I kind of stopped for a bit. Tracey went through a similar thing with her writing, because she was very affected by my illness too. I think we both felt we were writing fairly run-of-the-mill songs. We went out instead and started touring, and it wasn't until we got off that tour that the floodgates seemed to open. I found myself writing stuff very fluidly again. It seemed to come out in a fresh burst, and I wasn't paying too much attention to verses and choruses. I just wrote what came out, and that was the impetus behind the songs on *Amplified Heart*.

A lot of your strongest songs seem to be about separation. Does it help you lyrically to direct these songs at a specific person?

W: I think a sense of dialogue is always important, but the main problem is that for the listener, the tendency is always to assume that it's between two people. Sometimes it can be between two states of mind. Sometimes it's not necessarily autobiographical. But I do think that the dialogue between a resolution to the problem and being unable to resolve the problem is where the tension resides, and that's where people get the excitement and meaning from. The tension between what you wish could be and what really is. A lot of people have asked us, "How autobiographical are you records?" To a certain extent, they are, but at the same time, a lot of the songs are dialogues with myself, or between states of mind, and they can be interpreted in different ways. You want songs to have room for people to interpret. All I really want to be as a songwriter is a reflection of you the listener. I don't really want people to step right into my life and say "Oh, that's about Ben." It's not. It's about what you see of yourself in the songs.

Neil Tennant

West End Girls ✫ What Have I Done To Deserve This?
✫ Nothing Has Been Proved

Interview conducted in 1996

"Technology is about making the records, not writing the songs."

We have grown accustomed to thinking of the singer-songwriter as a lone man or woman on a simple stage, strumming an acoustic guitar or leaning into chords on their piano as they wrench emotional truths from the soul in an earnest voice. But that definition excludes Neil Tennant.

Without a guitar or piano, he links himself to the electronic pulse of a beatbox and wraps himself in the cool cloak of programmed synths and sequencers. He sings in a deadpan voice under the diamond rain of disco balls and lasers. Emotional connection is still a goal, but not at the expense of infectious melodies and eminently danceable grooves. Though some may disagree, Tennant, one half of the British duo Pet Shop Boys, is by his own estimation, "a very traditional singer-songwriter." Indeed, even stripped of their lush sheen and baroque frills, Pet Shop Boys' best-known songs such as "West End Girls," "Opportunities (Let's Make Lots Of Money)," "It's A Sin," "What Have I Done To Deserve This?" and "Domino Dancing" are solidly written pop songs.

Tennant was born July 10, 1954 in Northumberland, England. While in school, he played cello and absorbed the sounds of everything from The Beatles to Broadway musicals. Fresh from London Polytechnic University, he went into journalism, first as an editor at Marvel Comics, then as a staffer for the pop paper *Smash Hits*. But writing about other people's music couldn't quell Tennant's yearning to make his own.

In 1981, he met Chris Lowe, a cabaret pianist, who shared his enthusiasm for dance beats married to pop melodies. After a few years of misses and minor club successes, the duo of Tennant and Lowe hit paydirt with "West End Girls." It reached #1 in both the U.S. and UK, launching the Pet Shop Boys to international fame.

Since then, they've racked up gold, platinum and multi-platinum records all over the world. In 1987, they helped the legendary Dusty Springfield make a comeback by featuring her on their worldwide smash, "What Have I Done To Deserve This?" then penning and producing the UK hits "In Private" and "Nothing Has Been Proved" for her. They have also written songs for Liza Minelli and Tina Turner.

There's a perception that The Pet Shop Boys are very technology-oriented. How much of a part does technology play in the writing process for you?

Not that much really. There are three ways Chris and I write songs together. Firstly, we play together, as it were, in the studio. Secondly, Chris writes music at home and I put words to it, or maybe add a middle bit. And thirdly, I write more or less completed songs at home on the piano, and then Chris maybe changes the rhythm track. My things sound kind of singer-songwriter-y sometimes and he kind of grooves them up. So technology is not really the whole point. Technology is about making the records, not writing the songs.

A lot of your songs are so strong on groove I wondered if you ever had a drum machine in the room when you were writing.

I don't, no. But Chris will start a rhythm, or he'll suddenly think of some chord change he wants to try out. In terms of writing music, a new sound on a new keyboard can inspire a whole song or point you in a new direction. A loop can take a song in a different direction. I don't think it necessarily changes its melodic or lyrical content really. But sometimes, if you start from scratch or you're

improvising, that's when it can have an effect. You can create a different atmosphere for a song if your starting point is a kind of fast jungle rhythm or if it's a gentle hip-hop groove.

What other musical influences affect you?

We always have a compromise. Chris' main interest is dance music. Chris ideally would like a song to have one chord in it [laughs], or two or three chords, really simple, because that's what dance music is. A groove has to have a simple chord change, really. Otherwise it gets complicated. I always tend to come up with more songwriter-y things. I'm trying to be Stephen Sondheim, or I want it to have an orchestra. So it's a compromise between those two approaches. I'm very much a traditional songwriter in terms of structure and things. But then I try to screw up the structure because I think it's too old-fashioned or something like that. So it's really a marriage of opposites. I think it's very good to be open minded about music.

What inspired the writing of "West End Girls"?

It started off as a rap and was very much intended to be a rap record. I'd been watching a film late at night over at my cousin's house. It was this James Cagney gangster film and just as I was doddering off to sleep, the lines "Sometimes you're better off dead/There's a gun in your hand that's pointing at your head" came into my head. So I wrote it down and thought it was quite good. And the rhythm is very strong, a rap rhythm, and I just thought about it and wrote more lyrics. Then ultimately we put that to music. It was just this kind of beautiful sounding thing, and it occurred to me that you could rap the verses and have a sung chorus. But it started as a lyrical idea and that's how it normally works with me.

Do you think people missed the humor in "Opportunities (Let's Make Lots Of Money)"?

Yes. In America, a lot of people took that song very seriously. Every year we get requests for it to be used when companies are having conventions and all that [laughs]. I just turned one down. That song was meant to be a satire on those kinds of 80s attitudes, and people took it as a statement of them, which is sort of appalling really.

Did you have Dusty Springfield in mind when you wrote "What Have I Done To Deserve This?"

That song is unusual because we wrote that with Allee Willis, a successful American songwriter who was managed by our manager for awhile. On the demo of the song it was a duet between me and her. So when we came to record it, we needed a woman to sing it and Dusty Springfield was our favorite female singer. We managed to track her down and she did it. Since then, having worked with Dusty, we've written things specifically for her. We did a single in England called "In Private." Chris wrote this melody and I said, "That's a Dusty tune." Dusty never sings a verse or chorus of a song the same. She sings every one differently, and she builds the song to a climax in her vocal by bending the melody.

What was your experience in writing the song "Confidential" for Tina Turner?

They asked us to write a song for her and we listened to her greatest hits album, and Chris already had a little piece of music which was the basis of the song. But it helped to actually listen to her voice as we were writing it. I was writing the melody with her voice in my head, which kind of took the melody to places that I normally wouldn't have gone. But having said that, when she got the song she liked it, but we had to make a demo with the vocal line played on the piano. She found the vocal line incredibly complicated. When I actually played it on the piano, I thought, "God, this vocal line goes all over the place, I can't believe it." It was written very quickly, and I could see why it wasn't the sort of thing she normally sings. The chorus has an incredible range.

Lets talk about a few more specific songs. "Electricity"

It is actually about a drag queen. This phrase came into my head one day when I was walking down the street – "It's the greatest show with the best effects/Since Disco Tex and The Sex-o-Lettes" [laughs] – and I scribbled it down in my little notebook. Later we were improvising this particular track and I thought, "Wow, we can make this into our Disco Tex song." The drag queen in that song has kind of a tough life, and it's kind of wearying doing a whole show lip-synching and dancing. I often think drag queens have to be pretty tough. It's a song about lip-synching, which is funny, because in the 80s, we were always on television lip-synching to things [laughs], and we still do occasionally. Years ago, before we had any success, we used to do these little tours of places like Belgium and lip-synch in bars. It's a pretty weird experience.

"Up Against It"

Chris wrote the music, and I needed a four-syllable phrase and I couldn't think of anything for ages. I have thousands of books at home and when I can't think of anything, I'll just glance along the books until I come to a phrase that gives me an idea. *Up Against It* is a screenplay written by the playwright Joe Orton for The Beatles, and it was never made. Actually The Beatles were meant to be in drag in it [laughs], and Brian Epstein was absolutely appalled. It never got made but the screenplay was published. So I came across this book and I thought, "Wow, that's a good title. Four syllables." Then I immediately thought of the lyrics with the idea of looking back at the wars in England and how people had to always tighten their belts to get by. I'd been reading books about London during the war. It was easy to write once I had the title.

The song "Step Aside" seems to be more ambitious lyrically than many of your songs.

I was trying to compare my life – and where I am in the Pet Shop Boys, and also being in a relationship – with the lives of people who always seem to have to struggle for either a political utopia or a spiritual utopia. It was inspired by going to Santiago di Compastella in Spain where they have a famous cathedral, and all these pilgrims walk 150 miles from France to Spain. If you do this pilgrimage it means you've got salvation guaranteed. It's an ancient Catholic thing [laughs]. So the people walk all this way and when they get there, they're happy because it means they're going to go to heaven when they die. I just couldn't imagine having that kind of certainty in my life. So I compared that with my own lack of certainty. Then I went through Budapest a few months later and I was looking at these people who have tough lives in a Communist country. It just struck me that at one time they were all waiting for Communism to save them, and now they're waiting for the free market to save them. Again, comparing it to my own life and how I don't believe in certainties. Then I tried to connect that to whether I believe in being in love with someone. It's a lot to distill into a little four-minute song [laughs], and I didn't want it to sound pretentious, particularly with the starting point about the pilgrims. I wrote that verse about 15 times. I didn't like using the word "pilgrim," because I think it sounds a bit pretentious. Actually, I'm still not sure if I'm happy with the first verse, but we had to record something. You should never notice the words of a song. They should fit so perfectly that you don't notice them, then later on they get into your head and you notice what they're about. That's an example of a song on that level that doesn't work. You probably do notice the words because they're not necessarily musical words.

If you're writing a song and you keep running into a brick wall where the chorus should be, what helps?

Wow, that's difficult, because that does happen. On the *Bilingual* album, there's a song "Red Letter Day," where we were trying to write something very anthemic and we were writing it in C major, which is a very anthemic key. We based the song on the chord change of "Song Of Joy" from Beethoven's Ninth Symphony. We noticed that a song called "Go West" by The Village People was the same chord change as Pachelbel's Canon, the very famous piece. So we thought, "Wow, what a great idea. Let's think of a famous classical piece, take the chord change and put it to a dance beat" [laughs]. Anyway, it was a better idea than it was a reality. If you're stuck, I think it's good to undermine it. Even if you've gone a long way with something. We always try to do that, undermine it or subvert it so suddenly where it started off as a happy song, now it's a sad song. Suddenly what was major becomes kind of minor. It makes it more intriguing and that can be a way forward definitely. Another thing is to try playing on an instrument that you don't really play very well. Like if you're a guitarist, try a keyboard and chances are, you'll play something quite interesting. So you make mistakes and the mistakes are interesting. It makes you think of the melody in a different way. It can change the entire way you think about the song.

k.d. lang

Constant Craving ✱ Miss Chatelaine ✱ If I Were You

Interview conducted in 1995

"My whole life is based on the fact that I'm a singer. I know that is my purpose."

Pushing boundaries has always been at the center of k.d. lang's existence as an artist. Whether subverting the conventions of country music with her androgynous image or fusing disparate musical genres into the brilliant style of *Ingenue*, she continues to be one of the most intriguing and challenging artists in pop music today.

Her catalog of country-flavored albums, *A Truly Western Experience*, the rockabilly-flavored *Angel With a Lariat*, *Shadowland* (produced by legend Owen Bradley) and *Absolute Torch And Twang*, stands as some of the most soulful music made in that genre.

When lang decided to move beyond country, she and her co-writer Ben Mink, created *Ingenue*, a masterful record they described as "postnuclear cabaret." Drawing on folk, jazz, country, pop and torch, lang and Mink fashioned a song cycle about obsession and love. The first single, "Constant Craving," went Top 40. The campy second single, "Miss Chatelaine," along with its accompanying bubble-and-moonlight video, made lang a household name. At the 1993, Grammy Awards, the album racked up three nominations, and one "Best Pop Vocal Performance" trophy for "Constant Craving." It remains her masterpiece.

The follow-up, *All You Can Eat*, continued that sonic adventure and found her adding a little Memphis soul, 60s psychedelia and Brit-pop to the palette.

What were some of the discoveries you made about songwriting while making All You Can Eat*?*

I think the most important step in the evolution of maturity for me as a songwriter were the lyrics. I wanted to achieve simplicity and directness, but make it interesting and memorable and not too watered down. I've always written very metaphorically and used a lot of imagery and been very romantic. *Ingenue* is that way, very wordy. But for this record, I really wanted to write in-your-face direct lyrics. I sometimes referred to it as "Ricki Lake-speak" [laughs]. The kind of language that goes on on the "Ricki Lake Show," you know. That was the biggest change for me. Also, I think our [approach to] form changed a lot. In the past, we wouldn't even write a chorus sometimes. But on this record, I was super chorus conscious. I wanted strong choruses. I was influenced a lot by British pop bands like Blur, Oasis, Elastica and Radiohead – there's some sort of irreverence about the pop song but at the same time it's a complete tribute to it. At the same time, I can't be that way because my voice kind of dictates what I do. I can't sing alternative music. It doesn't quite work with my voice, although I may think alternative and I may consider myself alternative. So we were very conscious of bridges, verses and choruses, and we tried to build songs with more sections than ever before.

I've read that you and Ben sometimes go on record buying sprees and use that as a kind of a basis for songwriting.

When we find ourselves at an inspirational lull, we go out and we just sort of listen to everything from Burt Bacharach to Bjork, from one extreme to the other, just to see where we sit. Sonically, as producers we do that too. Definitely, we spent a few dollars on CDs this year.

Was "Season Of Hollow Soul" on Ingenue *inspired by Mary Hopkins' "Those Were The Days"?*

Yes, definitely. It was also inspired by "Is That All There Is?" by Peggy Lee, and by Lotte Lenya and Kurt Weill. It was all in that vein. We never try to steal, but songs like "Season Of Hollow Soul" are kind of put together. We love so many different types of music.

The All You Can Eat *album can be read as a sort of linear look at getting into a new relationship. Did you have much of a road map before starting the writing process?*

No, not at all. It originally started off that I was really set on doing some sort of fucked-up opera, somewhere between Yma Sumac and Bjork. But it didn't turn out that way at all [laughs]. But that's the journey of songwriting. Everyday there's something that triggers you in a different direction – a sound, a lyric, a guitar part, anything can do it. Food can do it. I really wrote the lyrics day to day, but then in sequencing I just had this one minute where I took all these post-its and went, bang, bang, bang, that's it. I played the record for a friend of mine and she said, "I just love how the first five songs are all these questions," and I was totally unaware of it.

How would you describe the first steps in yours and Ben's writing process?

First, we probably waste a good hour babbling and not doing anything, just talking about where we're at emotionally, or if we saw a good movie, or what video's really bugging you [laughs], something like that. Then generally, we'll hunker down to business. Ben's generally on guitar and I kind of bounce around between keyboards or anything – like this old banjo. I kind of doodle around with melodies while he's doodling around with chords. So I have a lot more freedom on the instrument than him. That's one way we begin. Another way is we'll be listening to music and we'll find one moment in a song that'll make us go, "What is really cool about this?" Then we'll figure out it's a riff, a drum beat or that one chord that sets this section up. Then we'll explore different ways of doing that same thing, taking the seed of inspiration from someone else and going from there.

Can you talk about your lyric writing process a bit.

A track has to speak to me. I cannot write lyrics until the track tells me what the lyrics are. I can't go, "Okay, I want this song to be about acquiescing." It's not like that. I listen and listen and listen to the tracks and I'll wait. The melody will have a rhythm and a word just pops out. In "If I Were You", the tag on that one spoke to me. I didn't know what it meant, this phrase "if I were you." Then you have to explore what it means. Then you have to listen to how the melody is and it has to sing right. You know, I'm really bad at talking about songwriting because it's very unintellectualized for me.

255

Is it usually a while after you get one of those phrases before you discover what the song is about?

Yes, but sometimes it can happen in a flash. The song "Maybe" was always a song about balance because the original guitar riff, which we never ended up using, was this kind of see-saw back and forth, so obviously it's like this question bouncing back and forth with this balancing procedure. So I spent like hours and hours over a period of weeks thinking "On one hand there's you, on one hand there's me, what comes between the two, a simple point of view," which was the original lyric. It just wasn't working. Then one day, I wasn't happy and I started from scratch again and I was actually paging through a book of Jean Michel Basquiat paintings. He painted words over and over and over again; his paintings are very repetitive. And I thought, "Why as songwriters are we so absorbed with not using repetition?" I've always had this fear of using the same word over. It wasn't a goal, but I wanted to try and use the word "maybe" in every line. You say maybe a lot when you're trying to decide about a lover. Maybe I'll sleep with her, maybe I won't. Maybe I'll go on a date. You say maybe a lot in your mind when you're talking to yourself. So that was a big turning point for me, to sort of let go of my preconceived notions of what to do and what not to do as a lyricist.

You've said that you'll retune your guitar while you're writing to put yourself more into a world of instinct. Are there things you do during other parts of the writing process to help you go on instinct?

I think probably one of the most beneficial things about me is that I'm really naive. I don't understand music, I don't know chords, I don't understand harmony. And lyrically, I really am just a listener. I'm emotional. Ben's more technical, more analytical. But also when we write, we really try to eliminate our heads from it. We talk in different terms. I'll go, "No, make the chord bigger and to the left" [laughs], and he knows what I mean, which is the beauty of our relationship. There's one chord we call "lime sherbet" because it sounds sweet and sour and clean, like lime sherbet. But I really am quite naive and primitive in my approach to songwriting and rely on my instincts, I would say wholly.

With melody writing as well?

As a songwriter, I really write for my voice. I have a classic sound-ing, crooner styled voice, so as a songwriter, I go for classic, roman-tic melodies. If I was writing for Bjork, I don't know if I would write classic sounding melodies. I have to re-write a lot of the melodies I write when I start narrowing in on lyrics and seeing the emotional content. I rewrote a lot of the choruses because they were too strict, too confining, too traditional. I would just kind of allow myself as a singer to completely ignore the songwriter and see what happened.

Your melodies have a lot of unexpected surprises in them – chromatic notes and interval leaps. Is that something you've always been attracted to?

I'm attracted to interesting movement. I'm interested in dissonance. I'm interested in sidestepping, but I don't know where that came from. I'm the youngest of four kids and my oldest sibling was 11 years older than me. They all studied classical piano seriously all through my upbringing. I listened to hours and hours of them prac-ticing classical music. Running around the house, getting ready for supper after school, there was always someone playing Chopin or Beethoven or Schubert or Strauss. I listened to it all, over and over, so I really think that that's where my initial development came from. Both my pitch reference and my melodic references.

That's a purely environmental shaping, but I sometimes wonder why certain people are attracted to say, darker, more dissonant music.

The biggest question I've been pondering for years is, "Are we attracted to certain things because they're familiar, or is it because they're unexplored in our soul, in our past, in our minds?" Why are we attracted to a painting or not attracted to a painting? Where does taste come from? I think there's an attraction gene. I think it has a lot to do with generations and heritage too. I've also been very inter-ested in why my voice sounds like it does, why it has the qualities it does. Is it because I like that music or do I like that music because my voice sounds like that music? I don't know. I think I probably like this kind of classic sounding music because my voice sounds like that. When I listen to Sarah Vaughan or that style of singing, I think, I like this music. Then I think, is it because my voice is that way – and honestly, I'm not trying to say I'm as good a singer as

Sarah Vaughan – but I mean that my voice tends to fit in that style of music. It's a hard one to figure out. Sometimes I think I was born in the wrong era, and then other times I think I was born to carry it on in a way. Strange thing, my voice, because as I said earlier, it dictates what I do as a songwriter. It's the leader.

I think bottom line, ultimately, my whole life is based on the fact that I'm a singer. I know that that is my purpose in a way and so my whole lifestyle, my whole thought process, my whole value system is based on protecting my gift, because it is exactly that, a gift, and I have a huge responsibility to treat it with the utmost respect I can. I am on a constant path of trying to learn how to sing deeper and deeper with less physical strength and to develop power from the internal, from the spiritual plane and not from the physical plane.

From what else do you draw inspiration?

I think that there's this whole realization, and it's not new, but there's a common realization amongst great artists that the real source of inspiration is, to quote a hyper-therapy term, "the child inside of you," the one that doesn't know criticism, that doesn't know judgment, that doesn't know editing, that doesn't second guess itself. Sometimes it's embarrassing, sometimes it may be very, very evil. Some of your thoughts can be devastating, you wouldn't even tell your best friend. Some can be so sexually explicit, some can be violent, some can be completely geeky. You really have to be able to accept all of those, because they're all there and they can all lead you somewhere. I mean, I often write from two different extremes – either from a real dark point of view or from an extremely spiritual place. It's really extreme, and I always second-guess myself at the beginning. But to start at an extreme is actually a good place to start. You can always smooth things out. But if you start from a mediocre point of view, then you're kind of stuck there.

Aimee Mann

Voices Carry ✫ I Should've Known ✫ Save Me

Interview conducted in 1993

"I know there's nobody who will ever get this, but in case there is, I'm going to put up a little signpost."

Aimee Mann is a survivor. She has spent more than half her career suffering in silence while lawyers, managers and record executives untied the Gordian knot contracts which have prevented her from doing what she loves best: writing songs and making records.

In times of upheaval and uncertainty, Mann has often done her most affecting work, transforming her frustrations with the business into sterling pop music. "Songwriting has always been a way that I can actually explain myself, a way to define things that I've found hard to define," she says.

Her professional career began in 1985, with a success that was almost overnight. Til Tuesday, an MTV-galvanized band, zoomed to stardom on the new wave wings of "Voices Carry," a catchy hit she wrote and sang. The song's video focused on Mann's spiky blond hair and alluring good looks. Of course, her record label, Epic, wanted to stick to a winning formula. Mann had other ideas, namely to become a more serious songwriter. Result? The decline and fall into oblivion of Til Tuesday, despite two subsequent albums, *Welcome Home* and *Everything's Different Now*. The latter, a great undiscovered masterpiece, features "The Other End Of The Telescope," a songwriting collaboration between Mann and Elvis Costello. (Costello later recorded the song for his *All This Useless Beauty* album.)

259

The band broke up, but Epic wouldn't let Mann go. She spent four years in legal limbo. She wrote songs and waited for her fate to be decided. Her flagging spirits were lifted when she met producer Jon Brion. Their collaboration resulted in the brilliant arrangements on *Whatever*, Mann's first solo album. On standout tracks such as "Fifty Years After The Fair," "Could've Been Anyone" and "Mr. Harris," fuzz guitars churn, flanged cymbals swirl and exotic, forgotten instruments like the mellotron and chamberlain float seductively around Mann's compelling voice. The result is a songfest that's as exhilarating as a ride in a newspaper taxi through Pepperland.

After "That's Just What You Are" gained some radio attention by way of its inclusion on the *Melrose Place* television show soundtrack, Mann released her second album, 1996's *I'm With Stupid*, which contained a baker's dozen of perfect pop songs, but didn't have the hit the label (Geffen) demanded. On the album's last track, "It's Not Safe," she wrote the first of her anti-music industry missives. It opens with the lines: "All you want to do is something good / So get ready to be ridiculed and misunderstood."

Geffen was taken over by Seagram's and Mann's third album was frozen in the merger. Two years passed. Interscope stepped in and signed her. Despite the first blush of love between artist and label, the deal quickly soured with the dreaded line, "We don't hear a single." Mann ended up buying back the master for what became *Bachelor No. 2*, and she started her own web-based label, Superego Records. The brave decision brought a wave of good fortune. Young gun director Paul Thomas Anderson built *Magnolia*, his epic film about dysfunctional relationships, around her fatalistic love songs, and Mann earned an Academy Award nomination for her song "Save Me." In the meantime, she sold loads of copies of *Bachelor No. 2* through her site, and made various licensing deals around the world to get it in stores. With her husband Michael Penn, she hit the road with the successful Acoustic Vaudeville tour. Having sworn off major labels for good, Mann is finally in control of her career and much happier.

"It's a huge relief to be working outside the strictures of the major label system," she says. "I'm doing better than ever. I mean, I have to pay for everything. If we have some idea for marketing or we do a tour, we pay for it all ourselves. There's no subsidized tour support. I hire a publicist, and photographers for press photos, all that stuff, and that's usually what the record companies would pay for. But you get to make your own decisions."

Mann's songs have also been featured in the films *Jerry Maguire* and *Cruel Intentions*. Her song "Put Me On Top" (from *Whatever*) was covered by Marti Jones. And she collaborated with Elvis Costello for a second time on the song "The Fall Of The World's Own Optimist." "I like the idea of sending him things when I'm really having trouble, when I feel like I need to be bailed out," she says.

Was there one thing that made you want to write your own songs?

I don't know. When you first start, if you're brought up in the tradition of Bob Dylan and The Beatles, you just think that's what you do. Later on, it becomes something else. I think at some point, the good songwriters are separated from the not-so-good songwriters by virtue of what it begins to mean to you.

Did you start young?

When I was 16, I started trying to write and it was miserable. I'd say that I started writing songs seriously on the second Til Tuesday record. When we were touring for the first record, I had a lot of time in hotel rooms to work on my writing.

Did the success of "Voices Carry" affect your outlook on writing?

I thought I was a pretty good songwriter then, until I started writing better songs. It's like anything, the more you learn, the more you realize you have a lot to learn.

Have you learned a lot by listening to and analyzing other people's songs?

Up until recently, I never really did that. But when I was exposed to seeing people work, like seeing Jules Shear and seeing the way his lyric structures were, and that kind of thing, and then Jon Brion on my first record, seeing the way he wrote was very instructive. It's also instructive being around Jon, because he's really listened to a lot of music, and so I started getting interested in some different albums I'd never heard. The Kinks' *Village Green Preservation Society*, for example. It's incredible. The Zombies' *Odessey & Oracle*. We'd sit hunched over the speakers together, listening to this stuff. I'd say, "Wow, this is exactly what I want to do. Listen to that drum sound." So I started getting interested in listening more closely.

What's the hardest thing about songwriting for you?

Usually, it's the music, and worrying if I'm repeating myself. With lyrics, there's always a way to get around it, which is to know what you're saying. There are ways of trying to remind yourself of what you're trying to say. You can call somebody up and say, "I'm trying to write this song and it's about how I feel about this and that." And you realize a lot of times, as soon as you say it, that that's the line. But music is different. Your hands tend to go in patterns they're familiar with. It's more of a challenge to keep things interesting.

Are you a careful line-by-line kind of writer?

It usually comes in a moderate hunk, then I'll go back. The lyrics and melody are usually born together. But once you have a melody with lyrics, that usually solidifies the melody. For me, it's always by virtue of starting at the beginning. Okay, what do I want to say? I can never backtrack. That's harder.

Is there a message that you want to convey?

Not to the public at large. But for me, half of it is, here's a message to somebody who does not exist, but maybe they do, and when they hear this, they'll understand. I know there's nobody who will ever get this, but in case there is, I'm going to put up a little signpost, and maybe I'll luck out.

What's the weirdest way a song has arrived?

One time I was washing dishes and this song popped into my brain. It turned out to be one of those songs that had a life of its own. I couldn't really explain it too well, but I kind of knew what it was about. It was more about a kind of feeling than a situation. I usually don't like songs like that, but I was washing dishes and this line came into my head with a melody. I kept thinking, "Why is this coming into my head now? I have dishes to wash [laughs]. Okay, I'll take off the rubber gloves and put this idea down."

Tell me about "Fifty Years After The Fair."

That's written as if it's by someone who was around during the 1939 World's Fair, which was particularly focused on how great the future would be with all these futuristic things. So I started writing it from that point of view, but the future is never as futuristic as you think it's going to be.

"Say Anything"

I wrote that with Jon. He had the line, "Say anything, cause I've heard everything," and boy, did I know exactly what he was talking about. So for the lyric, I immediately got a picture of someone who's listening to explanation after explanation that they know is a lie. As a focus point of the lyric, there was a Lewis Carroll poem that goes, "The jury said to a mouse that he mend the house / Come let us go to law, I will prosecute you / I'll be judge and jury" – and it's in the shape of a mouse's tail. I always remembered that, so I used that imagery for the song.

"The Other End Of The Telescope"

I had this music, but the lyrics weren't coming. I had the line "I know it don't make a difference to you / But oh it sure made a difference to me." And I just sent that off to Elvis [Costello], and I said, "I just have these two lines and I don't know if they mean anything to you." He totally knew what I was getting at. He sent it back really quickly – I think he wrote it on a plane flight – and he made a few changes.

I'm curious, were you a Smiths fan?

I think Morrissey is a really clever lyric writer. I really like him taking lines that ordinarily you wouldn't hear in the context of a song and putting them in. That's a really great skill, because I don't think people listen to themselves talk. They sit down to write a song and they fall into this rock speak, which is terrible. Melodically, it was all kind of two notes though.

What advice would you give to a songwriter who has experience but is looking for a break?

I wouldn't know. I don't feel like I can offer advice. I have friends who are really great songwriters, but I don't know what to do for them. Depending on what kind of songwriter you are – if you're a

real commercial pop writer, then I'm sure it's possible to get a publishing deal and be a writer. But for somebody like Elvis Costello, if
I knew him and he didn't have a deal and he was unknown, I wouldn't
know how to advise him. There's not much of a place for really
talented people. It's kind of depressing. Where do you go? There
aren't enough good songwriters.

Suzanne Vega

Luka ☆ Tom's Diner ☆ Marlene On The Wall

Interview conducted in 1994

"There was a boy named Luka who lived upstairs from me...I wanted to write from the point of view of a nine-year-old boy."

First impressions can be misleading. Take the case of Suzanne Vega. When she emerged from the Greenwich Village folk scene with her debut record in 1985, she earned a reputation as being a shy, sensitive poetess who sang sotto voce songs of love's darker side, such as "Small Blue Thing," "Marlene On The Wall" and "The Queen And The Soldier."

To some fans and critics, uninformed or unwilling to accept what she's become, Vega remains that delicate waif folkie. The delightful truth of the matter is that Suzanne Vega has spent years evolving in all sorts of unpredictable directions.

From folk roots, her musical tree has branched out to include Beatlesque power pop, synthesized mood pieces and even hip-hop (thanks to her encounter with British rappers DNA on "Tom's Diner," which went Top 5 on the *Billboard* charts). On her *99.9 F* album, her experimental bent lured her into dense aural landscapes bursting with industrial clangs, funky bass loops, and mad calliope swoops. She even sang through a fuzzbox.

Through all of Vega's experimentation, there has remained a constant: top-notch songwriting. Finely detailed and hard-hitting, her songs are as potent for what they say as for what they leave unsaid. Think of her best-known song, "Luka," a #3 hit from 1987's *Solitude Standing* album. In a few bold

265

strokes, she created a character and lured the listener into a mystery story. Inspired by heroes such as Leonard Cohen and Lou Reed, she is a master of this style of evocative portraiture in song.

Is songwriting something that comes naturally to you?

Yeah. I always felt I had an ability to rhyme words, even when I was very young. When I would write poetry, that was the kind of poetry that came the most easily to me – the stuff with rhyme and rhythm. So I do think it comes naturally, though it doesn't always come easily.

Was there a point when you decided to become a songwriter?

I was 11 when I first picked up the guitar. I tried to write songs for about two years before I wrote one that I was satisfied with. So I was 14 when the first one was finished. But with some of the early ones, the structure's there, you can kind of see it.

How do song ideas make themselves known to you most often?

There are different ways. Some of them are straightforward, you know, you see something in the street or something occurs to you. Others have a stranger way of making themselves known to you. Some of them come in dreams or some come just by the words themselves. You'll see a word or a phrase and suddenly that will appeal to you. I think the song "Left Of Center" was an example of that. I wrote it from the title on down. And "Cracking" was something like that too. I also use things like medical textbooks, science textbooks and various bits of information.

Do you do a lot of editing in your head before you start to write the idea?

Lately I'll write out the general idea in longhand and then eventually the whole thing gets whittled down. So I wouldn't say that I edit it first, but I try to make sure that it's at least a good idea or something worth pursuing. Sometimes those initial longhand ideas come out in rhyme and in meter, but some of them don't. For example, "The Queen And The Soldier," I had been thinking about that song for months and months, and when I finally sat down to write, it came out in rhyme and in meter, and in surprising ways. Ways that I hadn't expected. The rhymes would suggest themselves to me, that's the way it seemed. Whereas a song like "Rock In The Pocket," I must have had about three or four pages written out of the storyline before I finally boiled it down to the three verses that it is.

Do you have any feelings about songs that are completed quickly versus those that may take years?

The weird thing is that the songs that take the longest are sometimes the quickest ones to write, because you can spend months, as I said before, thinking about an idea and then when you sit down to write it, it'll take an hour or two. "The Queen And The Soldier," even though it took months of thinking about it, took about three hours to write. Same thing with "Luka." It took me months circling that idea, then I wrote the whole thing in about two hours.

Tell me about how a character song like "Luka" evolves.

Well, a character song is a tricky thing because, for me, there's always a connection between what I'm writing about and something that I'm feeling. So it's never abstract. I never just pluck somebody off the street and say "I'll write about that person." There's always something about that situation that I'm writing about that's true about my own life. Even if it's not the exact same thing, it's close. So in the case of "Luka," there was a boy whose name was Luka who lived upstairs from me, who seemed like a happy child. Not exactly happy, but he was not abused, as far as I knew. But I would watch him and he seemed sort of set apart from the other kids when he was playing, and I remember thinking I would take his character and use it for that particular idea. Write it from his voice, because in that way I wanted the song to stand up on its own. Because I wanted to write from the point of view of a nine-year-old boy, I was making it as simple as possible. I was also aware that the audience in the song is the neighbor. So it was kind of like writing a play. First of all, how do you introduce the character? You do that by saying, "My name is Luka, I live on the second floor." And then you get the audience involved, saying, "I live upstairs from you. So you've seen me before." You're incriminating the audience. You're pointing the finger without really doing it. You're unfolding this story and you're involving the audience in it and that was what I wanted to do.

Did you try different musical settings for "Luka"?

No, not at all. The idea of making it sad by putting it in a minor key, making it melancholy, just seemed really sentimental and horrible to me. I wanted it to be a song that was matter of fact. I did not intend for it to be cheerful and uplifting. I wanted it to be as matter of fact as the boy's voice would be. When I sing it alone on the acoustic guitar, I think it does come out that way. I think when we produced it for the album, it came out the way it did because of the drums and the chiming of the synthesizers. It gave it a more uplifting effect than I intended [laughs].

I read that the idea for "Tired Of Sleeping" was something you found in a notebook from eight years earlier. Is that typical of the way you write?

Yeah, definitely. I think that life – my life anyway – doesn't seem to go in any particular straight line. It seems to go round in circles, so something that was important to me when I was much younger is still important to me. Things repeat themselves. That's how you know if it's a good idea, if it's still relevant years later.

Are there certain tests that a song has to pass before you'll consider it finished?

I really think about the subject matter a lot, because to me, you have to really be careful about writing about things that are trendy. Humor doesn't seem to sit well in my songs, for example. Something that I think is funny doesn't wear well. So I try to look at it from different angles and the different moods I might be in. And I've learned over the years that it's better to have some kind of formal structure rather than thinking you're being inventive and deciding to do away with the melody all together for example. I think in my early-20s I thought I was being clever by saying I don't need to write with a melody or I don't need to write with this or that, but it's better to stick to some kind of structure. To have a chorus, to have a melody, to have rhymes. Formal guidelines.

You mentioned humor. I've read other interviews with you where you said you feel like sometimes people missed the humor in your songs. Can you explain that?

I guess the first thing that comes to mind is a song like "Small Blue Thing," which to me had a humorous element, and was meant to be more playful than it's been interpreted. It was meant to be almost like a cartoon, like a question that you'd ask a child. If you were to describe how you felt, what would you be like? Or, if you were a small blue thing, what would you be? That to me isn't side-splittingly funny, but it has an element of whimsy that some people don't look at. I have to say that most of the songs that I wrote as overtly angry, bitter songs don't wear well with me. Most of them I don't sing anymore, whereas the really sad ones seem to always go very well for me, I don't know why that is. The really sad ones like "The Queen And The Soldier" and "Cracking" are the ones that people really respond to.

Were you conscious from the beginning about the kinds of words and phrases you use in your songs? They're very identifiable – those short, hard-sounding words.

I don't know why I decided to adopt that particular way of writing but I think it's because I felt that a lot of songs were really romantic and I wanted to do something different that was more urban. That's one reason. Those shorter phrases seemed to hit harder. They were more satisfying to sing. But the other thing that I've discovered is that I think I tend to sing in short phrases because I've had asthma for a long time and couldn't really breathe and hold the long notes. So I developed my writing style to accommodate my voice uncon-sciously. I didn't intend to do it, I was just trying to write like a good writer, to the point and punchy, in words that were vivid.

Were there any authors that influenced your writing style?

John Steinbeck was someone who wrote in that simple style. I started to read poetry. I was reading Sylvia Plath, and I just really like the way she writes, because it's always startling and always interesting and she tends to use those short phrases with uncomfortable images.

I've heard you comment that there's a lot in your lyrics that you don't understand.

Yeah, some of it is like that because it comes to me and then I write it down. It's like getting a message on a telephone. Sometimes it comes in clearly and sometimes it doesn't. Sometimes you don't understand all the bits. That's what I mean by that. It's like a dream, where some-times you don't quite understand it. Songs are in that world.

Did the course that "Tom's Diner" took surprise you?

Well, yeah, because it was such a small idea that became such a big thing. It was like a whimsical thing. I was thinking of my friend Brian and I was thinking of writing through his eyes and I sort of had this tune in my head, then I put the whole thing down. It became sort of a signature thing

Was that an actual place?

Yeah, there's a place called Tom's Restaurant on 112th Street and Broadway, right near the Cathedral of St. John the Divine. Everyone from school would go there and eat. There's nothing really special about it. It's a very ordinary place, which is why I liked it.

After the DNA rap version of that song, did you feel like it set you free as an artist to experiment?

Yeah, I think it was something I would've done eventually anyway. The DNA version of "Tom's Diner" was not something I would've done myself, but I liked it when I heard it. I thought it was funny. And it did make me feel more free, but as I said, I think I would've eventually gotten there, because I was starting to feel very hemmed in by the production techniques we were using.

Your singing style is instantly recognizable. How did you develop it?

Mostly I took what I liked. When I was a kid, the voices I loved were voices like Astrud Gilberto. And I didn't like the adult ways of singing. I didn't like the vibrato – that didn't mean anything to me. I preferred voices that were very direct. And I loved Leonard Cohen's voice. And I liked Lou Reed's voice, Lotte Lenya's voice, the voices that are straightforward. So that's what I tried to do. I just tried to make my voice come out in the simplest way possible, with no pretending that I'm a fine singer or anything. I wasn't interested in being a fine singer, I didn't care about that.

Did you decide to mix in spoken word with melody?

Well, melody is something that I've had to work on very hard, because the thing that comes naturally to me is rhythm and rhyme in the songwriting. Melody is something I've had to really sit down and consciously work on. To figure out how a melody develops. You can't just repeat something over and over again. A melody is its own idea, but I didn't know that. So I mixed in spoken words, because I thought I was being experimental. Actually it was kind of a weakness of mine. Melody is my weakness, rhythm and rhyme are my strengths.

What do you do to develop your melodic sense?

If I'm listening to a classical piece I'll try to be aware of what the melodic line is, because I have a hard time remembering melodies or singing them. So sometimes I'll just try to make myself think of a melody. If I'm listening to classical or jazz, I think, "Where is the melody, how does it deviate?" Or I listen to Elvis Costello, who seems to have endless variations and all kinds of melodies, and I'll follow his thinking. It's the same way when I'm reading John Steinbeck – you just don't read it for the story, you get into the language. You take the sentences apart to see what he's done and how he's done it. So I try and do that a little bit with people like Elvis Costello, who seems to have a natural gift.

"When Heroes Go Down" and "In Liverpool" have an Elvis Costello sound to them.

Especially "When Heroes Go Down." I was looking for something that was melodic, short and punchy, and I was thinking of Elvis Costello. "In Liverpool" was a mixture. I was trying to teach myself how to play "Almost Blue" [a Costello song]. That's where the verses came from. Then the chorus was just something else. And I jammed the two things together. At first, I thought maybe it was really corny or it had a feeling like a campfire song [laughs], but then I realized that it worked. Another example of that is I was trying to teach myself how to play the Chrissie Hynde song "Kid." And I realized that the reason her songs sound classic is because she uses those chords that you hear from all the 1950s songs. They are songs that you would sing around the campfire, but because of the production, it's much cooler than that. But there's still a classic element to what she does because of those chords. That made me not afraid to use plain, simple chords like E and A and B7, chords that I felt like everybody used.

Do you ever feel like your audience wants to restrict you?

Yeah, certainly, all the time. But on the other hand, my audience seems to change constantly. In 1985, it was like, "Oh, she's a folkie." Then in 1987, I suddenly was accused of having all kinds of yuppie audiences, which I thought was kind of odd. Things change, and I find the audience changes. I think to some degree, I have been somewhat misinterpreted, but I'm not complaining about it. I'm just saying that I'm difficult to categorize. I look a certain way and sound a certain way, but I'm not that way. I may look like a sort of Irish maiden, but I grew up in New York City under very unusual circumstances, so I'm not what I appear to be. So some people will stick with me in the long run, and other people will find other people. That's just the way it is.

272

Matthew Sweet

Girlfriend ✶ Sick Of Myself ✶ The Ugly Truth

Interview conducted in 1995 and 1997

"If I talk about how carefully I craft my songs, that's kind of a lie...It would be a real sham for me to act like I knew what I was doing."

Matthew Sweet understands that a big part of writing great songs is staying connected to the child inside.

On the cover of his album *100% Fun* there's a photo of the singer/songwriter, age ten, his bright smiling face framed by a ridiculously large pair of hi-fidelity headphones. He's leaning back in the comfort of a typical suburban living room, listening to one of his favorite songs and balancing the LP cover on his J.C. Penney Toughskins.

This idyllic picture not only reminds any of us who grew up in the rock era of the joy of discovering music, but it says a lot about Sweet's overall musical approach. Sweet's three-and-a-half minute, unapologetically pop creations make you forget the troubles and woes of the world.

Born October 6, 1964 in Lincoln, Nebraska, Matthew Sweet was attracted by the sounds of The Beach Boys, The Beatles and The Rolling Stones, as well as late 1970s new wavers such as Elvis Costello and The Records. He started writing his own songs in high school. Upon graduating, he headed for Athens, Georgia, home of R.E.M. and mecca of alternative music.

After brief stints in two bands, Oh-OK and Buzz of Delight, Sweet moved to New York, where he was signed to a record deal. His first two releases,

Inside and *Earth* were art-rock efforts, promising but unfocused. Then, in 1991, he hit his stride with *Girlfriend*, a pop meisterwork that defined his sound and style. *Rolling Stone*, *MOJO* and many other publications have hailed it as one of the greatest pop-rock albums of the 1990s, and its title track was a major radio hit on both mainstream rock and alternative rock stations.

Altered Beast (1993), an unfairly maligned record (critics wanted *Girlfriend II*), found Sweet exploring a darker side of his music and personality on standout songs such as "Someone To Pull The Trigger" and "Devil With The Green Eyes." *100% Fun* (1995) merged Sweet's darker and poppier styles, and the tracks "Sick Of Myself" and "We're The Same" brought Sweet back to rock radio.

What's your latest discovery about songwriting?

That it's really hard to say how I do it. A lot of people are really intellectual when they talk about their songwriting. They think about it a lot, and they second guess what they're doing, and they think, "How can I make this better?" I tend to write in a much more haphazard, gut level way, where either I'm in a mood and it just kind of spurts out, or I'm not in that mood and I'm not writing. To some extent, it's kind of a mystery to me. Sometimes I'll have a riff or something for a long time that I haven't made into a song yet, and those will tend to be a little more worked out. Sometimes I'll have things that don't have words for a long time and I'll have to make myself finish the words. And then other times, the words and music will come really fast, out of nowhere. But very rarely will I sit down to have a writing session because I need to write songs. It's more that I build up ideas, then I find time to make demos and flesh them out.

Can you describe how you work when the songs come really fast?

I definitely try to stay out of the way. It's like magical to me. It's hard to talk about because I don't want it to sound like, "Oh yeah, songwriting's nothing to me and they just fall out" [laughs]. But if I talk about how carefully I craft my songs, that's kind of a lie too. It would be a real sham for me to act like I knew what I was doing [laughs]. Usually if a song comes like that, it ends up

being one that over time seems to be good, at least to me. Songs that I wrote that way were "You Don't Love Me" or "Someone To Pull The Trigger," and those are among my favorites that I've written. "Not When I Need It" was totally all at once – I even had the tag part with all the harmonies in my head from the minute I wrote it. That was exciting because it came out so exactly the way it was in my head.

How do you develop a lyric?

Because my songs have this real personal feeling about them, and because I write so much in the "me and you" kind of form, people really imagine that I have something that goes wrong in my relationship that day and I sit down to write a song about it. Very rarely do I do that. Usually a song has a real general feeling about it to me, and the words are almost like a fill in the blanks kind of thing. Certain words will be there, but I won't even know exactly what it really means, then I kind of fill it in until it makes some kind of sense. I like it when it's general enough where it's hard to pin down, but it's specific enough where it feels like real words rather than some kind of poetry.

Did you evolve into that kind of writing?

Early on when I wrote songs, I was writing much more impressionistic, R.E.M. kind of lyrics where it feels like it means something but it could be nonsense [laughs]. It's much more of a poetic way of doing it. After a few bands, when I became a solo artist and I got a record deal, I got into trying to write songs that said something more concrete and literal. But I still think there's value in a song not coming out and saying everything. An R.E.M song or a Nirvana song can be a very potent thing. Because it doesn't really say something that clearly, it might actually be more powerful. But if you do something that's personal that says something real, people can really relate to that. On the one hand, I have fans who get so into the lyrics. They'll get all deep into it and it really moves them. Then I have people who criticize me for that very thing, like "His lyrics have never been as strong as his melodies" [laughs]. I felt embarrassed when I wrote lyrics that were just wordplay, and I felt embarrassed when I wrote lyrics that really said something in a specific way, so I just ultimately thought it's gutsier to try to say something.

What's the story behind "Winona"?

I wrote the song, and it had nothing to do with Winona Ryder. In fact, it wasn't even called that. When I was looking for a title, actually Lloyd Cole, who I was hanging around with at that time, suggested I call it "Winona" because he knew that I liked her in *Heathers*. You have to realize that I had no conception of anyone caring anything about me when I did that song. I was so far from success. It was like if I named a song after a person from a movie, it was just inconceivable that it would mean anything. It was more just an in joke with me and Lloyd. Then what happened, when the record was in limbo for months and months, a guy who I knew at *Rolling Stone* did an interview with her for a cover story, and he sent her a tape of stuff that he liked. He included that song because it had her name on it. It was like the most exciting thing to happen to me that year – a movie star had heard my song! So in the credits for the record, I thanked my friends for sending the song to her, and then when the record came out, people read the credits and said, "Oh yeah, it is about Winona Ryder." I think even she thought it was about her in the beginning, but I kept saying to people who were relatives and friends of hers, "Tell her it's not about her." It's just about a lonely guy who has this fixation on this girl he's met and he's going way too far with it, but he doesn't care because he's so lonely.

So the whole thing went on and I did a billion interviews and said it's not about her. Finally, there was this *USA Today* request for an interview just about that song, and I thought, great, I can finally put this to rest. I told the whole story, then months went by and this story shows up in *USA Today*. The headline was "Ryder Inspires Sweet Song," with a big picture of Winona Ryder, then it quotes stuff I said, but it makes it sound like I'm lying, that it really is about her. Then they quote Lloyd at the end of the article saying, "Well he did have a big thing for Winona Ryder." So the song is going to be perpetually about her even if I say otherwise until I'm blue in the face.

That song, as well as "I Almost Forgot" from 100% Fun *makes me think you might be a big country fan.*

I would say I am. I'm not into a wide range of country. Gram Parsons was really my introduction into that whole world. He's my largest influence. Getting into him, I started listening to some of his influences like Lefty Frizzell, The Louvin Brothers, Johnny Cash, Merle Haggard, Hank Williams. That sort of stuff kills me. I love the form. The whole glitzy world of country today I don't know much about, though there are a few people who I think are good. Jim Lauderdale, The Mavericks.

Tell me a few songs you wish you wrote.

"Thousand Dollar Wedding," by Gram Parsons. "'Til I Die," by Brian Wilson from the *Surf's Up* album. A few of his – "God Only Knows," "The Warmth Of The Sun," that one kills me. I wish I wrote "Unchained Melody," that song kills me. "Everybody's Got Something To Hide Except Me And My Monkey," by The Beatles. I wish I made that record. That recording is really cool and bizarre. I wish I did the whole *Plastic Ono Band* record. "Like A Rolling Stone" by Dylan. "Gimme Shelter" by The Stones.

Sheryl Crow

All I Wanna Do ☆ Leaving Las Vegas
☆ Every Day Is A Winding Road

Interview conducted in 1993

"Songwriting

is never easy

or hard. It's

either joyful or

painful."

Tuesday Night Music Club, the title of Sheryl Crow's debut album, is more than just a catchy phrase. It explains how the songs within were written. For a year, almost every Tuesday night, Crow jammed with a group of musicians including David Baerwald (of David & David), Kevin Gilbert (Toy Matinee) and producer Bill Bottrell (Tom Petty, Traveling Wilburys). These informal sessions, held in Bottrell's studio, deliberately ignored any thoughts about radio formats, record company desires, and even proper song structure. The only intent was to have fun, jam on new ideas and put the results down on tape.

This relaxed vibe permeated the album, and it became a massive success. The single "All I Wanna Do" reached #2 on the Billboard chart, and Crow won a Grammy as Best New Artist of 1994. Her success has since continued its upward arc, with platinum albums *Sheryl Crow* and *The Globe Sessions*, and Top 40 hits such as "If It Makes You Happy," "Everyday Is A Winding Road" and "My Favorite Mistake." A respected writer, Crow's songs have been recorded by Wynonna Judd, Celine Dion, Eric Clapton, Bette Midler, Holly Cole, Faith Hill and Stevie Nicks. Her songs have appeared in movies such as *Kalifornia, Message In A Bottle, Big Daddy* and *Erin Brockovich*, and with Mitchell Froom, she co-wrote the theme song for the James Bond movie, *Tomorrow Never Dies*.

Can you remember when you first got the songwriting bug?

I remember discovering I could play by ear. I was maybe six years old, and there was a Harry Nilsson song called "Me And My Arrow," and I remember learning to play it on the piano and not knowing why I could play it, but just being able to figure it out. From that point, I always tinkered around writing my own melodies. I didn't really get into lyric writing until later on. The first real song I wrote was when I was 13. They had a music contest for kids across Missouri for a state theme song and you had to actually write out the music and the whole thing. That was the first time I wrote out lyrics, staff line, the whole thing [laughs] but I don't remember what it was called.

So you've been writing a long time. Has it gotten easier?

For me, songwriting is never easy or hard, it's either joyful or painful. It doesn't have anything to do with the strenuousness of it. For me, my best stuff comes from when I'm not thinking about it and when I don't have any sort of deadline or there's no demand for me to write. I've learned over the years how to craft a good song, and I know all the formulas for writing songs, and on *Tuesday Night Music Club*, we didn't adhere to any of those rules, which made for a much more honest and free-spirited record.

The songs on that record are credited to you plus one or more other writers. What was your role in the songwriting process?

It was the very first time I'd ever gone in with a bunch of people and just jammed and wrote. We generally started off with a theme, something that I really wanted to write about. We'd talk about it to a certain extent, then just goof around on it. The way we did it was if you were in the room, whether you contributed two notes or one word, you still got publishing credit on it. So, generally, since it was my record, I wrote most of the lyrics and all of the melodies and played on all the tracks, jammed along. Everyone contributed to some extent on some of the lyrics. It kind of varied with each song. It was really musical and a really charmed way to make a record.

What effect did David Baerwald have on your writing?

The one really great thing that David did was convince me that my stories were interesting enough to write about. A lot of times you just overlook the simple experiences that people might be able to relate to or might even be able to learn from. As I would sit around with him and just casually talk about stuff that's happened in my life, he'd say, "You ought to write about that." Also, he's really good at writing in a narrative fashion and I think he made me stretch out that way. You know, when you're writing with other good writers, it's like having quality control. You get a lot less lazy about it, and you don't let things go by without really thinking about them. That was one good thing about having him and Kevin Gilbert around. Kevin Gilbert was with Toy Matinee and is a great lyricist. So when you're around people like that, it makes you strive to make things better.

If you came up with a line that felt really good to sing, but you weren't sure what it meant, would you keep it?

I think a lot of times when you're writing subconsciously, you don't know exactly what you're writing about. It's truly from the subconscious. And those are some of the best lyrics ever. I think that's where music is really healing and really spiritual. I went through a period of feeling like everything had to be symbolic and an art piece. Sometimes simple, very clear meaning is what moves people to relate it to their own lives. So that's kind of where I'm at right now. Most of my stuff I think is very clear and it doesn't take a brain surgeon to figure out what I'm saying. The lyrics that are great are the ones that ring a bell in my subconscious and either show me some truth that might have always been lurking around, or open my eyes to something I hadn't acknowledged in myself.

Tell me about writing "Leaving Las Vegas."

"Leaving Las Vegas" was the first thing we wrote for *Tuesday Night Music Club*. Vegas for me is quite metaphorical. I was living in L.A., and I was really, really sick of it. I felt pretty beat up by the whole scene. I think L.A. and Las Vegas are similar in that people move there for a very specific reason – fame and fortune and that sort of thing. So that's what the song is about. It was recorded in a very spontaneous way. We played it a few times, worked a few things out, then recorded it. Most of the characters on my record are based on me and my experiences, even though I'm not the woman in the song. I think that if you write in a narrative way and use characters, it keeps the listener from being intimidated. People can relate better to a character.

The song that strikes me as being autobiographical is "We Do What We Can."

Yeah, definitely. That's the story of my folks, really. My parents were both in a big band and they played until I was about eight or ten years old. There was always music in my house, from James Taylor to The Beatles to Stan Kenton to classical stuff. *Madame Butterfly*, everything. There was always music on the Magnavox. So I was telling Bill about that and he said you should write a song about it. Again, those are things that I wouldn't think would be very interesting to people, but in some ways I guess they are.

Sarah McLachlan

Interview conducted in 1994

"Songwriting

is such

therapy for

me. It's given

me so much,

as far as

learning about

myself"

Thoreau once said that every writer's duty was to give, first and last, a simple and sincere account of his or her own life.

More than his sage words reached singer/songwriter Sarah McLachlan. In preparing the songs for her breakthrough album, *Fumbling Towards Ecstasy*, the Canadian songstress, inspired by Thoreau's Walden experience, retreated to an isolated cabin in the mountains for nearly seven months of meditation and soul-searching. The results of this temporary sabbatical were intensely personal, emotionally rich songs like "Good Enough," "Plenty," "Possession," and "Circle." Listening to these songs, one can hear McLachlan going through cathartic changes, making discoveries about herself and her life.

Born on January 28, 1968, in Halifax, Nova Scotia, Sarah McLachlan studied classical guitar and piano as a child at the Nova Scotia Royal Conservatory. Outside of the classroom, she remembers being drawn to the sounds of seminal folk/rock artists such as Cat Stevens, Joan Baez, and Simon & Garfunkel. Later, as she reached her teens, it was Peter Gabriel's music that touched her most. "The emotional response you get from his songs, because of the honesty, really inspired me to find my own voice and write from that point of view," she says.

283

At 19, she signed a recording contract with Nettwerk Records. The first ten songs she wrote comprised her debut album, *Touch* (1988). Signed to Arista, she released *Solace* in 1991, and embarked on a 16-month world tour that laid the groundwork for future success and sharpened her intimate, moving vocal power and evocative songwriting gifts.

In 1994, *Fumbling Towards Ecstasy* went triple platinum, despite never cracking the Top 50. In 1996, Sarah created the Lilith Fair, a celebration of women in music. She was inspired by a dispute she'd had with promoters after she requested Paula Cole to be her opening act. "No one's going to pay to see more than one female artist on a concert bill," she was told. Obviously, they were very wrong. Lilith Fair, featuring McLachlan, Cole, Sheryl Crow, Bonnie Raitt, and a host of others, became one of the biggest-grossing tours for four consecutive summers. And 1997's multi-platinum *Surfacing* placed Sarah high in the firmament of the pop world, powered by radio hits such as "Building A Mystery," "Sweet Surrender" and "Adia."

You said that it took about six years to learn how not to edit yourself and remain open in your music. What kinds of things can a songwriter do to reach that place in his or her writing?

Well, for me on *Fumbling Towards Ecstasy*, it was mainly secluding myself, being away from society and being away from everything. I locked myself up in a cabin in the mountains and stayed there for seven months. It was just an amazing time for me to really focus on a lot of stuff that had sort of been lurking behind the scenes in my brain but never had the time to come out. Also I think, I got incredibly in tune with the earth, with nature, like I hadn't before. I couldn't write a thing for three months. My brain was eating itself. It was terribly cold out and I couldn't do anything creative. I was just frozen. Everything was churning around inside but nothing would come out. Then spring happened and everything totally opened up. I was blossoming as well. Most of the songs – I had written four previous to going to the cabin – were written then, about seven of them, between April and May. I finally got to a place where I was totally happy and peaceful and living in the present tense instead of in the future.

The opening lines of your songs are always captivating and they seem to contain the germ of the whole song in just a few words.

I figure the first two lines usually tell the whole story of a song. The first two lines are what comes out first when I'm writing, and they basically tell which direction the song is going to go lyrically. Sometimes those two lines will sit for months by themselves, until they find a completion to the story. Most of the song titles come from the last word in the second line [laughs].

Say you have those two lines and the music wants to continue. Will you let it go on without words?

Unfortunately, I often try to fill it in. I'm still a bit stuck to that convention of writing a song with a four-line verse, the more traditional phrasing of a stanza or whatever. So if there are only two lines, they usually end up being four lines. But when I go in the studio, Pierre [Marchand, her producer] is great at editing. He'll say, "Why don't you just not sing that line, do you really need to say that?" That is something that I can't really do, because I'm not as objective about it. And I don't see things from the same direction that he does, which is why he's so good to work with.

Do you ever write with just a groove?

I never have before. I'm pretty lazy as far as technology, and I think it's something I'll probably have to get more into, because I'm sort of exhausting the instruments that I'm using, or exhausting the inspiration that they give me. I can go back and forth, but I don't have a piano, so I end up doing a lot of stuff on guitar. But when I was in Montreal I did, so a lot of that record came from piano because it was such an exciting thing, a new sound, a new instrument. That happened with electric guitar as well. I started writing with that, because it was a new sound. So maybe I will get into the drum machine. I just have to learn how to use the damn thing first [laughs]. I always fight against technology. I want to be grass roots and I want where it comes from to be organic.

A lot of your songs have an air of mystery and darkness. Is there something you do during the writing process to conjure this mood?

I sort of like the effect of two sides of things – one being really pretty and one being really ugly, like when you lift up a pretty rock and there's all these mites and worms underneath it [laughs]. I think that sort of came from this one poem I read in grade nine. It's funny, the little things that stick with me my whole life. Wilfred Owen is a World War I poet and he wrote about being in the field in the war

285

and all the horrors that went on. But somehow, without glamorizing or romanticizing it, he made it incredibly beautiful. In the same breath, he'd be talking about something horrendously grotesque. I just really loved that. That's actually where the title of the record, *Fumbling Towards Ecstasy*, came from. It was taken from a line in one of his poems –"Quick boys, in an ecstasy of fumbling we fit the masks just in time." I thought that was amazing. It was so beautiful, and since grade nine I've been trying to fit "in an ecstasy of fumbling" into something [laughs]. I sort of have a little library of phrases and words in my head that I like. Language is such a beautiful thing, and words are so amazing.

What was the inspiration behind "Good Enough"?

A lot of things. That song has been such an amazing experience for me because I've learned so much from it. There are so many different stories that I attach to it now. But initially it sort of came from really missing my best girlfriend. It started out as fiction, about a couple in which the woman was pretty much alienated by just about everybody, because her husband was really abusive and domineering, which somewhat mirrors my mother and father's relationship. And basically, I am the friend coming in, saying, "Hey, you deserve more than this, why don't you come with me and I'll take care of you."

For a couple years, every time I'd see my mom, I'd say, "You know, you deserve more, you deserve to be happier than you are. Why are you putting up with this?" Basically telling her that the only thing she knew sucked. So she never wanted to see me, and I wondered why. I couldn't understand it, then I wrote that song. Around the same time, I tried reverse psychology and didn't hassle her anymore. Then she opened up. She completely changed and she started saying, "I'm not going to accept this anymore, I'm changing this and this and this." It was fantastic, because I wasn't beating it into her, she was doing it on her own. That song taught me that. I have a lot of emotional attachment to that song.

Is it difficult for you to keep emotional connection with your songs over the course of a tour?

It does fluctuate. The good thing is that I usually can remember the places that they came from when I sing. I don't remember what they're about so much as the place that they came from, the mood that I was in, the strong, quiet place that I was in when I was writing it. And that gives me a lot of happiness. Sometimes I'm going through emotions, singing the songs and not even listening to the words, but having some weird memory of sitting under a tree and feeling happy [laughs]. Other times I'm thinking about my laundry list. The weirdest things go through my head when I'm singing.

One night – and I never, ever watch TV – but I've become involved in hockey, and it's really fun. So I was watching a game before a show and when I got out there on stage, the TV had sucked all my memory away. Before every line of every verse and chorus, I was terrified that I'd forgotten it. It just freaked me out. Not too many people noticed it in the audience because I'd hit most of the lines. But I asked an actress friend of mine and she said that it had happened to her before. You've just got to trust that it's there. You're just blocking it because of your fear. You've got to get rid of that fear, so think about that laundry list, think about mowing the lawn, and it'll be there.

What would you like to accomplish as a songwriter?

I'd like to keep trying to be able to work through things. Songwriting is such therapy for me. It's given me so much, as far as learning about myself. That's everything to me, just being able to work through things. I guess an offshoot of that is other people listening to it and being able to get something for themselves.

Do you have the sense that what you're doing will last?

Yes, it certainly will last for me. I'd like to think I'll keep writing and getting better and better. I'm really proud of what I've done so far, and that pride hasn't diminished in any way.

What advice would you give to someone looking to make music their career?

I'd tell them to go read *Letters To A Young Poet* by Rainer Maria Rilke, because his advice is better than any advice I could ever give.

Tori Amos

Interview conducted in 1993

"We are the poets who are going from town to town trying to remind the populace that everything is straying away from the heart."

Tori Amos takes her job as a songwriter seriously. On her debut album, 1991's *Little Earthquakes*, the fiery songstress confronted some difficult personal subjects: a woman's struggle for self worth ("Silent All These Years" and "Crucify"), buried anger ("Precious Things"), death ("Happy Phantom") and rape (the chilling, a cappella "Me And A Gun"). The result of this self-therapy was a striking, unconventional record, teeming with gorgeous melodies and stirring arrangements. In the hands of a lesser artist, these themes could have easily degenerated into a whining and venting session, but Amos delivered her messages with poetic lyrics, playfulness and a flamboyant, Lolita sexuality.

Little Earthquakes went gold, and Amos' passionate performing style set the pop world buzzing. Her follow-up album, *Under The Pink*, is a compelling collection of songs that are at once haunting, delicate, abrasive and beautiful. Though she's often compared to Kate Bush, Jane Siberry and Laura Nyro, Tori Amos has carved out her own unique spot on the musical map.

You've been writing songs for over 20 years. Has it gotten any easier?

I think it's harder than it was in the first ten years that I was doing it, because there was judgement then. With *Under The Pink*, all the songs

289

kind of showed up to me complete and then I had to write them. All these girls showed up, all dressed up – and all the songs are girls; don't take this wrong, some of them have heavy male energy, but they're all babes – and they all come in different shapes, sizes, and colors. Some of them aren't even human looking, but they're in a form that feels kind of female. And they would come and say "It's time for you to put down in music my essence and what I'm trying to tell you." I don't know if you've ever had a dream where you've written a song and you really love it. It's great, then you wake up and you can't remember it. This is kind of the same thing except I'm awake. I was going to take a year off, but the songs just demanded that I tell their story, and their story was about life under the pink. That's why the album is called *Under the Pink.*

What does that expression "under the pink" mean to you?

Well if you ripped everybody's skin off, we're all pink, the way I see it. And this is about what's going on inside of that. That's what I'm really interested in, not the outer world but the inner world. There are many other songs that live under the pink. These are just a few of them, these are just the girls who decided to come to the party.

To make that a successful party, do you have to keep a pretty disciplined schedule?

Well, they haunt me, these songs. You see, I've been doing it since I was a little kid. I can't even remember when I started writing, I was always making up my little ditties. So it's kind of a part of my day. As far as the discipline goes, I'm a pretty disciplined person anyway, and I'm pretty ruthless, as far as what stays and what goes in a song. I always listen to my tummy.

Can you explain that?

Beyond the logical mind there is the tummy. And I really believe this, because we can overthink everything. Hey, I'm not writing things for some genius that's sitting trying to criticize. I'm writing from the tummy, because that goes beyond what somebody else's concept of cool is. I'm so sick of cool. If this world has one more megameter of cool, we're just gonna explode. So it's about allowing yourself the freedom to express. Then the other step is the craft of it, the skill. It's about how you use what you know. I think you can stay on one chord for five minutes and make it incredibly interesting, if you know what you're doing. The more that I open my mind to different possibilities musically and lyrically, then the more places I can go.

I remember reading how you prepared yourself for one writing session by sitting in the center of a kind of circle of lyric fragments and song titles. Do you always do meditations like that to conjure up a song?

Yes. For *Under The Pink*, I was in New Mexico for the writing and recording of it. And I would go out into the desert and just sit until the soul of the song came and visited me. When it would come, I would start to get to know who this being was, and what they were trying to say to me. Of course all these beings are just parts of me, parts of you. So I would sit and try to just feel what I was feeling. So many times, I think I'm supposed to feel a certain way, and that's no good. That's not very interesting, in your normal life or your creative life. So I would sit by the Rio Grande and try to stop all the voices. I still had to deal with it as much as last time. "Silent All These Years" was just a beginning but the outside voices didn't get quieter, they just got louder. The previous record [*Little Earthquakes*] was about finding my voice again. So that was kind of different because I had just stumbled onto things that I hadn't dealt with in 15 years. Whereas this record is about how to struggle to stay awake, to stay conscious, to be present. Because once you go, "Yeah this happened to me; yeah, I was violently held hostage and sexually and emotionally violated; yeah I was a minister's daughter and I denied how I buried my true beliefs for all these years" – when you first deal with those realizations, it's kind of like the whole earth opens up. A week later, a year later, you don't have the firecrackers like you did, but you're still healing and dealing with things. So this one was a bit trickier, because when you first come to a realization, it's like a kid in a candy shop. Obviously I can't write "Me And A Gun" again, because how can you write that again? This record is working through not being a victim anymore. I had to sit out there in the desert and listen to what my inner being was really saying, not what I wanted it to say to me.

Do your lyrics arrive in a stream of consciousness?

Lines here and there do, but there's a lot of re-working that I do. I'm pretty ruthless with lyrics. I don't let anything slide. The music is more stream of consciousness and it's always done first, with a line here and a line there. Again, a line of lyric will come for a verse, then I have to craft around what the line means. What am I trying to say here? It gets tricky because I'm not in that trance anymore. I'm just sitting, me and my chair, me at the piano, going "What is this girl trying to tell me?" even though this girl is me. So I'm sitting there by myself and I have to try to go into the inner world. It's all about the inner world, songwriting is. Even if you're talking about the outer world, you have to go into the inner world to see the outer world with any interesting viewpoint.

Your lyrics are kind of free verse, yet by not having perfect rhymes, I think they hit you harder in a way.

I'm not a big believer in rhyme. Who decided that rhyming was the way to do it, who was that guy? Let's go find him and have a little chat because this has really cramped writers for a long, long time. Believe me, when I wrote, "We'll see how brave you are / we'll see how fast you'll be running / we'll see how brave you are, yes Anastasia," I didn't think of it as an assonance, though it is if you do it tonally. But it's about content, it's not about the rhyme. Everything is tone to me, like what a word feels like. There's certain words that I love, like "lemon pie." How it feels in my mouth.

What's the happiest accident that's ever turned into a song for you?

I don't know if this is happy, but it's kind of worth mentioning. The song "Pretty Good Year." I got a letter from a guy named Greg. He's a fan, and this letter just happened to get to me, because a lot of times I don't get them. But he's from the north of England and he drew this picture, a self-portrait of himself. It was a pencil drawing and Greg had glasses and long hair and he was really, really skinny. He had this drooping flower in his hand. And he wrote me this letter that touched me to the core about how at 23, it was all over for him. In his mind, there was nothing. He had become numb. He just couldn't find a way to put his desires and his visions into anything tangible, except this letter. How many people today, before they even reach 30, have just numbed themselves? I don't know the answer. It's not my job to come up with an answer. Nobody wants to hear an answer from me. Nobody asked. The point is, what I tried to come up with is the feeling we all feel. Shaking us out of the numbness. I was just telling Greg's story and Greg affected this singer so much that it brought my own stuff into it, and that was kind of a neat surprise.

Talk about the inspiration behind your song "God."

When I wrote that I was having a complete conversation with the concept of what God is. Not necessarily what I think God truly is, but what the institution, whether it be educational or what have you, has made of God. To me, it's the root of all problems, that song right there. For me, it's one of the most important things I've ever done. You can call it my prayer if you want.

You've called your performance style "confrontational." Do you think it's necessary to be shocking in some way these days to get people to listen to you?

I don't know. Shocking can be a bit boring, My performance style is more based on my relationship with the songs and what I need to express that night. I play the piano in a pretty passionate stance. My right leg supports my whole body. That's one big reason why it's swung back behind me. And the left foot is on the pedal because it supports my diaphragm and my whole body and I can play with ten times the power while I'm singing than I could in any other way. The deal is that I have a responsibility to give all of my being, which I make a commitment to. I go into a meditation and a trance to expose myself. I call a lot of energy into the room. I'm not alone. There's like thousands of spirits hangin' out. So I'm usually pretty supported when I walk out there and the whole live performance is about the transformation of myself. I go and find different parts of myself each night. Sometimes it's joy. Sometimes it's my violent side or whatever, and we work through it. The audience dictates to me what I'm going to go deal with, because I tune into them and everybody there that night is changing the atmosphere. I honor my audience and they're pretty wonderful people. They're all interesting characters; they all bring stuff to the party.

How does a songwriter shed layers and expectations and find their own sound?

First of all, songwriters need to understand what our role is. We are documenting a time. That's what we're doing. Music can do that in a way that nothing else can. We love painters and we love dancers, totally groovy. But sound goes into the being. I think it changes the DNA, I think it can shift somebody's whole molecular structure. I really believe that. So what is our job? Our job is to get in touch with ourselves. If we're not in touch with ourselves, how can we possibly give something to the people out there? My big worry is that we as songwriters aren't doing our job, because we're letting these people who run the industry, who run the critics' sheets, who run the radio stations, dictate what we're going to talk about. There's no excuse for this schlocky shit out there, there's no excuse. This is not about an inner experience or even somebody else's inner experience that they stole. This is about listening to another song on the radio that was a hit and formulating it. Hey, if that works for you as a writer and you make lots of money, go knock yourself out.

But what is our role? We are the poets who are going from town to town and trying to remind the populace, with all the stuff going on – information, whether it's television, movies, all this media – that everything is straying away from the heart. Everything is really straying away from what's inside of yourself. And that's what people are starving for. In a sense, songwriters are the mirrors, just like the poets were in another time. The poets of the late 19th century, especially the French poets, were the voice of their time. So what are we? I think there are a lot of us who are trying to remember why we're doing what we're doing. Our job is a real special one, because we're either supporting a media that would like us to forget about our feelings or we go against the media and say, no, we want to remind the people that they can form their own belief systems. It's about encouraging each individual to be your own bird. That's our job.

Photo Credits

Publicity photo, Shel Secunda (page 50); Motown Records publicity photo, James Hicks (page 88); Sugar Hill Records publicity photo, Jim Harrington (page 133); publicity photo, Lynn Goldsmith (page 162); Columbia Records publicity photo, Kevin Mazur (page 170); Virgin Records publicity photo, Annie Leibovitz (page 149); Atlantic Records publicity photo, Andy Gotts (page 182); Mercury Records publicity photo, Samuel Bayer (page 196); Atlantic Records publicity photo, Brad Branson (page 247); Atlantic Records publicity photo (page 236); Volcano Records publicity photo, Johnny Buzzerio (page 275); Atlantic Records publicity photo, Terry Richardson (page 288)

About The Author

Bill DeMain is a songwriter and one half of the pop duo Swan Dive. His songs have been recorded by Marshall Crenshaw, Jill Sobule, Amy Rigby, Marti Jones and others. As a journalist, he's written for *MOJO*, *Musician*, *Entertainment Weekly* and *Performing Songwriter*. He also contributed liner notes to Rhino Records' Grammy nominated box set, *The Look Of Love: The Burt Bacharach Collection*.